MW00781916

Verse by Verse Commentary on the Book of

REVELATION

Enduring Word Commentary Series
By David Guzik

The grass withers, the flower fades,
but the word of our God stands forever.
Isaiah 40:8

Commentary on the Book of Revelation
Copyright © 2001 by David Guzik
Printed in the United States of America
ISBN 1-56599-043-9

Enduring Word Media
23 West Easy Street, #204
Simi Valley, CA 93065
Phone (805) 527-0199
Fax (805) 577-0388
www.enduringword.com
Electronic Mail: ewm@enduringword.com

Scripture references, unless noted, are from the New King James Version of the Bible, copyright © 1979, 1980, 1982, Thomas Nelson, Inc., Publisher.

Table of Contents

For Chuck and Bobbie Carlson - thanks for your friendship and partnership in God's work

Revelation 1 - Introduction; A Vision of Jesus

A. The introduction and prologue to the Book of Revelation.

1. (1-2) The writer of the Book of Revelation.

The Revelation of Jesus Christ, which God gave Him to show His servants; things which must shortly take place. And He sent and signified *it* by His angel to His servant John, who bore witness to the word of God, and to the testimony of Jesus Christ, to all things that he saw.

a. **The Revelation of Jesus Christ**: The ancient Greek word translated "**Revelation**" is *apokalupsis* (apocalypse). The word simply means "a revealing, an unveiling." What does the Book of Revelation reveal? It is the **Revelation of Jesus Christ**. This book is Jesus' **Revelation** in the sense that *it belongs to Him*, He is the one doing the revealing. It is also Jesus' **Revelation** in the sense that *He is the object* revealed; Jesus is the person revealed by the book.

i. From the outset, we are given the most important truth about the Book of Revelation. This book shows us the Antichrist, it shows us God's judgment, it shows us calamity on the earth, it shows us Mystery Babylon in vivid detail. Most of all, it is the **Revelation of Jesus Christ** to us. If we catch everything else, but miss Jesus in the book, we miss the Book of Revelation.

ii. How we *need* a revelation of Jesus! "The great fault of many professors is that Christ is to them a character upon paper; certainly more than a myth, but yet a person of the dim past, an historical personage who lived many years ago, and did most admirable deeds, by the which we are saved, but who is far from being a living, present, bright reality." (Spurgeon)

b. **Which God gave Him to show His servants**: This is an important reason *why* God gave this **Revelation of Jesus Christ**. He gave it **to *show***

His servants. God gave this revelation that it might be shown, not hidden. This is an *apocalypse* - a revelation, not *apocrypha* (something hidden).

c. **Things which must shortly take place**: This describes *when* the events of this book will **take place** - they will happen **shortly**, and they **must** happen **shortly**. This means that the Book of Revelation is a book of *predictive* prophecy. It speaks of things that will happen in the future - at least future from the time of its writing.

> i. Not all prophecy is predictive, but this prophetic book clearly is predictive. It describes things that **must shortly take place**. *The time is near* (Revelation 1:3) for the fulfillment of these things, but the time was not present at the time of writing.

> ii. Some would say that we should not be concerned with prophecy, that it is a frivolous exercise - but if God was concerned enough to talk about it, we should be concerned enough to listen. "Some tell us that what is yet future ought not to be examined into till after it has come to pass. I can hardly realize that this is seriously meant." (Seiss)

d. **Shortly take place**: When John says these things **must shortly take place**, what does he mean? How short is short? How near is near? "**Short**" and "near" are relative terms, and this is God's timetable, not man's. Yet for 2000 years, history has been *on the brink* of the consummation of all things, running parallel to the edge, *not* running towards a distant brink.

> i. **Shortly** is the ancient Greek phrase *en tachei*, which means " 'quickly or suddenly coming to pass,' indicating rapidity of execution after the beginning takes place. The idea is not that the event may occur soon, but that when it does, it will be sudden." (Walvoord)

e. **He sent and signified it by His angel to His servant John**: This describes *how* the message is delivered in the Book of Revelation. It is a book of signs: the angel *sign*-**ified** this message to John. It is a book that communicates in signs.

> i. Why does God use so many signs in Revelation? After all, they have been the main cause of difficulty with the book. Does God play a game of "guess this mystery?" in Revelation? Not at all. The signs are necessary because John expresses things of heaven, which Paul said he heard with *inexpressible words* (2 Corinthians 12:4). John describes things he saw, so he can only use symbolic images to explain it. To us, this book is prophecy. But to John, he simply recorded history unfolding before him, as he saw it. "John had visions from heaven; but he described them in his own language and manner." (Clarke)

> ii. The signs are also necessary because there is tremendous power in symbolic language. It is one thing to call someone or something evil

or bad. It is far more vivid to describe the image of a woman *drunk with the blood of the saints* (Revelation 17:6).

iii. Though it is filled with signs, the Book of Revelation *is* accessible to those who have an understanding of the first 65 books of the Bible, and especially an understanding of the first 39 books of the Bible, the Old Testament. The Book of Revelation is rooted in the Old Testament. It contains more than 500 allusions to the Old Testament, and 278 of the 404 verses in Revelation (that is almost 70%) make some reference to the Old Testament.

f. **By His angel to His servant John**: This tells us *who* wrote the Book of Revelation. It was **His servant John**, and the best evidence points to this being the Apostle John, the same writer of the Gospel of John and the books of 1, 2, and 3 John.

i. **By His angel**: Many of the signs and visions of the Book of Revelation came to John through the supervision of an angel (Revelation 5:2, 7:2, 10:8 to 11:1, and 17:7 are some examples).

g. **Who bore witness to the word of God**: In this prologue, we see John knew this book was Holy Scripture, **the word of God**. We often wonder if the apostles knew they were writing Holy Scripture. At least in this case, John knew.

i. He knew it was Holy Scripture because he calls it a **revelation** from God. He knew it came from the Father through Jesus, and not from any mere human.

ii. He knew it was the Holy Scripture because he calls it the **word of God,** as an Old Testament prophet would say. He also calls it the **testimony of Jesus Christ**.

2. (3) A blessing to the reader and keeper of this book.

Blessed *is* he who reads and those who hear the words of this prophecy, and keep those things which are written in it; for the time *is* near.

a. **Blessed is he who reads . . . and keep those things which are written in it**: The Book of Revelation offers a particular and unique blessing to those who *read* and *keep* the message of this book. This is the first of seven beatitudes of Revelation (Revelation 1:3, 14:13, 16:15, 19:9, 20:6, 22:7, and 22:14).

i. Because they neglect the book Revelation, many people miss this blessing. For example, the Anglican Church virtually omits Revelation in its regular schedule of readings for both public worship and private devotions. This is a typical attitude towards the Book of Revelation.

Many people believe that only fanatics want to dig deep into this book, but really, it is a book for anyone who wants to be **blessed**.

ii. Fortunately, John didn't say that we had to *understand* everything in the Book of Revelation to be **blessed**. There are some difficult things in this book that may only be understood as we look back at fulfilled prophecy; but we can be blessed by *reading* and *hearing* even when we don't understand.

b. This promise gives more reasons to know John believed this book was Holy Scripture. First, the words **he who reads and those who hear** show that this book was intended to be read publicly, just as other books of accepted Scripture. Second, the promise of *blessing* itself shows that John regarded this book as Holy Scripture. In the Jewish world, such a blessing could never be pronounced on a merely human book.

i. All of these things together show that beyond doubt, the Book of Revelation *claims* to be Holy Scripture. A critic can agree or disagree with that claim, but it can't be denied that Revelation makes the claim.

c. **Keep those things which are written in it**: The Book of Revelation gives us much more than information for prophetic speculation. It gives us **things** to **keep**. If we understand the Book of Revelation, it will *change the way we live*.

d. **"He who reads"** is in the *singular*. It speaks of one person who reads. **"Those who hear"** is in the *plural*. It speaks of many people hearing. The idea is probably from custom of the early church, where attention was given to the public reading of Scripture, which was often then explained. In our modern way of speaking, John might say, "Blessed is the pastor who teaches Revelation, and blessed is the congregation who hears it." Most of all, pastor or congregation, **blessed** are those who **keep those things which are written in it**.

i. "Neither must we only live up to the words of this prophecy, but die for it also, and be content to be burned with it, if called thereto; as that holy martyr, who when he saw the Revelation cast into the fire with him, cried out 'O blessed Revelation, how happy am I to be burned in thy company!' " (Trapp)

3. Since so much controversy has risen over the interpretation of the Book of Revelation, it is helpful to know the four basic approaches people have used through the centuries to understand Revelation.

a. *The Preterist View*: This approach believes that Revelation deals only with the church in John's day. In the *Preterist* approach, Revelation doesn't predict anything. John simply describes events of his current day, but he puts them in symbolic code so those outside the Christian family couldn't understand his criticism of the Roman government. In the *Preterist* view, the Book of Revelation was for *then*.

b. *The Historicist View*: This approach believes that Revelation is a sweeping, disordered panorama of all church history. In the *Historicist* approach, Revelation predicts the future, but the future of the "church age" - not the future of end-time events. In the *Historicist* view, Revelation is full of symbols that describe *now*.

> i. For example, many of the Reformers called the Pope the beast of Revelation chapter 13, but they didn't necessarily want to believe that the end was very near. So they believed that Revelation spoke of *their* time, without necessarily speaking to the *end* times.

c. *The Poetic View*: This approach believes that Revelation is a book full of pictures and symbols intended to encourage and comfort persecuted Christians in John's day. In the *Poetic* or *allegorical* view, the Book of Revelation isn't literal or historic. Revelation is a book of *personal* meaning.

d. *The Futurist View*: This approach believes that beginning with chapter four, Revelation deals with the end times, the period directly preceding Jesus' return. In the *Futurist* view, Revelation is a book that mainly describes the *end* times.

e. Which approach is correct? *Each one* is true in some regard. The Book of Revelation did speak to John's day. It speaks to church history. And it does have meaning for our personal life. So while elements of the first three approaches have their place, we can't deny the place of the *futurist* view. We can know the Book of Revelation speaks with clarity about the end times because of two central principles drawn from Revelation 1:1-3.

> i. First, we believe that the Book of Revelation *must mean something*. This is a book that Jesus gave *to show His servants* something. It isn't a book of meaningless nonsense. It has a promise of blessing, not a promise of confusion.

> ii. Secondly, we believe that Revelation definitely claims to contain *predictive prophecy*. John made it clear: *things which must shortly take place . . . the time is near*. John wrote about events that were still future to him.

B. Greeting.

　1. (4-5a) A greeting of **grace** and **peace**.

John, to the seven churches which are in Asia: Grace to you and peace from Him who is and who was and who is to come, and from the seven Spirits who are before His throne, and from Jesus Christ, the faithful witness, the firstborn from the dead, and the ruler over the kings of the earth.

a. **To the seven churches which are in Asia**: This letter was originally addressed to these **seven** selected **churches** of **Asia**. This was the Roman province of **Asia**, which is the western part of modern day Turkey.

b. **From Him who is and who was and who is to come**: John brings a greeting from *God the Father*, who is described with this title. **Him who is and who was and who is to come** speaks to the eternal nature of God. It has the idea of a timeless Being, and is connected with the name *Yahweh* found in the Old Testament (Exodus 2:14).

> i. The ancient Greek construction of **who is, who was and who is to come** is intentionally awkward in the ancient Greek. It seems that John searched for a phrase to communicate the Old Testament idea of *Yahweh*.

> ii. It is never enough to just say that God **is**, or to just say that He **was**, or to just say that He **is to come**. As Lord over eternity, He rules the past, the present, and the future.

> iii. The description **Him who is and who was and who is to come** applies to God the Son and God the Holy Spirit as much as it does to God the Father. In fact, the title *Yahweh* describes the Triune God, the One God in Three Persons. Yet it seems that John focuses on God the Father with this title because he specifically mentions God the Son and God the Holy Spirit in the following words of this verse.

c. **From the seven Spirits who are before His throne**: John brings a greeting from *God the Holy Spirit*, who is described with this title. **The seven Spirits who are before His throne** speaks to the *perfection* and *completion* of the Holy Spirit. John uses an Old Testament description of the Holy Spirit.

> i. The idea of the **seven Spirits** quotes from the Old Testament. Isaiah 11:2 describes seven aspects of the Holy Spirit: *The Spirit of the LORD shall rest upon Him, the Spirit of **wisdom** and **understanding**, the Spirit of **counsel** and **might**, the Spirit of **knowledge** and **fear of the Lord**.* It isn't that there are seven different spirits of God, rather the Spirit of the LORD has these characteristics, and He has them all in fullness and perfection.

d. **From Jesus Christ, the faithful witness, the firstborn from the dead, and the ruler over the kings of the earth**: John brings a greeting from *God the Son*, who is described by *who He is* and by *what He has done*.

> i. Jesus is the **faithful witness**: This speaks to Jesus' utter reliability and faithfulness to His Father and to His people, even unto death. The ancient Greek word translated **witness** is also the word for a *martyr*.

ii. **Firstborn from the dead**: This speaks to Jesus' standing as *pre-eminent* among all beings, that He is first in priority. **Firstborn from the dead** means much more than that Jesus was the first person resurrected. It also means that He is pre-eminent among all those who are or will be resurrected. Jesus is *the firstborn among many brethren* (Romans 8:29).

iii. The use of **firstborn** does not mean that Jesus had a birth date and is therefore a created being, and not God. The ancient Rabbis called Yahweh Himself "Firstborn of the World" (Rabbi Bechai cited in Lightfoot's commentary on Colossians). Rabbis also used **firstborn** as a Messianic title. "God said, 'As I made Jacob a first-born (Exodus 4:22), so also will I make king Messiah a first-born' (Psalm 89:28)." (R. Nathan in *Shemoth Rabba*, cited by Lightfoot in his commentary on Colossians)

iv. Jesus is the **ruler over the kings**. Before the Book of Revelation is over, Jesus will take dominion over every earthly king. At the present time, Jesus rules a kingdom, but it is a kingdom that is not yet of this world.

e. In this greeting, with its systematic mention of each Person of the Trinity, we see how the New Testament presents the doctrine of the Trinity. It doesn't present it in a carefully defined, "systematic theology" kind of way. It simply weaves the truth of the Trinity - that there is One God in Three Persons - throughout the fabric of the New Testament.

2. (5b-6) A statement of praise to Jesus.

To Him who loved us and washed us from our sins in His own blood, and has made us kings and priests to His God and Father, to Him *be* glory and dominion forever and ever. Amen.

a. **To Him who loved us**: What a beautiful title for Jesus! When **loved** is used, in the *past tense*, it points back to a particular time and place where Jesus **loved us**. It should be pointed out that many translations have *loves us* (such as NASB, NIV, and NLT), but there is something beautiful about **loved us**. It looks back to *the cross*. Every believer should be secure in God's love, not based on their present circumstances (which may be difficult), but based on the *ultimate demonstration of love* at the cross. This is worth praising Jesus about.

i. Paul put it like this in Romans 5:8: *But God demonstrates His own love toward us, in that while we were still sinners, Christ died for us.* The work of Jesus on the cross for us is God's ultimate proof of His love for you. He may give additional proof, but He can give no greater proof.

ii. No wonder many believers are not secure in knowing the love of Jesus towards them - they look to their *present circumstances* to measure His love. Instead, they need to look back to the cross, settle the issue once for all, and give praise to Jesus, **to Him who loved us**.

b. **And washed us from our sins in His own blood**: This is what happened when Jesus **loved us** at the cross. He **washed us** - cleansed us from the deep stain of sin, so that we really are *clean* before Him. This is worth praising Jesus about.

i. If we understand our own deep sinfulness, this seems almost too good to be true. We can stand clean before God - clean from the deepest of stains. No wonder the same Apostle John would write, *If we confess our sins, He is faithful and just to forgive us our sins and to cleanse us from all unrighteousness* (1 John 1:9).

ii. **In His own blood**: If there were any other way to wash us from our sins, God would have done it that other way. To wash us **in His own blood** meant the ultimate sacrifice of God the Son. God wouldn't do it this way unless it was the only way. "The priests could only cleanse with blood of bulls and goats; but he has washed us from our sins 'in his own blood.' Men are willing enough to shed the blood of others. How readily they will enter upon war! But Christ was willing to shed his own blood, to pour out his soul unto death, that we might be saved." (Spurgeon)

iii. Notice the order: first **loved**, then **washed**. It wasn't that God washed us out of some sense of duty and then loved us because we were then clean. He **loved us** while we were dirty, but then He **washed us**.

iv. In fact, washing *proves* love. If you had an old pair of pants, and got them *covered* in paint, you would only wash them and keep them for two reasons. First, you might wash them and keep them if you *were poor*. You can't or won't spend money on another pair of pants, so you wash them and keep them. Second, you might wash them and keep them if you *really loved* those old pants. Money isn't the issue. You could go down and buy a new pair of pants any time; but you love that pair so much that you spend the time and the effort to clean them, and use them again. God loves us so much that He **washed us**. God certainly is not poor. With merely a thought, He could obliterate every sinner and start over with brand-new creatures. But He doesn't. He loves us so much that He **washed us**.

v. Some scholars believe that John wrote *and loosed us from our sins*. There is only one letter different between the words **washed** and *loosed* in the ancient Greek language. Both words show up in ancient manuscripts, so it's hard to say which one John wrote. Nevertheless, both are true - we are both **washed** and *loosed* **from our sins.**

c. **And has made us kings and priests to His God and Father:** This is status Jesus gives to those whom He **loved** in His work on the cross and who are **washed . . . in His own blood.** It would have been enough just to love them and cleanse them. But He goes far beyond, and makes **us kings and priests to His God and Father.** This is more than Adam ever was. Even in the innocence of Eden we never read of Adam among the **kings and priests** of God. This is worth praising Jesus about.

i. We are **kings,** so we are *God's royalty* - this is privilege, status, and authority. We are **priests,** so we are *God's special servants.* We represent God to man and man to God. We offer sacrifice unto Him (Hebrews 13:15). We have privileged access to God's presence (Romans 5:1-2).

ii. **Kings *and* priests:** In the Old Testament, it was forbidden to combine the offices of king and priest. King Uzziah of Judah is an example of a man who tried to combine the two offices, and paid the penalty for it (2 Chronicles 26:16-23). But under the New Covenant, we can be like Jesus in the sense that He is both King and High Priest (Luke 1:31-33; Hebrews 4:14).

d. **To Him be glory and dominion forever and ever:** In light of all that Jesus has done for us, shouldn't we praise Him? Shouldn't we honor Him with all **glory and dominion forever and ever?** When we say this, we aren't *giving* Jesus **glory and dominion.** We are simply *recognizing* that He has it, and honoring Him for it.

i. To recognize the **glory** of Jesus is to come out-and-out for Him. "Some of you are very like a mouse behind the wainscot. You are in the Lord's house, but you are not known as one of the family: sometimes you give a little squeak in your hiding-place, and sometimes come out at night, as the mouse does, to pick up a crumb or two, without being seen. Is this worthy of yourself? Is it worthy of your Lord and Master?" (Spurgeon)

ii. To recognize the **dominion** of Jesus is to let Him truly rule over us. "Again, if we truly say, 'To him be glory and dominion,' then *we must give him dominion over ourselves.* Each man is a little empire of three kingdoms - body, soul, and spirit - and it should be a united kingdom. Make Christ king of it all. Do not allow any branch of those three kingdoms to set up for itself a distinct rule; put them all under the sway of your one King." (Spurgeon)

e. **Amen**: This word - in the ancient Greek language, brought over from the Hebrew of the Old Testament - simply means "*Yes.*" It isn't a wish that it *may* be so, but it is an affirmation that, through God, it *will* be so. Jesus *will be praised.*

> i. Jesus has done all this and more for you. You have much to praise Him for - so praise Him! "Would you not wish to be in heaven when your life on earth is over? The time will come when you must die; would you not desire to have a good hope of entering then into the felicities of the perfected ones? I am sure you would; but if you are at last to be numbered amongst the redeemed host on high, you must here learn their song. You cannot be admitted into the choirs above without having practiced and rehearsed their music here below." (Spurgeon)

> ii. "The Greek word *amen* is a transliteration of a Hebrew word of similar sound meaning 'truth' or 'faithfulness,' hence the meaning 'be it true' or 'so be it.' " (Walvoord)

3. (7) An opening description of the return of Jesus.

Behold, He is coming with clouds, and every eye will see Him, even they who pierced Him. And all the tribes of the earth will mourn because of Him. Even so, Amen.

a. **Behold, He is coming**: This is a command to *look* - to *check it out.* John moves from praising Jesus to describing His return. He wants *us* to **behold** the coming of Jesus. Jesus said that we should watch and wait for His coming (Matthew 24:42). It is something to *keep before the eye of our mind*, to **behold**.

> i. This wasn't a supernatural vision of Jesus' return. That supernatural vision will come later. This description is based from John's understanding of Old Testament promises of the Messiah's return and Jesus' own words about His return. For example, John knew that Jesus was **coming** because Jesus said He was **coming**. Jesus said, *I will come again and receive you to Myself* (John 14:3).

> ii. "Christ has not gone to heaven to stay there. He has gone for the church's benefit; and for his church's benefit he will return again." (Seiss)

b. **He is coming with clouds**: When Jesus comes, He will be surrounded by **clouds**. This will be true literally, because when Jesus left this earth, He was taken up into a cloud, and God said that He would return in the same manner (Acts 1:9-11). It will also be true figuratively, because multitudes of believers are called **clouds** in a figurative manner (Hebrews 12:1).

Clouds are commonly associated with God's presence and glory (Exodus 13:21-22, 16:10, 19:9, and 24:15-18), relating to the Old Testament cloud of glory called the *Shekinah*.

> i. Understanding this connection with the glory of God, it is fitting - and wonderful - that the multitude of believers is called a *cloud*. God's people are His glory. They are His "cloud," His *Shekinah*.

> ii. John didn't need a special vision to know **He is coming with clouds**. He knew this from the Old Testament (Daniel 7:13-14) and from Jesus' own words: *I say to you, hereafter you will see the Son of Man sitting at the right hand of the Power, and coming on the clouds of heaven* (Matthew 26:64).

c. **And every eye will see Him**: When Jesus comes, it won't be a "secret" coming. Everyone will know. At His first coming, Jesus was somewhat obscure. During His earthly ministry, He never made front-page news in Rome. But when Jesus comes again, **every eye will see Him**. The whole world will know.

> i. John didn't need a special vision to know **every eye will see Him**. John heard Jesus Himself say, *Therefore if they say to you, "Look, He is in the desert!" do not go out; or "Look, He is in the inner rooms!" do not believe it. For as the lightning comes from the east and flashes to the west, so also will the coming of the Son of Man be* (Matthew 24:26-27).

d. **Even they who pierced Him**: When Jesus comes, it will be a particularly meaningful revelation for the Jewish people. Of course, it was not the Jews alone **who pierced Him**. But we know John has in mind the revelation of Jesus to His own people because this is an allusion to Zechariah 12:10.

> i. When Jesus reveals Himself to His own people, the Jews, it will not be in anger. By that time, the Jewish nation will have turned to Jesus, trusting in Him as their Messiah (Matthew 23:39, Romans 11:25-26). When they see Jesus, and His **pierced** hands and feet, it will be a painful reminder of their *previous* rejection of Him. It will fulfill the scene of Zechariah 12:10: *And I will pour on the house of David and on the inhabitants of Jerusalem the Spirit of grace and supplication; then they will look on Me whom they pierced. Yes, they will mourn for Him as one mourns for his only son, and grieve for Him as one grieves for a firstborn.*

> ii. John didn't need a special vision to know **even they who pierced Him**. He could read it in Zechariah 12:10.

e. **All the tribes of the earth will mourn because of Him**: When Jesus comes, it won't be only the Jewish people who **mourn** because of their previous rejection of Jesus. Since there will be people saved from **all the**

tribes of the earth (Revelation 7:9), everyone will have a part in this mourning. We will all look at His scars and say "We did this to Him."

> i. John didn't need a special revelation to know **all the tribes of the earth will mourn because of Him**. He just needed to remember what Jesus said at Matthew 24:30: *Then the sign of the Son of Man will appear in heaven, and then all the tribes of the earth will mourn, and they will see the Son of Man coming on the clouds of heaven with power and great glory.*

4. (8) An introduction from Jesus Himself.

"I am the Alpha and the Omega, *the* Beginning and *the* End," says the Lord, "who is and who was and who is to come, the Almighty."

> a. **I am the Alpha and the Omega**: In many translations, and in "Red-Letter" editions, these words are in red. This shows that the translators believed that these were the words of Jesus. John is finished with his introduction, and now Jesus introduces Himself. After all, it is His revelation (*the Revelation of Jesus Christ*, Revelation 1:1), so it isn't strange that He introduces it.

> > i. Some wonder if it is God the *Father* or God the *Son* speaking here. We suspect it is the *Son*, Jesus Christ, and we believe this for many reasons. First, since it is Jesus' Revelation, it seems appropriate that He introduces it. Second, the titles **Alpha and Omega** and **the Beginning and the End** are titles claimed by Jesus (Revelation 22:13). Third, though the title **who is and who was and who is to come** is used of God the Father in Revelation 1:4, it is also true of God the Son, and seems to be directed to Jesus in Revelation 11:17 and 16:5.

> b. **The Alpha and the Omega, the Beginning and the End**: The idea behind these titles for Jesus is that He is *before* all things and will remain *beyond* all things. **Alpha** was the first letter of the ancient Greek alphabet, and **Omega** was the last letter. Jesus says, "I am the 'A to Z,' **the Beginning and the End.**"

> > i. If Jesus is both the **Beginning** and the **End**, then He also has authority over everything in-between. This means that Jesus does have a plan for history, and He directs the path of human events toward His designed fulfillment. Our lives are not given over to blind fate, to random meaninglessness, or to endless cycles with no resolution. Instead, Jesus Christ who is **the Alpha and the Omega, the Beginning and the End** directs all of human history and even our individual lives.

> c. **Who is and was and who is to come**: As shown in the comments on Revelation 1:4, this phrase communicates the *idea* behind the great Old

Testament name for the Triune God, *Yahweh*. It reflects His eternal nature and His unchanging presence. Jesus has this eternal nature just as much as God the Father does. Micah 5:2 prophetically expressed it this way: *Whose goings forth are from of old, from everlasting*. Hebrews 13:8 expressed it this way: *Jesus Christ is the same yesterday, today, and forever.*

d. **The Almighty**: This word **Almighty** translates the ancient Greek word *pantokrater*, which literally means "the one who has his hand on everything." It speaks of the great sovereign control of Jesus over everything - past, present, and future.

i. This great word **Almighty** is used ten times in the New Testament, and nine of the ten times are in the Book of Revelation. This book has a striking emphasis on God's sovereignty, the understanding that He has His hand on *everything*.

C. John is commanded to write.

1. (9) John on the Island of **Patmos**.

I, John, both your brother and companion in the tribulation and kingdom and patience of Jesus Christ, was on the island that is called Patmos for the word of God and for the testimony of Jesus Christ.

a. **I, John . . . was on the island that is called Patmos**: The island of **Patmos** was a like an Alcatraz Island in the Roman Empire. It was used as a prison island and functioned as a jail without bars. The island was rich in marble, and most of the prisoners were forced laborers in marble quarries. **Patmos** was a rocky, desolate island about 10 miles long and 6 miles wide.

i. "John was at the time in exile, upon a lonely and desolate island. But neither seas, nor Alps, nor ages, can sever the bonds by which Christians are united to each other, or to Christ, their Lord. Less than a year ago I passed that island. It is a mere mass of barren rocks, dark in colour and cheerless in form. It lies out in the open sea, near the coast of Western Asian Minor. It has neither trees nor rivers, nor any land for cultivation, except some little nooks between the ledges of rocks. There is still a dingy grotto remaining, in which the aged Apostle is said to have lived, and in which he is said to have had this vision. A chapel covers it, hung with lamps kept burning by the monks." (Seiss)

ii. Barnes describes Patmos as "Lonely, desolate, barren, uninhabited, seldom visited, it had all the requisites which could be desired for a place of punishment; and banishment to that place would accomplish all that a persecutor could wish in silencing the apostle, without putting him to death." Yet this exile *didn't* silence the Apostle John.

b. **For the word of God and for the testimony of Jesus Christ**: Most scholars assume that John was on **Patmos** because he was arrested and imprisoned in persecution from the Romans. This is probably the case, especially because John says that he is **your brother and companion in the tribulation and kingdom and patience of Jesus Christ**. However, it is also possible that John was on **Patmos** as a missionary to the prisoners there.

i. The ancient Christian historian Eusebius says John was imprisoned at Patmos under the reign of the Roman Emperor Domitian. (*Church History*, III.18, 20 - from the *Nicean and Post Nicean Fathers Series 2*, Volume 1, pages 148-149)

ii. "According to Victorinus, John, though aged, was forced to labor in the mines located at Patmos. Early sources also indicated that about A.D. 96, at Domitian's death, John was allowed to return to Ephesus when the Emperor Nerva was in power." (Walvoord)

2. (10-11) John is commanded to write.

I was in the Spirit on the Lord's Day, and I heard behind me a loud voice, as of a trumpet, saying, "I am the Alpha and the Omega, the First and the Last," and, "What you see, write in a book and send *it* to the seven churches which are in Asia: to Ephesus, to Smyrna, to Pergamos, to Thyatira, to Sardis, to Philadelphia, and to Laodicea."

a. **I was in the Spirit on the Lord's Day**: What does John mean by saying he **was in the Spirit**? This seems to have more meaning than simply saying he was walking "in the Spirit" as opposed to being "in the flesh" in the sense Paul means in Galatians 5:16. The idea isn't simply that John was *walking in the Spirit*, but that he received unique revelation from the Holy Spirit. This was a unique spiritual experience for John, what some might call an *out of body experience* - though of course, without the occult or spiritism such experiences are associated with today.

i. Walvoord defines **in the Spirit** like this: "Carried beyond normal sense into a state where God could reveal supernaturally the contents of this book."

ii. There are four references to John being **in the Spirit** in the Book of Revelation. First at Patmos (Revelation 1:10), then in heaven (Revelation 4:2), then in the wilderness (Revelation 17:3), and finally on the mountain of God (Revelation 21:10).

b. **On the Lord's Day**: When is **the Lord's Day**? Among the pagans of the Roman Empire, the first day of each month was called "Emperors Day" in honor of the Roman Emperor. Perhaps Christians proclaimed their allegiance to Jesus by honoring the first day of the *week* as their own **Lord's Day**.

> i. This is *not* the same term used for *The Day of the* LORD in the Old Testament, nor is it the same idea. The Book of Revelation will deal with the idea of *The Day of the* LORD, but it doesn't do it here.

c. **I heard behind me a loud voice**: The **loud voice** John heard was clear and striking as the sound of a **trumpet**. The **loud voice** belongs to the **Alpha and Omega**, the **First and the Last**, who is the beginning and the end of all things. Since Jesus introduced Himself with these titles in Revelation 1:8, we know this was the **loud voice** of Jesus.

> i. Clarke on the phrase **as of a trumpet**: "This was calculated to call in every wandering thought, to fix his attention, and solemnize his whole frame."

> ii. **The First and the Last** is a title that belongs to the LORD, Yahweh, the God of Israel (Isaiah 41:4, 44:6, and 48:12). The title **Alpha and the Omega** has the same *idea* as **First and the Last**. This is one of the New Testament passages where Jesus *clearly* claims to be God.

d. **What you see, write in a book**: Here, John is commanded to write what he sees. He will be commanded to **write** eleven more times in the Book of Revelation. We get the sense that unless John was commanded to **write**, he would have just kept it to himself. It's always best to keep visions and revelations to one's self unless *commanded* otherwise.

e. **Send it to the seven churches which are in Asia**: John is commanded to write to **seven churches** in seven cities. Each of these churches is in the region of the Roman province of **Asia**. But these were not the *only* cities with churches in this region. For example, there was a church in the city of Colosse (to which the Apostle Paul wrote the letter of *Colossians*), but the city of Colosse isn't included in this list of **seven churches**. Why were these specific **seven churches** chosen?

> i. Some suggest that it is because they are arranged in a roughly circular pattern. Others think it was because these were postal districts in the Roman province of Asia. Many believe **seven churches** were chosen because in the Bible, the number **seven** often represents completeness, and these letters - and all of the Book of Revelation - are written to the *complete* church, not *only* these **seven churches**. Seiss writes, "The churches of all time are comprehended in seven," and quotes many modern and ancient commentators that agree with this perspective.

> ii. "It is the opinion of very learned writers upon this book, that our Lord, by these *seven churches*, signifies all the churches of Christ to the

end of the world; and by what he saith to them, designs to show what shall be the state of churches in all ages, and what their duty is." (Poole)

iii. Interestingly, the Apostle Paul also wrote to **seven churches**: Rome, Corinth, Galatia, Ephesus, Colosse, Philippi, and Thessalonika.

D. John's vision of Jesus.

1. (12-13) Jesus in the midst of the **lampstands**.

Then I turned to see the voice that spoke with me. And having turned I saw seven golden lampstands, and in the midst of the seven lampstands *One* **like the Son of Man, clothed with a garment down to the feet and girded about the chest with a golden band.**

a. **I turned to see the voice**: We can only imagine what went through John's mind as he **turned**. The voice he heard was probably not exactly the same sound as he remembered Jesus' voice to be (John described it *as of a trumpet*, Revelation 1:10). Yet he knew from the voice's self-description (*Alpha and Omega*) that it was Jesus. This was John's opportunity to see Jesus again, after knowing Him so well during the years of His earthly ministry.

b. First, John didn't see Jesus. He **saw seven golden lampstands**. These were not candlesticks, they were not menorahs, but they were free standing oil lamp stands. The lamps set *on* these **lampstands**.

i. There were **seven** separate **lampstands**. This is an image that *reminds* us of the *golden lampstand* that stood in the tabernacle and the temple (Exodus 25:31-37). Yet this is different. The Old Covenant lampstand was *one lampstand* with *seven lamps* on it. Here in the New Covenant, we see **seven lampstands**. "In the Jewish tabernacle there was on golden candlestick, and seven lamps, to give light . . . John here seeth seven. God had but one church of the Jews, but many among the Gentiles." (Poole)

ii. The light doesn't come from the **lampstands**. The light comes from the oil lamps themselves. The stands merely make the light more visible. Therefore, the **lampstands** are a good picture of the church. We don't produce the light, we simply display it.

iii. "A lamp is not *light in itself*, it is only the *instrument* of dispensing light, and it must receive both *oil* and *fire* before it can dispense any; so no Church has in itself either *grace* or *glory*, it must receive all from Christ its head, else it can dispense neither light nor life." (Clarke)

c. **And in the midst of the seven lampstands One like the Son of Man**: Jesus is there in the midst of these lampstands, as the **Son of Man**, a figure of glory looking back to Daniel 7:13-14. Though the title **Son of**

Man sounds like a humble title, in light of the Daniel passage, it is not a humble title at all.

d. Clothed with a garment down to the feet and girded about the chest with a golden band: The clothing of Jesus indicates that He is a person of great dignity and authority. Long garments were only worn by those who didn't have to work much, so they were a picture of great status and authority. The **golden band** around **the chest** probably hints at the garments of the high priest (Exodus 29:5).

> i. Exodus 39:1-5 says that there were golden threads in the band that went around the chest of the high priest of Israel. Jesus' **band** has more than a few golden threads. It is all gold! How much greater is the eternal, heavenly priesthood of Jesus!

> ii. One of the duties of the Old Testament priests was to tend the golden lampstand in the tabernacle. Every day they had to fill the oil, clean the soot, and trim the wicks. They had to closely inspect and care for the lamps so they would burn continually before the Lord. Here is Jesus, our High Priest, in the **midst of the seven lampstands**, carefully inspecting and caring for the lamps, helping them to always burn brightly before the Lord.

2. (14-16) John describes Jesus.

His head and hair *were* white like wool, as white as snow, and His eyes like a flame of fire; His feet *were* like fine brass, as if refined in a furnace, and His voice as the sound of many waters; He had in His right hand seven stars, out of His mouth went a sharp two-edged sword, and His countenance *was* like the sun shining in its strength.

a. His head and hair were white like wool: The **white** hair speaks of old age, and is therefore in that culture connected with the idea of great wisdom and timelessness. The phrase **white as snow** also emphasizes the idea of purity (Isaiah 1:18).

> i. The white hair and head also connect Jesus with the Ancient of Days in Daniel 7:9. "The term of *Ancient of Days* belongs to God the Father, yet it also agreeth to Christ, who is equal with the Father as to his Divine nature." (Poole)

> ii. "When we see in the picture his head and his hair white as snow, we understand the antiquity of his reign." (Spurgeon)

> iii. "This was not only an emblem of in *antiquity*, but it was evidence of his *glory*; for the *whiteness* of splendour of his head and hair doubtless proceeded from the *rays of light* and *glory* which encircled his head, and darted from it in all directions." (Clarke)

b. **His eyes like a flame of fire**: **Fire** is often associated with judgment in the Scriptures (Matthew 5:22, 2 Peter 3:7). Jesus' eyes display the **fire** of searching, penetrating judgment.

c. **His feet were like fine brass**: Since **fire** is connected with judgment, these **feet like fine brass, as if refined in a furnace** speak of someone who has been through the fires of judgment and has come forth with a refined purity. Jesus has been through the "Refiner's Fire."

> i. **Brass** is a metal connected with judgment and sacrifice. Israel's altar of sacrifice was made of brass (Exodus 27:1-6), and it was called the "brazen altar."

> ii. **Brass** is also a strong metal, the strongest known in the ancient world. Therefore **feet . . . like fine brass** are "An emblem of his *stability and permanence, brass* being considered the most durable of all metallic substances or compounds." (Clarke)

d. **His voice as the sound of many waters**: This means that Jesus' voice had the power and majesty of a mighty waterfall.

e. **He had in His right hand seven stars**: The **seven stars** speak of the leaders or representatives of the *seven churches* mentioned in Revelation 1:11 (Revelation 1:20). The **stars** are securely in the hand of Jesus. Since **seven** is the number of completion, we can say that "He's got the whole church in His hands."

f. **Out of His mouth went a sharp two-edged sword**: This is a heavy **sword** (the ancient Greek word *rhomphaia*), used to kill and destroy. Sometimes the New Testament speaks of a smaller, more tactical sword known in the ancient Greek language as the *machaira*. Hebrews 4:12 uses the term for this smaller, more precise sword.

> i. The idea of it coming **out of His mouth** is *not* that Jesus carries a sword in His teeth. The idea is that this **sword** is His word. His weapon - and ours also - is the Word of God (Ephesians 6:17).

> ii. Barnes says that John didn't necessarily *see* a sword coming out of Jesus' mouth. "He heard him speak; he felt the penetrating power of his words; and they were *as if* a sharp sword proceeded from his mouth."

> iii. It is **a sharp two-edged sword**: "There is no handling this weapon without cutting yourself, for it has no back to it, it is all edge. The Word of Christ, somehow or other, is all edge." (Spurgeon)

g. **His countenance was like the sun shining in its strength**: The glory of Jesus is so great, so shining, that it is hard to even look upon Him. Jesus has the same glory as in His transfiguration, when *His face shone like the sun* (Matthew 17:2).

> i. "His face was like the disk of the sun in the brightest summer's day, when there were no clouds to abate the splendour of his rays." (Clarke)

> ii. "What do you see in Christ's right hand? Seven stars; yet how insignificant they appear when you get a sight of *his face!* They are stars, and there are seven of them; but who can see seven stars, or, for the matter of that, seventy thousand stars, when the sun shineth in his strength? How sweet it is, when the Lord himself is so present in a congregation that the preacher, whoever he may be, is altogether forgotten! I pray you, dear friends, when you go to a place of worship, always try to see the Lord's face rather than the stars in his hand; look at the sun, and you will forget the stars." (Spurgeon)

> iii. Everything in this vision speaks of strength, majesty, authority and righteousness. There is an impressive difference between this vision of Jesus and the many weak, effeminate portrayals of Jesus seen today. But the Jesus that John saw is the *real* Jesus, the Jesus that lives and reigns in heaven today.

> iv. We should consider the fact that this is the only physical description of Jesus given to us in the Bible. The only other description that comes close is in Isaiah 53:2: *He has no form or comeliness; and when we see Him, there is no beauty that we should desire Him.*

> v. In our modern pictures of Jesus, we like to think of Him as He *was*, not Jesus as He *is*. We prefer to see and know Jesus after the flesh. But Paul said, *Even though we have known Christ according to the flesh, yet now we know Him thus no longer* (2 Corinthians 5:16).

3. (17-18) John's reaction and Jesus' assurance.

And when I saw Him, I fell at His feet as dead. But He laid His right hand on me, saying to me, "Do not be afraid; I am the First and the Last. I *am* He who lives, and was dead, and behold, I am alive forevermore. Amen. And I have the keys of Hades and of Death."

> a. **When I saw Him, I fell at His feet as dead**: John was overwhelmed by this awesome vision, even though he was an apostle who knew Jesus on this earth. Even the three years John spent with Jesus on this earth did not really prepare him to see Jesus in His heavenly glory. At this moment, John knew what a miracle it was that Jesus could shield His glory and authority while He walked this earth.

> > i. "Blessed position! Does the death alarm you? We are never so much alive as when we are dead at his feet." (Spurgeon)

ii. "It matters not what aileth us if we lie at Jesus' feet. Better be dead there than alive anywhere else." (Spurgeon)

b. **He laid His right hand on me**: First, Jesus comforted John with a compassionate touch. Perhaps the *touch* of Jesus felt more familiar than the *appearance* of Jesus. Then Jesus gave John a command: **"Do not be afraid."** John didn't need to be **afraid** because He was in the presence of Jesus, and Jesus clearly identifies Himself to John with three titles.

i. Jesus is **the First and the Last**, the God of all eternity, Lord of eternity past and eternity future.

ii. Jesus is the one **who lives, and was dead, and** is **alive forevermore**. He has the credentials of resurrection, and lives to never die again. The victory that Jesus won over sin and death was a permanent victory. He didn't rise from the dead just to die again.

iii. Jesus is the one who has **the keys of Hades and of Death**. Some imagine that the devil is somehow the "lord of Hell." Some imagine that the devil has authority or power to determine life or death. Clearly, they are wrong, for only *Jesus* holds **the keys of Hades and of Death**. We can trust that Jesus never lets the devil borrow **the keys**.

4. (19-20) Another command to write and an explanation.

"Write the things which you have seen, and the things which are, and the things which will take place after this. The mystery of the seven stars which you saw in My right hand, and the seven golden lampstands: The seven stars are the angels of the seven churches, and the seven lampstands which you saw are the seven churches."

a. **Write the things**: This second command to write gives us a structure to understand the Book of Revelation. John is commanded to **write** regarding the past, present, and future (looking from John's perspective).

i. **The things which you have seen**: This means that Jesus wanted John to write the things he had just **seen** in his vision of the glorious, heavenly Jesus.

ii. **The things which are**: This means that Jesus wanted John to write about the things of his present day, the things regarding the *seven churches which are in Asia*.

iii. **The things which will take place after this**: This means that Jesus wanted John to write about the things that would happen after the things regarding the *seven churches*, the things of the last days.

b. The Book of Revelation is arranged in this three-part structure.

• **The things which you have seen**: Revelation chapter 1

- **The things which are**: Revelation chapters 2 and 3

- **The things which will take place after this**: Revelation 4 through 22

c. **The seven stars are the angels of the seven churches, and the seven lampstands which you saw are the seven churches**: Jesus kindly interprets His own images. The **stars** in His hand represent **the angels of the seven churches**. The **lampstands** represent the **seven churches** themselves.

> i. Why would each church have its own *angel*, and why does Jesus hold these **angels** in His hand? Some believe these **angels** are the pastors of these seven churches. This idea is based on a literal understanding of the ancient Greek word translated angel, *aggelos*. That word literally means "messenger," and certainly pastors are "messengers" to churches. Others think the **angels** might be "guardian angels" over each congregation. Some suggest that the **angels** are not literal beings at all, but they just represent the "prevailing spirit" of each church. There are strengths and weaknesses to any of these interpretations, but we do know that in some way, these **angels** are *representatives* of each congregation.

> ii. Adam Clarke believed the **angel** of each church was its pastor. "*Angel of the Church* here answers exactly to that officer of the synagogue among the Jews called . . . the messenger of the Church, whose business it was to *read, pray*, and *teach* in the synagogue." (Clarke)

> iii. It is more important to notice *where* the **angels** are: the **right hand** of Jesus. This is a place of safety and strength. Even the "problem churches" that will be described in the next chapters are in the **right hand** of Jesus.

d. This was a spectacular vision, and many people wish they could have a spectacular vision like John had, but we *can* know the very same Jesus John saw. We can know His purity, His eternal wisdom, His searching judgment, His victory, His authority and His majesty. Each of these aspects of His nature are ours to know intimately.

> i. When the think of John's spectacular vision, we should remember where John is: imprisoned on Patmos. Jesus is often known most intimately in the midst of suffering and trials. Both John and Stephen (Acts 7:54-60) saw Jesus most clearly and gloriously in the context of suffering for the cause of Jesus. "The wrath of the wicked does but bring saints the nearer to the choice favours of God." (Seiss)

Revelation 2 - Jesus' Letters to the Churches

The letters to the seven churches share a similar structure. They each feature:

- An address to a particular congregation
- An introduction of Jesus
- A statement regarding the condition of the church
- A verdict from Jesus regarding the condition of the church
- A command from Jesus to the church
- A general exhortation to all Christians
- A promise of reward

We can see the state of each of these seven churches - and the state of our own walk with Jesus - by looking at what Jesus has to say to each church in each section.

A. Jesus' letter to the church at Ephesus.

1. (1a) The character of the city of **Ephesus**.

"To the angel of the church of Ephesus write,"

a. **To the angel**: As discussed under Revelation 1:20, this **angel** may be the pastor of the church at Ephesus, or an angel looking in on the workings of the church at Ephesus. In some way, this **angel** represents this church; but the letter isn't written just to the representative, but to the whole church.

i. "I consider what is spoken to this angel as spoken to the whole Church; and that it is not *his* particular state that is described, but the states of the *people* in general under his care." (Clarke)

b. **Ephesus** was a famous city in the ancient world, with an equally famous church. Paul ministered in Ephesus for three years (Acts 19:1, Acts 10, Acts 20:31). Aquilla and Priscilla, with Apollos ministered there (Acts 18:24-28). Paul's close associate Timothy (1 Timothy 1:3) served in Ephesus.

According to strong and consistent historic tradition, the Apostle John also ministered there.

> i. "Surely it was a place of great privilege, of great preaching." (Robertson)

c. **Ephesus** was also world-famous as a religious, cultural, and economic center of the region. Ephesus had the notable temple of Diana, who was a fertility goddess worshipped with immoral sex. This tremendous temple to Diana in Ephesus was regarded as one of the seven wonders of the ancient world. It was supported by 127 pillars, each pillar 60 feet tall, and it was adorned with great sculptures.

> i. "The Temple of Artemis was also a major treasury and bank of the ancient world, where merchants, kings, and even cities made deposits, and where their money could be kept safe under the protection of deity." (Longenecker in his commentary on Acts)

> ii. "Ephesus was a stronghold of Satan. Here many evil things both superstitious and satanic were practised. Books containing formula for sorcery and other ungodly and forbidden arts were plentiful in that city." (Gaebelein in his commentary on Acts)

2. (1b) Jesus describes Himself to the church at Ephesus.

These things says He who holds the seven stars in His right hand, who walks in the midst of the seven golden lampstands:

a. **He who holds the seven stars in His right hand, who walks in the midst of the seven golden lampstands**: These images are taken from John's vision of Jesus in Revelation 1. They emphasize the authority of Jesus in the Church (He **holds the seven stars**) and His immediate presence in the Church (He **walks in the midst of the seven golden lampstands**). This introduction stresses that Jesus is central to the church, and should be recognized as central to the church.

b. **Holds** (the ancient Greek word *kratein*) is an emphatic and complete word. Jesus has these churches, and **holds** them securely. The churches belong to Jesus, not the leaders of the churches or to the people of the churches. He **holds** them.

3. (2-3) What Jesus knows about the Christians of Ephesus.

I know your works, your labor, your patience, and that you cannot bear those who are evil. And you have tested those who say they are apostles and are not, and have found them liars; and you have persevered and have patience, and have labored for My name's sake and have not become weary.

a. **I know your works**: Jesus looks at His church, and He knows what is going on. It is no mystery to Him. There may be sin or corruption hidden in a congregation, but it isn't hidden to Jesus. He would say the same thing to us today, both as individuals and as a congregation: **I know your works**.

i. "There are also working Christians who do not approach to laboring; yet a lifetime of such work as theirs would not exhaust a butterfly. Now, when a man works for Christ he should work with all his might." (Spurgeon)

b. **Your works, your labor, your patience**: Jesus knows what this church is doing *right*. They work hard for the Lord and they have godly endurance. **Patience** is the great ancient Greek word *hupomone*, which means "steadfast endurance." In this sense, the church was rock-solid.

c. **You cannot bear those who are evil**: The Ephesian church pursued doctrinal purity. Paul warned the Ephesians in Acts 20:29-31: *For I know this, that after my departure savage wolves will come in among you, not sparing the flock. Also from among yourselves men will rise up, speaking perverse things, to draw away the disciples after themselves. Therefore watch, and remember that for three years I did not cease to warn everyone night and day with tears.* From this commendation of Jesus, we know that the Ephesians took Paul's warning seriously.

i. The church today, like the Ephesian church then, must vigorously test those who claim to be messengers from God - especially **those who say they are apostles**, because deceivers will speak well of themselves. The greater the evil, the more deceptive its cloak.

ii. "This was grand of them: it showed a backbone of truth. I wish some of the churches of this age had a little of this holy decision about them; for nowadays, if a man be clever; he may preach the vilest lie that was ever vomited from the mouth of hell, and it will go down with some." (Spurgeon)

d. **You have persevered and have patience, and have labored for My name's sake and have not become weary**: Also, the Ephesian church *continued* doing these things, without becoming **weary**. They showed a godly perseverance that we should imitate. By all outward appearances, this was a solid church that worked hard, had great outreach, and protected the integrity of the gospel.

4. (4) What Jesus has *against* the church at Ephesus.

Nevertheless I have *this* against you, that you have left your first love.

a. **Nevertheless I have this against you**: Jesus begins with a sobering word - **nevertheless**, which means "despite all that." Jesus took into full account *all the good* in the Ephesian church, yet *despite all that,* He had something **against** them.

> i. **Nevertheless** means that all the *good* in the Ephesian church did not cancel out the *bad* Jesus is about to describe.

b. **You have left your first love**: Despite all the good in the Ephesian church, there is something seriously wrong. They **have left** - not *lost* - their **first love**. They once had a **love** that they don't have anymore. This can be described as "a definite and sad departure." (Robertson)

> i. The distinction between *leaving* and *losing* is important. Something can be lost quite by accident, but *leaving* is a deliberate act, though it may not happen suddenly. As well, when we *lose* something we don't know where to find it; but when we *leave* something, we know where to find it

> ii. Though they had **left** their **first love**, *everything looked great on the outside.* If you would have attended a service of the church at Ephesus, you might have thought, "This is a happening church. They are doing so much, and they really guard the truth." At the same time, you might have had a vague, uneasy feeling - yet it would probably be hard to pin down. It wasn't hard for Jesus to see the problem, even though everything probably looked wonderful on the outside.

> iii. The problem was serious. Without love, all is vain. No wonder Jesus said, "**Nevertheless I have this against you**." "A church has no reason for being a church when she has no love within her heart, or when that love grows cold. Lose love, lose all." (Spurgeon)

c. **Left your first love**: What **love** did they leave? As Christians, we are told to love God and to love one another. Did they leave their love for God? Did they leave their love for one another? Probably *both* are in mind, because the two loves go together. You can't say you love God and not love His family, and you can't really love His family without loving Him first.

> i. The Ephesian church was a *working* church. Sometimes a focus on *working* for Jesus will eclipse a love relationship with Him. We can put *what we do* for Jesus before *who we are* in Him. We can leave Jesus in the temple, just as the parents of Jesus did (Luke 2:45-46).

> ii. The Ephesian church was a *doctrinally pure* church. Sometimes a focus on *doctrinal purity* will make a congregation cold, suspicious, and intolerant of diversity. "When love dies orthodox doctrine becomes a corpse, a powerless formalism. Adhesion to the truth sours into bigotry when the sweetness and light of love to Jesus depart." (Spurgeon)

d. **First love**: There is a definite, sure difference in their relationship with Jesus. Things aren't as they used to be. It isn't that we expect that we should have the exact same excitement we had when everything was brand new in the Christian life, but the newness should transition into a depth that makes the **first love** even stronger.

> i. A couple that has been married for a long time doesn't always have the same thrill of excitement they had when they first dated. That is to be expected, and is fine - if that excitement has matured into a *depth* of love that makes it even *better* than the **first love**.

> ii. There is nothing *wrong* with that initial excitement, or wanting it to remain or be restored. "When we were in our first love, what would we do for Christ; now how little will we do. Some of the actions which we performed when we were young Christians, but just converted, when we look back upon them, seem to have been wild and like idle tales." (Spurgeon)

5. (5-6) What Jesus wants the church at Ephesus to do.

Remember therefore from where you have fallen; repent and do the first works, or else I will come to you quickly and remove your lampstand from its place; unless you repent. But this you have, that you hate the deeds of the Nicolaitans, which I also hate.

a. **Remember therefore from where you have fallen**: The first step in restoration for the Ephesian church is for them to **remember**. They need to **remember from where you have fallen**. This means remembering *where they used to be in their love for the Lord and for one another.*

> i. When the Prodigal Son was in the pigpen, the first step in restoration was remembering what life was like back in his father's home (Luke 16:17-19). This is always the first step in getting back to where we should be with the Lord.

b. **Repent**: This is *not* a command to feel sorry, or really to *feel* anything. It means to change your direction, to go a different way. It is an "urgent appeal for instant change of attitude and conduct, before it is too late." (Robertson)

c. **Do the first works**: This means that they must go back to the basics, to the very first things they did when you first fell in love with Jesus. These are the things that we never grow beyond.

> i. What are **the first works**?

> > • Remember how you used to spend time in His Word?

> > • Remember how you used to pray?

- Remember the joy in getting together with other Christians?

- Remember how excited you were about telling others about Jesus?

ii. We might say that Satan does a masterful job in creating a sense of general dissatisfaction with these **first works**. Christians will run after almost every new, strange method or program for growth and stability. Our shortened attention spans make us easily bored with the truest excitement. Sometimes we will do almost anything *except* **the first works**.

d. **Or else I will come to you quickly and remove your lampstand from its place**: Jesus gives them a stern warning. **Unless** they **repent**, He will remove *their light* and *His presence*. When their **lampstand** is removed, they may continue as an organization, but no longer as a true church of Jesus Christ. It will be the church of *Ichabod*, where the glory has departed (1 Samuel 4:21).

i. Apparently, at least in the short term, the Ephesians heeded this warning. In the early second century (not too long after John wrote), Ignatius praised the love and the doctrinal purity of the Ephesians. "You, who are of the most holy Church of the Ephesians, which is so famous and celebrated throughout the world . . . you, being full of the Holy Spirit, do nothing according to the flesh, but all things according to the Spirit. You are complete in Christ Jesus." (*Epistle of Ignatius to the Ephesians*, Chapter 8. From the *Ante Nicean Fathers Volume 1*, page 52)

ii. From what Ignatius wrote, it seems that the Ephesians returned to their *first love* without compromising doctrinal purity. That isn't always an easy balance to keep, but the Ephesians apparently kept it, at least for a time.

e. **But this you have, that you hate the deeds of the Nicolaitans, which I also hate**: Jesus - probably so the Ephesians would not be overly discouraged - gives this church another commendation here. They are complimented because they hated **the deeds of the Nicolaitans** - but who are the **Nicolaitans** and what were their **deeds**? The *doctrine of the Nicolaitans* is also condemned in Revelation 2:15, and in that passage it is related to immorality and idolatry.

i. Irenaeus (writing in the late second century) described what he knew of the Nicolaitans: "The Nicolaitanes are the followers of that Nicolas who was one of the seven first ordained to the diaconate by the apostles. They lead lives of unrestrained indulgence. The character of these men is plainly pointed out in the Apocalypse of John, as teaching that it is a matter of indifference to practice adultery, and to eat things sacrifice to idols." (*Against Heresies*, book 1, chapter 26. From the *Ante Nicean Fathers Volume 1*, page 352)

ii. Hippolytus, a student of Irenaeus (writing in the early third century) associated the Nicolaitans with the Gnostics: "There are, however, among the Gnostics diversities of opinion . . . But Nicolaus has been a cause of the wide-spread combination of these wicked men. [He] departed from correct doctrine, and was in the habit of inculcating indifferency of both life and food." (*Refutation of all Heresies*, book 7, chapter 24; ANF volume 5, page 115)

iii. Others have emphasized the root meanings of the words that make up the name **Nicolaitans**. *Nikao-laos* means literally "to conquer the people." Based on this, some point to presumptuous claims of apostolic authority and to the heart that sets up hierarchies and separates the "clergy" from the "laity." Perhaps the **Nicolaitans** fulfilled all these aspects, being both an idolatrous immorality and a presumptuous, hierarchical, "hidden mysteries" system typical of Gnosticism.

iv. The **Nicolaitans**, like all deceivers that come from the body of Christ, claimed "not that they were destroying Christianity, but that they were presenting an improved and modernized version of it." (Barclay)

f. **Which I also hate**: These are powerful words, in that they come from our Savior who is so rich in love. Whoever exactly the Nicolaitans were, and whatever exactly they did and taught, we learn something from Jesus' opinion of them. We learn that the God of love hates sin, and wants His people to also hate sin.

6. (7a) A general exhortation to all whom will hear.

He who has an ear, let him hear what the Spirit says to the churches.

a. **He who has an ear**: This qualifies everyone - or at least everyone who will *listen*. This letter was not only written to the church at Ephesus in the Apostle John's day. It is written to us, and to all Christians throughout the centuries.

b. **Let him hear what the Spirit says to the churches**: Each one of these seven letters apply to all churches. We must hear what the Spirit says **to the churches** - not just to *one church*. These letters - each of them - were meant to speak to *you*, if you will only have an **ear** to **hear what the Spirit says**.

i. "There were not seven books written, but one book in which these seven epistles were, out of which each church, or the church in it several periods, might learn what concerned it." (Poole)

ii. "The churches of the land are sprinkled all over with bald-headed old sinners whose hair has been worn off by the constant friction of countless sermons that have been aimed at them and glanced off and hit the man in the pew behind." (H.W. Beecher)

7. (7b) The promise of a reward.

"To him who overcomes I will give to eat from the tree of life, which is in the midst of the Paradise of God."

a. **To him who overcomes**: Jesus makes this promise **to him who overcomes** - but what does this overcomer overcome? We usually think of overcoming in dramatic terms of overcoming sin and in spiritual warfare, but here Jesus seems to speak of overcoming of the coldness of their hearts and lack of love marked by leaving their first love.

b. **I will give to eat from the tree of life**: The promise for these overcomers is a return to Eden, a restoration, and eternal life. This is meant first in the eternal sense of making it to heaven, which was no small promise to a church threatened with the removal of Jesus' presence. It is also meant in the sense of seeing the effects of the curse rolled back in our own lives though walking in Jesus' redeeming love.

c. **In the midst of the Paradise of God**: Originally, the word **Paradise** meant "a garden of delight." Eventually, it came to mean "the place where God lives." Where God is, that is **Paradise!**

B. Jesus' letter to the church at Smyrna.

1. (8a) The character of the city of **Smyrna**.

"And to the angel of the church in Smyrna write,"

a. **Smyrna** was a large, beautiful, and proud city. It was a center of learning and culture, and was proud of its standing as a city. "Smyrna was an outstandingly beautiful city. It claimed to be the 'Glory of Asia.' " (Barclay)

b. **Smyrna** was a *rich* city. "Smyrna was a great trade city . . . Smyrna stood at the end of the road which served the valley of the river Hermus, and all the trade of that valley flowed into its markets and found an outlet through its harbor. It had a specially rich trade in wines. Smyrna, like Ephesus, was a city of wealth and commercial greatness." (Barclay)

c. We also know from history that it was a city deeply committed to idolatry and the worship of the Roman Emperor. On one famous street in Smyrna, called the "Golden Street," stood magnificent temples to Cybele, Apollo, Asklepios, Aphrodite, and a great temple to Zeus - but the worship of those pagan gods was dying out. The real focus was on the worship of the Roman Emperor.

i. In 196 B.C. **Smyrna** built the first temple to *Dea Roma* - the goddess of Rome, the spiritual symbol of the Roman Empire. Once the "spirit" of Rome was worshipped, it wasn't much of a step to worship the dead Emperors of Rome. Then it was only another small step to worship the living Emperors, and then to demand such worship as a evidence of political allegiance and civic pride.

ii. In 23 A.D. Smyrna won the privilege (over 11 other cities) to build the first temple to worship the Emperor Tiberius Caesar. Smyrna was a leading city in the Roman cult of Emperor worship.

iii. The Roman Emperor Domitian (81-96 A.D.) was the first to *demand* worship under the title "Lord" from the people of the Roman Empire as a test of political loyalty. According to ancient church history, it was under the reign of Domitian that John was banished to the Island of Patmos where he received this vision.

iv. "Emperor worship had begin as spontaneous demonstration of gratitude to Rome; but toward the end of the first century, in the days of Domitian, the final step was taken and *Caesar worship became compulsory*. Once a year the Roman citizen must burn a pinch of incense on the altar to the godhead of Caesar; and having done so, he was given a certificate to guarantee that he had performed his religious duty." (Barclay)

v. "All that the Christians had to do was to burn that pinch of incense, say, 'Caesar is Lord,' receive their certificate, and go away and worship as they pleased. But that is precisely what the Christians would not do. They would give no man the name of Lord; that name they would keep for Jesus Christ and Jesus Christ alone. They would not even formally conform." (Barclay)

2. (8b) Jesus describes Himself to the church at Smyrna.

These things says the First and the Last, who was dead, and came to life:

a. **The First and the Last**: Jesus chose this title from His initial appearance to John (Revelation 1:11, 1:17) to speak of His eternal character. **The First and the Last** are titles that belong only to the LORD, Yahweh, according to Isaiah 41:4, 44:6, and 48:12.

b. **Who was dead, and came to life**: Jesus chose this title from His initial appearance to John (Revelation 1:18) to remind the Christians in Smyrna that they serve the risen Lord, victorious over death. Death could not hold Jesus, and it cannot hold His people.

i. The association with death - and the victory of resurrection - is throughout this letter. The name *Smyrna* comes from the word *myrrh*, a sweet-smelling perfume used in embalming dead bodies.

3. (9) What Jesus knows about the Christians in Smyrna.

"I know your works, tribulation, and poverty (but you are rich); and *I know* the blasphemy of those who say they are Jews and are not, but *are* a synagogue of Satan."

a. **I know your works**: Jesus knew the works of the church in Ephesus also (Revelation 2:2). In Smyrna, Jesus also knew their **works, tribulation, and poverty**. He knows these hardships both in the sense that He saw what happened to them, and in the sense that He knew their hardships by His personal experience.

i. **Poverty**: According to history, Smyrna was a prosperous city. Yet the Christians there were poor. "The word used for 'poverty' is the word for abject poverty. They were not just poor." (Walvoord)

ii. The Christians of Smyrna knew **poverty** because they were robbed and fired from jobs in persecution for the gospel. Early Christians *joyfully accepted the plundering of your goods, knowing that you have an enduring possession for yourselves in heaven* (Hebrews 10:34). This kind of economic persecution was one important reason why Christians were poor in Smyrna. Even today, this is a common form of persecution against Christians.

b. **I know the blasphemy**: Jesus knew the abuse these Christians endured at the hands of "religious" men, **those who say they are Jews and are not.**

i. Historically, we are told there was a large and hostile community of Jews in Smyrna, but this tells us that a *true* Jew is one who trusts God and believes in Jesus Christ (Philippians 3:3). Others may be Jews ethnically - which still has its place before God - but they are not Jews spiritually before God.

c. **I know . . . I know**: In midst of this kind of affliction, it is easy to think God has forgotten - but Jesus knows.

4. (9) What Jesus thinks about the church in Smyrna.

But you are rich.

a. **Rich**: Every outward circumstance said that the Christians in Smyrna were poor, even destitute, but Jesus saw through the circumstances to see that they were really **rich**. "Sweet smelling Smyrna, the poorest but purest of the seven." (Trapp)

b. **Rich** is what Jesus thought of them, and if Jesus considered them **rich**, then they were **rich**. Our estimation of ourselves is far less important than God's estimation of us.

> i. In contrast, the Christians at Laodicea thought they were rich, but they were really poor (Revelation 3:17). Laodicea was a poor rich church. Smyrna was a rich poor church. Better to be a rich poor church than a poor rich church.

c. **And poverty (but you are rich)**: The contrast between material poverty and spiritual riches of the Christians in Smyrna reminds us that there is nothing inherently spiritual in being rich. Nevertheless, there is also nothing inherently spiritual in poverty.

> i. Material riches are an obstacle to the Kingdom of God, an obstacle that some do not overcome (Mark 10:23-25). There is nothing wrong with having money; the trouble is that money so easily "has" us.

> ii. Often, material riches are acquired and maintained at the *expense* of true spiritual riches. In the glory days of the Renaissance Papacy, a man walked with the Pope and marveled at the splendors and riches of the Vatican. The Pope told him, "We no longer have to say what Peter told the lame man: '*Silver and gold have I none.*' " His companion replied, "But neither can you say, '*rise up and walk.*' "

d. The church at Smyrna was also **rich** in leadership. One of the pastors of that church was named Polycarp. He was one of the Apostle John's disciples and served at Smyrna until 155 A.D. when he died heroically as a martyr.

5. (10) What Jesus wants the Christians in Smyrna to do.

"Do not fear any of those things which you are about to suffer. Indeed, the devil is about to throw *some* of you into prison, that you may be tested, and you will have tribulation ten days. Be faithful until death, and I will give you the crown of life."

a. **Do not fear**: Literally, this is better translated "stop being afraid." The Christians in Smyrna suffered under persecution, and they were afraid. Sometimes we think that Christians who endure persecution are almost super-human, and we sometimes don't appreciate the depths of **fear** they struggle with. There were **things which** they were **about to suffer**, and Jesus wanted them ready to stand against **those things**.

b. **The devil is about to throw some of you into prison**: Here, Jesus describes the nature of the persecution that would come against the Christians in Smyrna. Apparently, they would be imprisoned, and for a specific period of time (**you will have tribulation ten days**).

i. According to Jesus, the persecution about to come against the Christians of Smyrna was from **the devil**. At the same time it was measured and limited by God. Surely, **the devil** wanted to imprison them for a longer time, but God limited the **tribulation** to **ten days**.

ii. Being thrown **into prison** was severe persecution. In that day, **prison** was never used to rehabilitate someone, and rarely used to punish someone. Normally, you were thrown **into prison** as you awaited trial and execution.

iii. "For a man to become a Christian anywhere was to become an outlaw. In Smyrna above all places, for a man to enter the Christian Church was literally to take his life in his hands. In Smyrna the church was a place for heroes." (Barclay)

iv. "This 'tribulation' does not mean the common trials to which all flesh is heir. Some dear souls think they are bearing their cross every time they have a headache. The tribulation mentioned here is trouble they would not have had if they had not been Christians." (Havner)

c. **You will have tribulation ten days**: Commentators on the Book of Revelation have long debated the meaning of these **ten days**.

i. Some think that John really means **ten** *years* of persecution. "As the *days* in this book are what is commonly called *prophetic days*, each answering to a *year*, the *ten years* of tribulation may denote *ten years of persecution*; and this was precisely the duration of the persecution under *Diocletian*, during which all the Asiatic Churches were grievously afflicted." (Clarke)

ii. Others think that John really means persecution over the reign of **ten** *Roman Emperors*. "The *first* under Nero, A.D. 54; the *second* under Domitian, A.D. 81; the *third* under Trajan, A.D. 98; the *fourth* under Adrian [Hadrian], A.D. 117; the *fifth* under Septimus Severus, A.D. 193; the *sixth* under Maximin, A.D. 235; the *seventh* under Decius, A.D. 249; the *eighth* under Valerian, A.D. 254; the *ninth* under Aurelian, A.D. 270; the *tenth* under Diocletian, A.D. 284." (White, cited in Walvoord)

iii. Still others take strange and confusing approaches: "Others observe, that in ten days are two hundred and forty hours, which make up the number of years from 85, when the second persecution began, (under which John at this time was) to 325, when all the persecutions ceased." (Poole)

iv. Others say that **ten days** is simply an expression of speech: "The expression *ten days* is not to be taken literally; it is the normal Greek expression for a short time." (Barclay)

v. However, there is no compelling reason to believe it means anything other than **ten days** of severe persecution, with an emphasis on the idea that it is a limited time.

d. **That you may be tested**: If this attack came from **the devil**, then why couldn't these Christians in Smyrna just rebuke Satan, and stop the attack? Because God had a purpose in their suffering, and so He allowed it. God uses suffering to purify (1 Peter 1:6-7), to make us like Jesus (Romans 8:17), and to makes us truly witnesses of Him. In all ages, the blood of the martyrs has been seed for the church.

i. "The saints at Smyrna had not been given a pep-talk on 'How to Win Friends and Influence People.' They had no testimony on 'How Faith Made Me Mayor of Smyrna.' They were not promised deliverance from tribulation, poverty and reviling. In fact, the worst was yet to come." (Havner)

ii. Most specifically in this case, God allowed this attack so that they **may be tested**, in the sense of being *proven*. Through their suffering, God displayed the true riches of the church in Smyrna to everyone, including themselves - even though *He* knew they were rich already.

iii. The Christians in Smyrna would **be tested**, but they passed the test. This church, compared to the other six, has no evil spoken against it. Only this church among the seven survives today, and it has survived through centuries of Roman and Muslim persecution.

iv. **That you may be tested**: God is interested in testing us also. We may not have the same opportunity to suffer for Jesus that the Christians in Smyrna had, but we can have their same heart. We may never be in a place to die a martyr's death, but we can all live a martyr's life. But many Christians avoid persecution of any kind by conforming so much to the world that they are no longer *distinctively* Christians. This wasn't the case with the Christians in Smyrna. They were **tested** and they passed the test.

e. **Be faithful until death, and I will give you the crown of life**: What Jesus says to this church is important, but what He *doesn't say* is also important. Jesus didn't have a single word of rebuke or correction for the Christians in Smyrna. All He has is the promise of a **crown** - and the encouragement to **be faithful until death**, which is literally "become faithful until death." (Walvoord)

i. There are two different words for **crown** in the ancient Greek language. One described the kind of crown a *king* would wear, a crown of royalty. The other kind of **crown** - the *stephanos*, used here - is given as a trophy to a winning athlete. Jesus looks at the Christians of

Smyrna, and says to them: "You are My winners. You deserve a trophy."

ii. The *stephanos* was also the crown worn at marriages and special celebrations. The picture is of Jesus and His bride, each wearing their crowns.

iii. The promise of a **crown** would be especially meaningful for the Christians of Smyrna.

- The city of Smyrna had a "crown" of beautiful buildings at the top of Mt. Pagos
- In Smyrna, worshippers of pagan gods wore crowns
- In that culture, good citizens and winning athletes received crowns

iv. Jesus promises a special **crown** - the **crown of life**. A champion athlete received a crown of leaves, which would soon get brown and die. But Jesus' champions receive **the crown of life**.

v. "A crown without cares, corivals, envy, end. Kings' crowns are so weighty with cares, that oft they make their heads ache. Not so with this crown; the joys whereof are without measure or mixture." (Trapp)

6. (11a) A general exhortation to all whom will hear.

He who has an ear, let him hear what the Spirit says to the churches.

a. **He who has an ear**: Though **the Spirit** has something to say to us through every one of **the churches**, this letter to the Christians in Smyrna may apply least of all to modern, western Christians. To this point, we simply don't face the kind of persecution the Christians in Smyrna experienced. Polycarp was a remarkable example of both the persecution and the courage of early Christians.

i. The year after Polycarp returned from Rome, a great persecution came upon the Christians of Smyrna. His congregation urged him to leave the city until the threat blew over. So, believing that God wanted him to be around a few more years, Polycarp left the city and hid out on a farm belonging to some Christian friends. One day on the farm, as he prayed in his room, Polycarp had a vision of his pillow engulfed in flames. He knew what God said to him, and calmly told his companions, "I see that I must be burnt at the stake."

ii. Meanwhile, the chief of police issued a warrant for his arrest. They seized one of Polycarp's servants and tortured him until he told them where his master was. Towards evening, the police chief and a band of soldiers came to the old farmhouse. When the soldiers found him, they were embarrassed to see that they had come to arrest such an old, frail man. They reluctantly put him on a donkey and walked him back to the city of Smyrna.

iii. On the way to the city, the police chief and other government officials tried to persuade Polycarp to offer a pinch of incense before a statue of Caesar and simply say "Caesar is Lord." That's all he had to do, and he would be off the hook. They pleaded with him to do it, and escape the dreadful penalties. At first Polycarp was silent, but then he calmly gave them his firm answer: no. The police chief was now angry. Annoyed with the old man, he pushed him out of his carriage and onto the hard ground. Polycarp, bruised but resolute, got up and walked the rest of the way to the arena.

iv. The horrid games at the arena had already begun in earnest and a large, bloodthirsty mob gathered to see Christians tortured and killed. One Christian named Quintis boldly proclaimed himself a follower of Jesus and said he was willing to be martyred, but when he saw the vicious animals in the arena, he lost courage and agreed to burn the pinch of incense to Caesar as Lord. Another young man named Germanicus didn't back down. He marched out and faced the lions and died an agonizing death for his Lord Jesus. Ten other Christians gave their lives that day, but the mob was unsatisfied. They cried out, "Away with the atheists who do not worship our gods!" To them, Christians were atheists because they did not recognize the traditional gods of Rome and Greece. Finally, the crowd started chanting "Bring out Polycarp."

v. When Polycarp brought his tired body into the arena, he and the other Christians heard a voice from heaven. It said, "Be strong, Polycarp, play the man." As he stood before the proconsul, they tried one more time to get him to renounce Jesus. The proconsul told Polycarp to agree with the crowd and shout out "Away with the atheists!" Polycarp looked sternly at the bloodthirsty mob, waved his hand towards them and said, "Away with those atheists!" The proconsul persisted. "Take the oath and revile Christ and I'll set you free!" Polycarp answered, "For eighty-six years I've served Jesus; how dare I now revile my King?" The proconsul finally gave up, and announced to the crowd the crime of the accused: "Polycarp has confessed that he is a Christian."

vi. The crowd shouted, "Let the lions loose!" but the animals had already been put away. The crowd then demanded that Polycarp be burnt. The old man remembered the dream about the burning pillow, and took courage in God. He said to his executioners, "It is well. I fear not the fire that burns for a season and after a while is quenched. Why do you delay? Come, do your will."

vii. They arranged a great pile of wood and set up a pole in the middle. As they tied Polycarp to the pole, he prayed: "I thank You that You have graciously thought me worthy of this day and of this hour, that I may receive a portion in the number of the martyrs, in the cup of Your Christ." After he prayed and gave thanks to God, they set the wood ablaze. A great wall of flame shot up to the sky, but it never touched Polycarp. God set a hedge of protection between him and the fire. Seeing that he would not burn, the executioner, in a furious rage, stabbed the old man with a long spear. Immediately, streams of blood gushed from his body and seemed to extinguish the fire. When this happened, witnesses said they saw a dove fly up from the smoke into heaven. At the very same moment, a church leader in Rome named Iraenus, said he heard God say to him, "Polycarp is dead." God called his servant home.

b. Nevertheless, the day of martyrs is definitely not past. All over the world, Christians face persecution, especially in Asia, Eastern Europe, and in the Muslim world. Some people estimate that more Christians have suffered and died for their faith in the 20th Century than in all previous centuries combined.

i. A May 1994 news item illustrates this: THE GRUESOME MARTYRDOM of a pastor in central India led to several hundred conversions to Christianity. A former Hindu who had changed his name to Paul James was murdered by a crowd of extremists as he spoke in a field prior to a Feb. 20 church service in the Phulabani district.

"Jesus, forgive them," eyewitnesses said James called out as his assailants cut off his hands and legs, and severed his torso. The attackers also decapitated James, an outspoken believer who had planted 27 churches. The murder has drawn heavy media attention in the area, which is charged with Hindu-Muslim tensions. Some, but not all, of James' assailants reportedly have been caught.

The attackers' hatred and violence have left many Indians wanting to emulate the love shown by the victim, said K. Anand Paul, head of Gospel to the Unreached Millions. "The gospel is spreading because of persecution," said Paul, who has been beaten seven times and kidnapped once by fanatical religious groups. "We are risking our lives to do this. People need to pray for us." (*National and International Religion Report*, May 2, 1994)

7. (11b) The promise of a reward.

He who overcomes shall not be hurt by the second death.

a. **He who overcomes**: This is a promise for *overcomers*. This promises is for those who overcome the threat of persecution, and the presence of persecution.

i. We might say that we overcome by our close association with Jesus, who is the ultimate overcomer. As Jesus said, *In the world you will have tribulation; but be of good cheer, I have overcome the world* (John 16:33).

b. **Shall not be hurt by the second death**: Those who overcome in Jesus will never **be hurt by the second death**. The **second death** is hell, the lake of fire (Revelation 20:14 and 21:8). Though Satan threatened and attacked their life, Jesus promises His overcomers that death is conquered for them.

i. "The *second death* was a Jewish rabbinic expression for the *total extinction of the utterly wicked*." (Barclay)

ii. "All men died, but all are not killed with death . . . Oh, it is a woeful thing to be killed with death." (Trapp)

C. Jesus' letter to the church at Pergamos.

1. (12a) The character of the city of **Pergamos**.

And to the angel of the church in Pergamos write,

a. **Pergamos** was the political capital of the Roman Province of Asia the Less. When John wrote, Pergamos had been the capital city of the region for more than three hundred years. The city was a noted center for culture and education, having one of the great libraries of the ancient world, with more than 200,000 volumes.

b. **Pergamos** was also an extremely religious city. It had temples to the Greek and Roman gods Dionysus, Athena, Demeter, and Zeus. It also had three temples dedicated to the worship of the Roman Emperor.

i. Some 50 years before Smyrna won the honor of building the first temple to Tiberius, the city of Pergamos won the right to build the first temple to worship Caesar Augustus in the province of Asia.

c. **Pergamos** was especially known as a center for the worship of the deity known as Asclepios. Represented by a serpent, Asclepios was the god of healing and knowledge. There was a medical school at his temple in Pergamos. Because of the famous temple to the Roman god of healing, sick and diseased people from all over the Roman Empire flocked to Pergamos for relief.

i. "Sufferers were allowed to spend the night in the darkness of the temple. In the temple there were tame snakes. In the night the sufferer might be touched by one of these tame and harmless snakes as it glided over the ground on which he lay. The touch of the snake was held to be the touch of the god himself, and the touch was held to bring health and healing." (Barclay)

2. (12b) Jesus describes Himself to the church at Pergamos.

These things says He who has the sharp two-edged sword:

a. **He who has the sharp two-edged sword**: In Revelation 1:16, John observed of Jesus *out of His mouth went a sharp two-edged sword*. Now, Jesus "shows" this **two-edged sword** to the Christians in Pergamos.

i. The description of the sword in Revelation 1:18 helps us to associate it with the *mouth* of Jesus. Jesus will confront this church with His word, and they will feel the **sharp** edges.

b. **Sharp two-edged sword**: This reminds us of the passage in Hebrews 4:12: *For the word of God is living and powerful, and sharper than any two-edged sword, piercing even to the division of soul and spirit, and of joints and marrow, and is a discerner of the thoughts and intents of the heart.* Jesus will use this **sharp two-edged sword** to make some separation among the Christians in Pergamos.

3. (13) What Jesus knows about the church at Pergamos.

"I know your works, and where you dwell, where Satan's throne *is*. And you hold fast to My name, and did not deny My faith even in the days in which Antipas *was* My faithful martyr, who was killed among you, where Satan dwells.

a. **I know your works**: Jesus says this to each church. It is true of each one of us. He knows our **works**, even if there isn't much to know.

b. **And where you dwell, where Satan's throne is**: What does it mean that they lived **where Satan's throne is**? In many ways, Pergamos was a stronghold of Satanic power.

i. What made it such a stronghold? There are many different opinions. Some believe it is because Pergamos was a center of pagan religion, especially of *"Asclepios Soter"* or *"Asclepios Savior."* Some believe it was because Pergamos had a huge throne-like altar dedicated to the Roman god Zeus. Some believe it was because Pergamos was a center for the ancient Babylonian priesthood, but this is tough to prove conclusively. Others believe it was because Pergamos was the political center of the worship-demanding Roman government.

c. **And you hold fast to My name**: Despite the fact they live in such a difficult city, the Christians of Pergamos hold fast to their faith in Jesus (**hold fast to My name . . . did not deny My faith**).

> i. **Did not deny My faith**: Jesus praises the Christians of Pergamos because they did not deny *His* faith. It is always important to make sure that the faith we hold on to is the faith that belongs to Jesus.

d. **Antipas was My faithful martyr, who was killed among you**: One specific man among the Christians of Pergamos received a precious title (**faithful martyr**). This same title is held by Jesus also (Revelation 1:5). **Antipas** was a man who followed Jesus, who was like Jesus.

> i. **Antipas** is one of the great anonymous heroes of the Bible. History tells us nothing about him except for here. "It is much no ecclesiastical history makes mention of this martyr Antipas, which argues him to have been a person but of obscure note in the world; but Christ seeth and taketh notice of those little ones who belong to him, though the world overlooks them." (Poole)

> ii. **Antipas** lived **where Satan's throne** was. Yet he stood against the attacks and the evil around him. He fulfilled the meaning of his name, because **Antipas** means "Against All."

> iii. **Martyr** is the ancient Greek word *martus*. "*Martus* is a most interesting and suggestive word. In classical Greek *martus* never means a *martyr* in our sense of the term. It always means a *witness*. A *martus* was one who said: 'This is true, and I know it.' It is not until New Testament times that *martus* ever means *martyr*." (Barclay)

4. (14-15) What Jesus has *against* the Christians in Pergamos.

But I have a few things against you, because you have there those who hold the doctrine of Balaam, who taught Balak to put a stumbling block before the children of Israel, to eat things sacrificed to idols, and to commit sexual immorality. Thus you also have those who hold the doctrine of the Nicolaitans, which thing I hate.

a. **I have a few things against you**: The Christians in Pergamos were rightly praised for holding fast to the name of Jesus and keeping his faith. At the same time, their difficult environment did not excuse the **few things** Jesus had **against** them.

b. **You have there those who hold the doctrine of Balaam**: What is the **doctrine of Balaam**? Balaam was a prototype of all corrupt teachers. According to Numbers 22-24 and 31, Balaam combined the sins of immorality and idolatry to please Balak, the king of Moab, because he could not curse Israel directly.

i. When Balaam counseled Balak, he **taught Balak to put a stumbling block before the children of Israel**. The **stumbling block** was connected with idolatry (**to eat things sacrificed to idols**) and **sexual immorality**. If the church in Pergamos has those who **hold the doctrine of Balaam**, it shows they have tendencies towards both idolatry and immorality.

ii. Sexual immorality marked the whole culture of the ancient Roman Empire. It was simply taken for granted, and the person who lived by Biblical standards of purity was considered strange. To paraphrase the Roman statesman Cicero, cited in Barclay: "If there is anyone who thinks that young men should not be allowed the love of many women, he is extremely severe. I am not able to deny the principle he stands on. But he contradicts, not only with the freedom our age allows, but also with the customs and allowances of our ancestors. When indeed was this not done? When did anyone find fault with it? When was such permission denied? When was it that what is now allowed was not allowed?" To keep from **sexual immorality** in that culture, you really had to swim against the current.

c. **You also have those who hold the doctrine of the Nicolaitans**: In Revelation 2:6, Jesus praised the Ephesian Christians because they hated *the deeds of the Nicolaitans*. But the **Nicolaitans** also have their **doctrine**, and some among the Christians held **the doctrine of the Nicolaitans**.

i. What is the **doctrine of the Nicolaitans**? The title *Nico-laitans* has the idea of a proud authority and a hierarchical separatism. The name *Nikao-laos* literally means "to conquer the people." According to ancient commentators, the **Nicolaitans** also approved of immorality.

d. **You have those there . . . you also have those**: The rebuke is not only against those who **hold the doctrines of Balaam** and **those who hold the doctrine of the Nicolaitans**. The rebuke is also against those who allow them to continue (**you have there those . . . you have those**).

i. The Christians of Pergamos were like the Christians of Corinth as Paul wrote to them in 1 Corinthians 5:1-9. They were too tolerant and accepting of false doctrines and immoral living, and Jesus had to rebuke them. Satan couldn't accomplish much by persecution, because many did *hold fast*, like Antipas. So Satan tried to accomplish his goals by using deception. The strategy was first *violence*, then *alliance*.

ii. A difficult environment never justifies compromise. It is easy for a church in such difficulty to justify this compromise in the name of "we need all the help we can get" - but no church needs that kind of help.

5. (16) What Jesus wants the church at Pergamos to do.

Repent, or else I will come to you quickly and will fight against them with the sword of My mouth.

a. **Repent**: The simple word **repent** stands out. Five of the seven churches are commanded to repent. **Repent** is a command that applies to Christians, not only to those who first come to Jesus.

b. **Or else I will come to you quickly and will fight against them with the sword of My mouth**: Unless they do **repent**, the Christians of Pergamos will face the Jesus who has the two-edged sword. Judgment will begin at the house of God (1 Peter 4:17).

   i. **The sword of My mouth**: When Jesus comes **against** the Christians of Pergamos, He will confront them with His Word.

6. (17a) A general exhortation to all whom will hear.

He who has an ear, let him hear what the Spirit says to the churches.

a. **He who has an ear**: The danger of false teaching and immoral conduct still faces the church today. So does the danger of *allowing* false teaching and immorality, as was the problem with the Christians in Pergamos.

7. (17b) The promise of a reward.

To him who overcomes I will give some of the hidden manna to eat. And I will give him a white stone, and on the stone a new name written which no one knows except him who receives *it*.

a. **To him who overcomes**: The one who overcomes this spirit of accommodation to false teaching and living will receive **hidden manna**. This is God's perfect provision, the true bread from heaven (John 6:41).

b. **And I will give him a white stone**: In the ancient world, the use of **a white stone** had many associations. A **white stone** could be a ticket to a banquet, a sign of friendship, evidence of having been counted, or as a sign of acquittal in a court of law. Jesus may have any one of these meanings in mind, but at the very least we know that it has the assurance of blessing.

   i. Adam Clarke writes: "Others suppose there is an allusion here to conquerors in the public games, who were not only conducted with great pomp into the city to which they belonged, but had a *white stone* given to them, with *their name inscribed on it*; which badge entitled them, during their whole life, to be maintained at the pubic expense . . . These were called *tesserae* among the Romans, and of these there were several kinds." Clarke then gives examples of the different kinds: "*Tesserae conviviales*, which answered exactly to our *cards of invitation*, or tickets of admission to a public feast or banquet; when the person invited produced his *tessera* he was admitted . . . But the most remarkable of these instruments were the *Tesserae hospitales*, which were given as badges of *friendship* and *alliance*, and on which some device was engraved, as a testimony that a contract of friendship had been made between the parties."

c. **And on the stone a new name written which no one knows except him who receives it:** What is the meaning of this **new**, secret **name** promised to **him who overcomes**? Is it God's name, or is it the believer's name? This is probably the believer's new name, and the name itself is probably more important than the stone itself.

> i. One idea behind this new, secret name is that it shows what an intimate relationship we have with God. When a couple is close, they often have "pet names" for each other. This is the same idea.

> ii. Another idea associated with the new name is simply the assurance it gives of our heavenly destination. Your name is there, waiting for you. It is as if your "reservation" in heaven is made.

D. Jesus' letter to the church at Thyatira.

1. (18a) The character of the city of **Thyatira**.

And to the angel of the church in Thyatira write,

a. **Thyatira** was the smallest and least important of the seven cities Jesus addresses in Revelation 2 and 3. In history, we have no record that the Christians of **Thyatira** suffered any significant political or religious persecution.

> i. "The elder Pliny dismisses Thyatira in the almost contemptuous phrase 'Thyatira and other unimportant cities.' " (Barclay)

b. Still, **Thyatira** was an important center of *business* and *trade*. It had many active trade guilds, each having their own patron deity from the Greek and Roman pantheon of gods.

> i. Acts 16:14-15 mentions Lydia of Thyatira, who was a *seller of purple* cloth from the city of Thyatira. "Thyatira was famous for the manufacture of a purple dye, and numerous references are found in secular literature of the period to the trade guilds which manufactured cloth." (Walvoord)

> ii. "From the inscriptions which have been found in the neighborhood it is clear that Thyatira possessed more trade guilds than any other town of its size in Asia." (Barclay)

2. (18b) Jesus describes Himself to the church at Thyatira.

These things says the Son of God, who has eyes like a flame of fire, and His feet like fine brass:

> a. **These things says the Son of God**: Jesus first describes Himself with a title that emphasizes His *deity*. In Jewish thought, to be the *son of* a thing meant you had the nature of that thing. The *sons of the sorceress* (Isaiah 57:3) had the nature of the sorceress. The *sons of thunder* (Mark 3:17) had a nature like thunder. So the **Son of God** has the divine nature, the nature of **God**.

> b. **Who has eyes like a flame of fire**: Jesus chooses this description of Himself from the presentation in Revelation 1:14 to emphasize the idea that His **eyes** look with penetrating judgment.

> c. **His feet like fine brass**: Jesus chose this description of Himself from Revelation 1:15 to emphasize His *purity* because **brass** is pure and highly refined in the fire. It also emphasizes His *steadfastness*, because **brass** was the strongest known metal in the ancient world, and **feet like fine brass** would be strong and unmovable.

3. (19) What Jesus knows about the Christians in Thyatira.

I know your works, love, service, faith, and your patience; and *as* for your works, the last *are* more than the first.

> a. **I know your works**: Thyatira was the least significant city among the seven cities Jesus addressed, yet they were not hidden to Jesus. Like each one of the churches, Jesus said to the church at Thyatira "**I know your works.**"

> b. **Love, service, faith, and your patience**: In many ways, the church at Thyatira was a model church. They had four great essential qualities. They had **love**, both for the Lord and for one another. They knew **service**, and had **faith** and **patience** worth mentioning.

> c. **As for your works, the last are more than the first**: This is another compliment to the church at Thyatira. Not only do they *have* these **works**, but they have them in *increasing measure* - they are *growing* in **love, service, faith**, and **patience**.

4. (20-21) What Jesus has *against* the church at Thyatira.

Nevertheless I have a few things against you, because you allow that woman Jezebel, who calls herself a prophetess, to teach and seduce My servants to commit sexual immorality and eat things sacrificed to idols. And I gave her time to repent of her sexual immorality, and she did not repent.

a. **Nevertheless**: Despite all the good Jesus sees in the church at Thyatira, there are significant problems. The problems are big enough for Jesus to say **nevertheless**, which means "despite all the good, **I have a few things against you.**"

b. **Because you allow that woman Jezebel**: The center of the corruption at the church at Thyatira is a woman Jesus calls **Jezebel**. This may not have been her literal name, but a "title" that clearly represents a self-styled **prophetess** within the church, after the pattern of Jezebel in the Old Testament (1 Kings 16-21 and 2 Kings 9:30-37).

> i. The name **Jezebel** had a powerful association. If we call someone a Judas or a Hitler it means something strong. It's also a strong thing to call this woman **Jezebel**. "She was one of the most evil characters of the Old Testament, who attempted to combine the worship of Israel with the worship of the idol Baal . . . Jezebel herself had a most unenviable record of evil." (Walvoord)

> ii. Some ancient Greek manuscripts state the phrase **that woman Jezebel** as *your woman Jezebel* or *your wife Jezebel*. Based on this, some (like Dean Alford) think that **Jezebel** was the pastor's wife, or that Jesus meant **Jezebel** was the pastor's "woman" in a symbolic sense.

c. **Who calls herself a prophetess**: This "**Jezebel**" at the church of Thyatira wasn't really a **prophetess**, she only claimed to be one. Yet, it seems the Christians there *received* her as a **prophetess**, and that is why Jesus gave them this warning.

> i. Jesus said this would happen in Matthew 24:11: *Then many false prophets will rise up and deceive many.* Those words were first spoken with a view to the end times, but there have always been those who call themselves prophets in the church, but are not.

d. **To teach and seduce My servants to commit sexual immorality and eat things sacrificed to idols**: Here, Jesus describes the specific *sin* of this woman "Jezebel." Mainly, she was an *immoral* and *ungodly* influence on others, and led others into sin. Jezebel led others into immorality and idolatry.

> i. Because of the strong trade guilds in Thyatira, the **sexual immorality** and the eating of **things sacrificed to idols** was probably connected with the mandatory social occasions of the guilds. Perhaps a Christian was invited to the monthly meeting of the goldsmith's guild, and the meeting was held at the temple of Apollo. "Jezebel" would allow or encourage the man to go - perhaps even using a "prophetic" word - and when the man went, he fell into immorality and idolatry.

ii. The draw to the guilds and their meetings was powerful. "No merchant or trader could hope to prosper or make money unless he was a member of his trade guild." (Barclay) Nonetheless, Christians were expected to stand in the face of this kind of pressure. One ancient Christian named Tertullian wrote about Christians who made their living in trades connected to pagan idolatry. A painter might find work in pagan temples or a sculptor might be hired to make a statue of a pagan god. They would justify this by saying, "This is my living, and I must live." Tertullian replied, *Vivere ergo habes?* "Must you live?"

iii. **My servants**: This shows how terrible Jezebel's sin was. She corrupted the **servants** of Jesus, and they belong to Him. Jesus said, *But whoever causes one of these little ones who believe in Me to stumble, it would be better for him if a millstone were hung around his neck, and he were thrown into the sea* (Mark 9:42).

e. Later in this letter, Jesus will also reveal a link to the work of Jezebel and false doctrine: *this doctrine . . . the depths of Satan, as they say* (Revelation 2:24). It seems that this Jezebel led others in the church at Thyatira to discover *depths of Satan*.

i. In the days of the New Testament, many non-Christian religions (such as the Ophites and various Gnostic groups) said they knew the "deep things of Satan." The ancient Christian writer Tertullian said if you asked a Gnostic about their cosmic mysteries, they furrowed their brow and said, "It is deep." It may be deep - but deep into a dangerous hole.

ii. How could Christians ever fall for *the depths of Satan*? Perhaps the deceptive reasoning went this way: "To effectively confront Satan, you must enter his strongholds, and learn his depths in order to conquer him." People use similar reasoning in misguided spiritual warfare today.

f. **And I gave her time to repent . . . and she did not repent**: Jesus' greatest accusation is that this "Jezebel" **did not repent**. She apparently rejects the work of the Holy Spirit in her heart, calling her to repentance.

i. In these words we see both the *mercy* and *judgment* of our Lord. **Time to repent** shows *mercy*. God gives us **time to repent**, we should deal with others the same way. **And she did not repent** speaks to the *judgment* of God. God gives **time to repent**, but it is not an unlimited time. There is a time when God says, *My Spirit shall not strive with man forever* (Genesis 6:3). This means that when God gives us **time to repent**, we must *take advantage* of that time.

ii. " 'In space comes grace' proves not always a true proverb." (Trapp)

g. Because you allow: This shows the sin of the *church* of Thyatira. On the outside, they were a model church, showing *works, love, service, faith,* and *patience.* Yet there was significant corruption *inside* the church. The sin of the church was that they *allowed* this corruption.

> i. It wasn't necessarily a large group following Jezebel. A little leaven affects a whole lump of dough, and a few in immorality and idolatry will corrupt the whole church - especially if they influence others the way this Jezebel did.

5. (22-25) What Jesus wants the church at Thyatira to do.

Indeed I will cast her into a sickbed, and those who commit adultery with her into great tribulation, unless they repent of their deeds. I will kill her children with death, and all the churches shall know that I am He who searches the minds and hearts. And I will give to each one of you according to your works. Now to you I say, and to the rest in Thyatira, as many as do not have this doctrine, who have not known the depths of Satan, as they say, I will put on you no other burden. But hold fast what you have till I come.

> **a. I will cast her into a sickbed**: Before Jesus told the Christians in Thyatira what *they* must do, He first told them what *He* will do. Jesus will chastise this Jezebel, and **cast her into a sickbed**, along with **those who commit adultery with her**.

> > i. The reference to **adultery** is important. It speaks of both sexual **adultery** *and* spiritual **adultery.** When these Christians honored other gods, they were unfaithful to the Lord who saved them.

> > ii. For this reason, the figure of **a sickbed** is fitting. They were guilty of adultery, both sexual and spiritual. It is as if Jesus says, "You love an unclean bed. Here, I will give you one, and **cast** you **into a sickbed.**"

> > iii. What was the **sickbed**? It could simply be an image of affliction, or it could be literal sickness that Jesus allowed in the lives of Jezebel and her followers as chastisement. We know from passages of Scripture such as 1 Corinthians 11:30 that God can use sickness as a way to chastise us when we are in sin.

> > iv. The ancient Greek word used here for **bed** "is also the word for a *banqueting couch*; and if that meaning is taken, the meaning is: 'I will strike her down as she sits at her forbidden feasts.'" (Barclay)

> **b. Unless they repent of their deeds**: Jesus reveals the *purpose* for this chastening. First, it is to draw them to **repent of their deeds**. They wouldn't listen to Jesus before, so He has to speak louder through the **sickbed**.

Second, it is to give an example of holiness to other churches: **and all the churches shall know that I am He who searches the minds and hearts**.

> i. **Minds and hearts** is literally "hearts and kidneys." In the mind of the ancient Jews, the *heart* was the place of intellect, and the *kidneys* were the place of emotion. Jesus says, "I know your every thought and your every feeling."

c. **I will kill her children with death**: "All men die, but all are not killed with death . . . Oh, it is a woeful thing to be killed with death." (Trapp)

d. **Hold fast what you have till I come**: There were many faithful, uncompromising Christians in Thyatira. To them, Jesus simply says **hold fast**. They must not stop doing what is good. They must not become distracted or discouraged from what Jesus wants them to be and to do.

> i. Jesus also tells them *how long* to **hold fast: till I come**. We are to hang in there and stand strong for Jesus until He comes. It is only *then* that the battle will be over.

6. (26-28) The promise of a reward.

And he who overcomes, and keeps My works until the end, to him I will give power over the nations; "He shall rule them with a rod of iron; they shall be dashed to pieces like the potter's vessels"; as I also have received from My Father; and I will give him the morning star.

a. **He who overcomes, and keeps My works until the end**: Even when there is the immoral and idolatrous influence of a Jezebel, Christians can *overcome* and *keep Jesus' works until the end*. We must not become overly discouraged at immorality and idolatry around us, even among Christians. God's work will still go on through His overcomers.

b. **To him I will give power over the nations**: Jesus promises that His people will reign with Him. Here, there is a special promise to those who overcome the threat of immorality and idolatry. To them, Jesus offers a share in His own kingdom.

> i. **He shall rule them with a rod of iron**: This quotation from Psalm 2 speaks of the authority of the Messiah when He rules over the earth. In that day, righteousness will be enforced, and those who rebel against Jesus will be **dashed to pieces** like a clay pot hit with an iron bar. Jesus includes this here to give hope to the faithful Christians of Thyatira, who felt overwhelmed by the immorality and idolatry all around them. Jesus reminds them, "You're on My winning team."

> ii. "The word for 'rule' (Gr. *poimanei*) means literally 'to shepherd.' Their rule will not be simply that of executing judgment, but also that of administering mercy and direction." (Walvoord)

c. **I will give him the morning star**: Jesus offers them a reward greater than the kingdom. He offers them the reward of Himself, because He is the *Morning Star* (Revelation 22:16).

7. (29) A general exhortation to all whom will hear.

He who has an ear, let him hear what the Spirit says to the churches.

a. **He who has an ear**: This is a letter that applies to everyone. It applies to those who are like Jezebel, who lead others into sin. It applies to those who follow the teaching of a Jezebel, and follow others into sin. It applies to those who permit a Jezebel to work her wickedness. Finally, it applies to the faithful who must hold fast.

Revelation 3 - Jesus' Letters to the Churches (Continued)

A. To the church at Sardis

1. (1a) The character of the city of **Sardis**.

And to the angel of the church in Sardis write,

a. At the time Jesus spoke these words to John, the ancient city of **Sardis** had seen its best days and had started to decline. Yet it was a wealthy city, situated at the junction of several important roads and trade routes. The connection between **Sardis** and money - easy money - was well known in the ancient world.

i. "It is of interest to note that the first coinage ever to be minted in Asia Minor was minted in Sardis in the days of Croesus. These roughly formed electrum staters were the beginning of money in the modern sense of the term. Sardis was the place where modern money was born." (Barclay)

b. **Sardis** was also a city well known for its softness and luxury. It had a well-deserved reputation for apathy and immorality. In Sardis there was a large, stately temple to the mother goddess, Cybele. From the ruins of that temple we can see that its main columns were 60 feet high and more than 6 feet in diameter. This mother goddess was honored and worshipped with all kinds of sexual immorality and impurity.

c. The combination of easy money and a loose moral environment made the people of **Sardis** notoriously soft and pleasure loving. "The great characteristic of Sardis was that, even on pagan lips, Sardis was a name of contempt. Its people were notoriously loose-living, notoriously pleasure- and luxury loving. Sardis was a city of the decadence." (Barclay)

i. This softness, this lack of discipline and dedication, was the doom of **Sardis** on a few different occasions. The Greek historian Herodotus tells the story of the fall of Sardis in days of Cyrus. King Cyrus came to Sardis, and found the position of the city ideally suited for defense. There seemed to be no way to scale the steep cliff walls surrounding the city. He offered a rich reward to any soldier in his army who could figure out a way to get up to the city. One solider studied the problem carefully, and as he looked he saw a soldier defending Sardis drop his helmet down the cliff walls. He watched as the soldier climbed down a hidden trail to recover his helmet. He marked the location of the trail and led a detachment of troops up it that night. They easily scaled the cliffs, came to the actual city walls and found them unguarded. The soldiers of Sardis were so confident in the natural defenses of their city they felt no need to keep a diligent watch, so the city was easily conquered. Curiously, the same thing happened almost 200 years later when Antiochus attacked and conquered the overconfident city that didn't set a watch.

ii. "Although the situation of the city was ideal for defense, as it stood high above the valley of Hermus and was surrounded by deep cliffs almost impossible to scale, Sardis had twice before fallen because of overconfidence and failure to watch. In 549 B.C. the Persian King Cyrus had ended the rule of Croesus by scaling the cliffs under the cover of darkness. In 214 B.C. the armies of Antiochus the Great (III) captured the city by the same method." (Walvoord)

2. (1b) Jesus describes Himself to the church at Sardis.

These things says He who has the seven Spirits of God and the seven stars:

a. As Jesus describes Himself, He uses terms that emphasize His character as the Master of every spiritual power and authority. The repetition of the number **seven** helps indicate this because **seven** is the number of *completeness* in the Bible. Therefore, Jesus holds the fullness of the Spirit of God, and the fullness of the church.

b. **He who has the seven Spirits of God**: Jesus has the fullness of the Holy Spirit in Himself, and He also **has** the Holy Spirit in fullness to give to the Church.

c. **And the seven stars**: Jesus also has the fullness of the church in His hand. We know the **seven stars** represent the churches because of what Jesus said in Revelation 1:20: *The seven stars are the angels of the seven churches,* and through these letters, when Jesus speaks to the *angels of the seven churches,* He speaks not to one individual, but to the entire church through that individual.

3. (1c) What Jesus knows about the Christians of Sardis.

I know your works, that you have a name that you are alive,

> a. **I know your works**: As Jesus says to each church, He also says to Sardis. What a church *is* and what a church *does* is never hidden from Jesus.
>
> b. **That you have a name that you are alive**: Jesus knew the church at Sardis had **a name** - that is, a *reputation* - of life and vitality. If you looked at the church of Sardis, you would see signs of life and vitality. In the church of Sardis, like the city of Sardis, everything seemed alive and good.
>
> > i. "We are not to get the impression that Sardis was a defunct affair with the building a wreck, the members scattered, the pastor ready to resign. It was a busy church with meetings every night, committees galore, wheels within wheels, promotion and publicity, something going on all the time. It had a reputation of being a live, wide-awake, going concern." (Havner)

4. (1d) What Jesus has *against* the church at Sardis.

But you are dead.

> a. **Dead**: Despite their reputation of life, Jesus saw them for what they really were. **But you are dead** shows that a good reputation is no guarantee of true spiritual character. Despite their good appearance, Jesus saw them for what they really were.
>
> b. **Dead** indicates no struggle, no fight, no persecution. It wasn't that the church at Sardis was *losing* the battle. A **dead** body has *lost* the battle, and the fight seems over. In this letter Jesus doesn't encourage the Christians in Sardis to stand strong against persecution or false doctrine, probably because there simply *wasn't* a significant danger of these things in Sardis. Being **dead**, the church in Sardis presented no significant threat to Satan's domain, so it wasn't worth attacking.
>
> > i. Sardis is "A perfect model of inoffensive Christianity." (Caird) Their problem was not scandalous wickedness, but a decent death. Their image said "alive," but in substance they were dead.
> >
> > ii. "The church of Sardis was at peace - but it was the peace of the dead." (Barclay)

5. (2-4) What Jesus wants the church at Sardis to do.

Be watchful, and strengthen the things which remain, that are ready to die, for I have not found your works perfect before God. Remember therefore how you have received and heard; hold fast and repent. Therefore if you will not watch, I will come upon you as a thief, and you will not know what hour I will come upon you. You have a few names even

in Sardis who have not defiled their garments; and they shall walk with Me in white, for they are worthy.

a. **Be watchful**: This first instruction from Jesus tells them they need to examine and protect, strengthening what they have. **The things which remain** tells us that though the spiritual condition of the church of Sardis was bad, it wasn't hopeless. Spiritually, there were **things which remain** that could be strengthened. Jesus had not given up on them, and though it was late (**that are ready to die**) it was not *too* late.

i. In its history, the city of Sardis was easily conquered twice before. It wasn't that the attacking armies overwhelmed Sardis, but because over-confidence made them stop being **watchful**. The spiritual state of the church in Sardis was a reflection of the city's historical character.

b. **I have not found your works perfect before God**: This shows that their **works**, though present, haven't measured up to God's standard. The *presence* of **works** isn't enough because God requires a particular intent and purpose in all of our **works**. They should be done with a heart and in a manner that show them to be **perfect before God**.

i. Clarke on **I have not found your works perfect**: "They performed duties of all kinds, but not duty *completely*. They were constantly beginning, but never brought anything to a proper end."

c. **Remember therefore how you have received and heard; hold fast and repent**: What they must do is **remember** how they first **received and heard** the Word of God. Then they must **hold fast** to those things, and **repent** by turning and restoring the gospel and apostolic doctrine to authority over their lives.

i. Paul describes in 1 Thessalonians 2:13 the kind of reception of the word they needed to remember: *For this reason we also thank God without ceasing, because when you received the word of God which you heard from us, you welcomed it not as the word of men, but as it is in truth, the word of God, which also effectively works in you who believe.*

d. **Therefore if you will not watch, I will come upon you as a thief**: Jesus warns them of the great danger in failing to watch. If they ignore His command to **be watchful**, then Jesus will come upon them **as a thief**, at a time completely unexpected.

i. **I will come upon you**: How will Jesus **come upon** them? He could **come** in the sense bringing immediate judgment. Or, He could **come** in the sense of His coming at the rapture of the church (1 Thessalonians 4:16-17). Used in either sense, it shows He may come suddenly and unannounced, so they must **be watchful**.

ii. Winston Churchill said to Britain in the early days of World War II: "I must drop one word of caution, for next to cowardice and treachery, overconfidence leading to neglect and slothfulness, is the worst of wartime crimes." (cited in Bunch)

e. **You have a few names even in Sardis who have not defiled their garments**: Even among the dead Christians in Sardis, there was a faithful remnant, but only a **few names**. In Pergamos (Revelation 2:14) and in Thyatira (Revelation 2:20) there were a few bad among the good; in Sardis there are **a few** good among the bad.

i. **Even in Sardis: Even** shows that in some ways it was remarkable that there were **a few names** still faithful to the Lord. It may have been remarkable because of the city's notoriously immoral reputation. **Even** in a city that wicked, some among the Christians had not defiled themselves by joining in sin.

ii. **Who have not defiled their garments**: Why does Jesus refer to **defiled garments**? In the heathen worship of the day, the pagan gods could not be approached with dirty clothes. The analogy can work for the worship of Jesus because He gives His people white garments.

iii. "As sin is expressed under the notion of nakedness, so holiness is expressed under the notion of a garment." (Poole)

f. **And they shall walk with Me in white**: Jesus also promises that these pure ones will **walk with Me**. This picture of close fellowship and friendship is seen in Enoch, who *walked with God; and he was not, for God took him* (Genesis 5:24).

i. Of course, the garments Jesus gives are always **white**. Sardis was a church that was *dead* because of *sinful compromise*. They needed to receive and walk in the pure, **white** garment that Jesus gives. **White** was also the color of triumph to the Romans, so the **white** garments spoke of the believer's ultimate triumph in Jesus.

ii. **Walk with Me**: This is the greatest reward Jesus can give His followers. The Christians in Sardis who forsake the sinful compromise of their city will be rewarded with a closer, more intimate walk with Jesus. This reward is ultimately a better motivator than the fear of punishment or ruin from our sin.

iii. The pure can have greater intimacy with God not because they have *earned* it, but because they are simply more interested in the things of God. God promises to reward that interest: *Blessed are the pure in heart, for they shall see God* (Matthew 5:8).

iv. "But what shall be done with such persons as live in the church, but are not of it, having a name to live, but are dead? What shall be done with mere professors who are not possessors? What shall become of those who are only outwardly religious but inwardly are in the gall of bitterness? We answer, as good Calvin did once: 'They shall walk in black, for they are unworthy.' They shall walk in black - the blackness of God's destruction. They shall walk in black - the blackness of hopeless despair. They shall walk in black - the blackness of incomparable anguish. They shall walk in black - the blackness of damnation. They shall walk in black for ever, because they were found unworthy." (Spurgeon)

6. (5) A promise of a reward.

He who overcomes shall be clothed in white garments, and I will not blot out his name from the Book of Life; but I will confess his name before My Father and before His angels.

a. **He who overcomes shall be clothed in white garments**: Jesus identifies the overcomers with those *few names* who have not *defiled their garments* (Revelation 3:4). These overcomers will wear **white garments**, received from Jesus.

i. The difference between the dead majority with imperfect works (but who had a good reputation) and the *few names* who pleased God was *purity*, and the closeness with Jesus that is always related to purity. The deadness and spiritual facade of most of the Christians in Sardis was related to their impure lives, their embrace of the impurity and sin of the world around them. It's hard to say if the deadness came before the impurity or the impurity came before the deadness, but they are surely related.

ii. Jesus explained the absolute necessity of this being clothed by God with His garments of purity and righteousness in His parable of the wedding feast (Matthew 22:11-14). Real righteousness is receiving God's covering instead of trying to cover ourselves. Adam and Eve tried to cover their own sin (Genesis 3:21) but God provided them with a covering that came from sacrifice (Genesis 3:7).

b. **And I will not blot out his name from the Book of Life**: By this, the overcomers are assured of their heavenly citizenship. In the ancient world, death or a criminal conviction could **blot out** the name of an ancient citizen from the city's book of the living, which was the city register.

i. "In ancient times cities kept a register of their citizens; and when a man died, his name was removed from the register. The risen Christ is saying that, if we wish to remain on the roll of the citizens of God, we must keep our faith flamingly alive." (Barclay)

c. **Blot out his name from the Book of Life**: Does this mean that someone can lose their salvation? That someone is saved one day - their name is in **the Book of Life** - and another day, they have fallen away and their name has been blotted out **from the Book of Life**? We need to first see the context here in Revelation 3:5. The focus is *assurance*, so we should not think that names are being constantly erased and then rewritten. The focus here is not the idea that Jesus sits in heaven with a busy eraser. At the same time, we should carefully consider what the Word has to say about the Book of Life.

i. There is a **Book of Life**, and it will be opened and referenced on the Day of Judgement. This means that the Book of Life is *real*, and will be *read*.

And I saw the dead, small and great, standing before God, and books were opened. And another book was opened, which is the Book of Life. And the dead were judged according to their works, by the things which were written in the books. (Revelation 20:12)

ii. There is a **Book of Life**, and it determines if we go to heaven or hell. This means that the Book of Life is *important*.

And anyone not found written in the Book of Life was cast into the lake of fire. (Revelation 20:15)

iii. There is a **Book of Life**, and knowing our names are written there should bring us great joy.

Nevertheless do not rejoice in this, that the spirits are subject to you, but rather rejoice because your names are written in heaven. (Luke 10:20)

iv. There is a **Book of Life**, and there are five different references to people being blotted out of the book. This means that the *idea of being blotted out of the Book of Life should be taken seriously*. Perhaps it is only a symbol, and that person's name was never there to begin with. Even if that is the case, *the Lord still wants us to take it seriously*, because there are some who *by every human appearance* are saved, yet will not be in heaven.

Moses said to the Lord: Yet now, if You will forgive their sin; but if not, I pray, blot me out of Your book which You have written. (Exodus 32:32)

And the LORD said to Moses, "Whoever has sinned against Me, I will blot him out of My book." (Exodus 32:33)

Let them be blotted out of the book of the living, and not be written with the righteous. (Psalm 69:28)

He who overcomes shall be clothed in white garments, and I will not blot out his name from the Book of Life; but I will confess his name before My Father and before His angels. (Revelation 3:5)

And if anyone takes away from the words of the book of this prophecy, God shall take away his part from the Book of Life, from the holy city, and from the things which are written in this book. (Revelation 22:19)

v. A good example of how we should take this warning seriously is the life of a man named Charles Templeton. A generation ago he was deeply involved in the foundations of Youth for Christ and impacted the nation for Jesus. Many people received Jesus at his meetings, and Mr. Templeton was an associate with Billy Graham in the early years. Nevertheless, he renounced his belief in Jesus, renounced even his belief in God, and said he is an atheist. Charles Templeton totally renounces his early confessions of faith and wants to "rescue" the people he once brought to Jesus. Obviously, this man - in his present, apostate state - is not going to heaven. One may long debate if he was ever saved or if he lost his salvation, but at the end of the day there are two conclusions. First, at one time - by all human appearance - he was saved. Second, he didn't honor the warnings of the Bible telling us to keep walking, to keep trusting, and to keep persevering in the faith.

vi. In the genealogies of the Bible there are two books mentioned.

- *The book of the generation of Adam* (Genesis 5:1)
- *The book of the generation of Jesus Christ* (Matthew 1:1)

Being born of Adam doesn't guarantee that our name is written in the Book of Life. Being born again - born of Jesus Christ - gives us that assurance.

d. **But I will confess his name before My Father and before His angels**: This is an amazing promise. It simply makes sense that we should be willing to confess the name of Jesus, but it is amazing that He would not be ashamed to confess us!

i. It is important for us to accept Jesus. But it is far more important to know if Jesus accepts us.

7. (6) A general exhortation to all who will hear.

He who has an ear, let him hear what the Spirit says to the churches.

a. **Let him hear**: We must all hear what the Spirit says to the church at Sardis. It is easy to drift in sleepy apathy towards spiritual death, especially when you have a good reputation. Still, there is always hope for the dead church because Jesus knows how to raise the dead.

b. **What the Spirit says to the churches**: Sardis teaches us that we must beware of our success. The city was wealthy and knew easy living, but it made them soft and spoiled. Sardis also teaches us that we be watchful at our strongest points. Sardis thought it was unconquerable, and so it was conquered. Where we say "I would never do that" is the exact place we must guard against.

i. The British Field Marshal Montgomery used to say, "One man can lose me a battle." One corrupt or disobedient Christian can lose a battle for an entire church. First, they can lose a battle simply through their own point of failure. Second, they can lose a battle because they lead others into their same sin. Finally, they can lose a battle because they foster a spirit of accommodation to sin in the other members of the church. One man can lose a battle!

B. Jesus' letter to the church at Philadelphia.

1. (7a) The character of the city of **Philadelphia**.

And to the angel of the church in Philadelphia write,

a. **Philadelphia** (the name means *brotherly love*) was the youngest of the seven cities, and was originally founded as a missionary outpost for Hellenism, the culture of ancient Greece.

i. "The original purpose behind this key city was to make it a center for spreading Greek language, culture and manners throughout the Asian provinces." (Hocking)

ii. "Philadelphia had been built with the deliberate intention that it might become a missionary city. Beyond Philadelphia lay the wilds of Phrygia and the barbarous tribes; and it was intended that the function of Philadelphia should be to spread the Greek language, the Greek way of life, the Greek civilization, throughout the regions beyond." (Barclay)

iii. The city gained its name after its founder - Attalus the Second - who was nicknamed *Philadelphos*.

b. **Philadelphia** was a *prosperous* city. "Philadelphia commanded one of the greatest highways in the world, the highway which led from Europe to the East. Philadelphia was the gateway from one continent to another." (Barclay)

c. **Philadelphia** was also known for beautiful buildings (it was called the "little Athens") and her earthquakes, which required frequent evacuations.

i. "To walk through its temple-scattered streets was to be reminded of Athens, the center of worship of the Olympian gods." (Barclay)

2. (7b) Jesus describes Himself to the church at Philadelphia.

These things says He who is holy, He who is true, "He who has the key of David, He who opens and no one shuts, and shuts and no one opens":

a. **These things says He who is holy, He who is true**: Jesus reminds the church in Philadelphia that He is **holy** and **true**. These do not describe "tendencies" within Jesus, but His very being. They also show that Jesus is Yahweh, because He alone is **holy** in an absolute sense.

i. There are two ancient Greek words that we might translate **true**. One means "**true** and not *false*." The other means "**true** and not *fake*." The ancient Greek word used here for **true** (*alethinos*) is the second, with the idea of "real" or "genuine." Jesus is **true** in all of who He is; He is the *real* God and the *real* man.

b. **He who has the key of David, He who opens and no one shuts, and shuts and no one opens**: Jesus shows He is also the keeper of the keys and doors. In this quotation from Isaiah 22:20-23, Jesus expresses His power and authority, especially to admit and exclude.

3. (8) What Jesus knows about the church of Philadelphia.

I know your works. See, I have set before you an open door, and no one can shut it; for you have a little strength, have kept My word, and have not denied My name.

a. **I know your works**: Jesus says this to each of the seven churches. The church at Philadelphia had served God well in difficult circumstances, and Jesus knew it.

b. **I have set before you an open door, and no one can shut it**: The church in Philadelphia has an **open door** set before them. Often, an **open door** speaks of evangelistic opportunity (1 Corinthians 16:9, 2 Corinthians 2:12, and Colossians 4:3). Jesus tells them He has opened the **door** of evangelistic opportunity, and they must go through that door in faith.

i. In its history, Philadelphia had a great "evangelistic" calling. The city had the mission of spreading Greek culture and language through the whole region. Now Jesus opens the door for them to spread the culture of His kingdom through the whole region.

ii. Jesus tells them to **see** that they have this **open door**. Sometimes God sets an **open door** of evangelistic opportunity in front of us, but we don't **see** it. A man once came to Spurgeon and asked how he could win others to Jesus. Spurgeon asked him, "What are you? What do you do?"

The man said, "I'm an engine driver on a train."

"Then," said Spurgeon, "Is the man who shovels coal on your train a Christian?"

"I don't know," said the man.

"Go back," said Spurgeon, "and find out and start on him."

iii. Once we **see** the **open door**, we then have to *walk through it*. God wants us to take every evangelistic opportunity that He gives us.

iv. There may be another sense to this **open door**. It seems Christians in Philadelphia were excluded from the synagogue (Revelation 3:9). The **open door** may also speak of their opportunity to enter God's kingdom in contrast with exclusion from the synagogue.

c. **And no one can shut it**: The emphasis is on unhindered openness. There is nothing that can keep them from their access to this door. Since Jesus is *He who opens and no one shuts, and shuts and no one opens* (Revelation 3:7), He has the authority to keep this door open for the Christians in Philadelphia.

i. "David could *shut* or *open* the kingdom of Israel to whom he pleased. He was not bound to leave the kingdom even to his eldest son. He could choose whom he pleased to succeed him. The kingdom of the Gospel, and the kingdom of heaven, are at the disposal of Christ." (Clarke)

ii. God opens doors for ministry and ministers today. "I would like to bear witness that I have proved this Philadelphian promise of the open door through years of ministry and it has never failed. Promotion does not come from the south, east, or west, but from God; and if we commit our way unto Him and trust Him, He will bring it to pass . . . God's man is not dependent on religious talent scouts nor is his ministry in the hand of ecclesiastical officials. His headquarters is heaven and his itinerary is made up by the Lord of the Open Door." (Havner)

iii. Because Jesus has opened the door, He gets the glory for it. "Neither wealth or influence, neither promotional schemes nor the eloquence of its pulpit, nor the harmonies of its musicians can give it an effective ministry. The Lord alone has opened the door; the Lord alone 'giveth the increase.' " (H. Morris)

d. **For you have a little strength**: The term **a little strength** does not imply weakness, but *real* **strength**. They were weak enough to be strong in the Lord. We can be "too strong" or "too big" or too sure of ourselves for God to really use us. The church in Philadelphia had the poverty of spirit to know they really needed God's strength.

> i. "It is not a matter of great strength, not great ability but great dependability. Samson had great ability but poor dependability. A little strength faithfully used means more than much strength flashily and fitfully used." (Havner)

> ii. The Apostle Paul was a great example of this dynamic of weakness and strength. God's strength was made evident in his weaknesses (2 Corinthians 12:7-10).

e. **Have kept My word, and have not denied My name**: The church in Philadelphia was faithful to Jesus and His word. The idea behind **have not denied My name** is not only that they expressed their allegiance to Jesus, but that they *lived* in a way that was faithful to the name and character of Jesus.

> i. Some churches that claim great faithfulness to the **word** of Jesus deny His **name** - His character. They represent the manner and style of Jesus as something very different from what the Bible shows.

f. Look at the features of the church in Philadelphia:

- Evangelistic opportunity (**I have set before you an open door**)
- Reliance on God (**You have a little strength**)
- Faithfulness to Jesus (**have kept My word, and have not denied My name**)

In some ways, these features seem unspectacular. They should be commonplace among churches. Yet Jesus was *completely* pleased with this church. He has *nothing* negative to say to the church at Philadelphia.

> i. "The church of Philadelphia is commended for keeping the Word of the Lord and not denying His Name. Success in Christian work is not to be measured by any other standard of achievement. It is not rise in ecclesiastical position. It is not the number of new buildings which have been built through a man's ministry. It is not the crowds that flock to listen to any human voice. All of these things are frequently used as yardsticks of success, but they are earthly and not heavenly measures." (Barnhouse)

4. (9-10) What Jesus will do for the Christians of Philadelphia.

Indeed I will make *those* of the synagogue of Satan, who say they are Jews and are not, but lie; indeed I will make them come and worship before your feet, and to know that I have loved you. Because you have

kept My command to persevere, I also will keep you from the hour of trial which shall come upon the whole world, to test those who dwell on the earth.

a. **I will make those of the synagogue of Satan**: Apparently, the Christians in Philadelphia were persecuted by Jewish people (**the synagogue**). However, these persecuting Jews were Jews in name only (**who say they are Jews and are not, but lie**). In fact, they had no spiritual connection to Abraham or to the people of faith.

i. In this, Jesus does not speak against *all* Jewish people. It would be entirely wrong to speak of the Jewish people as a whole as **the synagogue of Satan** or those **who say they are Jews and are not**. Jesus spoke of this specific group of Jewish people in Philadelphia who persecuted the Christians during that period.

b. **I will make them come and worship before your feet**: In this, Jesus promised that He will vindicate His people and make sure that their persecutors recognize they are wrong, and that Jesus and His followers are right. The idea is of vindication before self-righteous "spiritual" persecutors. God promises that the church in Philadelphia will be vindicated before their persecutors.

i. God promised Israel that Gentiles would honor them and acknowledge their God (Isaiah 45:14). Now the tables are somewhat turned, and these Jewish people "will play the role of the heathen and acknowledge that the church is the Israel of God." (Mounce)

ii. 1 Corinthians 14:24-25 speaks of unbelievers falling down in the midst of Christians to worship God. This establishes that it isn't Christians who are being worshipped, but God is being worshipped in the *presence* of Christians.

iii. **And to know that I have loved you**: As those who were once their enemies worship along side them, they are destroyed as enemies. They now know that Jesus has **loved** these people they once persecuted. The best way to destroy the enemies of the Gospel is to pray that God would change them into friends.

iv. Persecuted people often long for justice against their persecutors (Revelation 6:10). A passage from a second century Christian shows this: "What sight shall wake my wonder, what my laughter, my joy and exultation? As I see all those kings, those great kings . . . groaning in the depths of darkness! And the magistrates who persecuted in the name of Jesus, liquefying in fiercer flames than they kindled in their rage against the Christians!" (Tertullian, cited in Barclay)

c. I will keep you from the hour of trial which shall come upon the whole world: Jesus also promises them protection from the **hour of trial** coming on the **whole world**.

> i. Most Bible scholars see this **hour of trial** as a prophetic reference to the Messianic woes, the Great Tribulation, which precede Jesus' earthly kingdom. Jesus promises to **keep** these Christians from that **hour of trial**.

d. To test those who dwell on the earth: The test is directed against **those who dwell on the earth**. This phrase is used nine times in the Book of Revelation, and it speaks of those who are *not* saved in Jesus. Revelation 17:8 makes the term synonymous with the lost: *And those who dwell on the earth will marvel, whose names are not written in the Book of Life from the foundation of the world*. This **test** is for *unbelievers*, not Christians.

> i. **Those who dwell on the earth** "refers not to believers but to unbelievers who are objects of God's wrath" throughout Revelation. (Johnson)
>
> ii. Christians are different. Though we walk on this earth, our dwelling place is in heaven. We have been seated in heavenly places in Jesus (Ephesians 2:6). We do not **dwell on the earth**, our life is hidden in Jesus (Colossians 3:3).

e. Does this promise to keep you from the hour of trial imply an *escape before* the Great Tribulation? Or does it promise *protection in* it? Each side believes this passage easily supports their position.

> i. Those who believe the church will be here on earth during this time of Great Tribulation focus on Jesus' **command to persevere**, and say the context demands seeing this as protection that enables the faithful to **persevere** in the period.
>
> ii. Those who believe that Jesus will come for His church before this time of Great Tribulation note that protection is promised from the very **hour of trial**, not just the trial itself. They also point to the world-wide, inescapable cataclysm predicted in the Great Tribulation (Matthew 24:21 and Revelation chapters 6, 8-9, 16).
>
> iii. However, **persevere** is in the past tense, showing it is something that the Christians had already done before the **hour of trial**, which has not yet come upon the world. The promise is a *reward* for past perseverance, not the *equipping* to persevere in the future. "As far as the Philadelphian church was concerned, the rapture of the church was presented to them as an imminent hope." (Walvoord)

iv. In addition, the ones tested by this **hour of trial** are not primarily believers, but **those who dwell on the earth** - whose home is this earth, who are not citizens of heaven (Philippians 3:20).

5. (11) What Jesus wants the church of Philadelphia to do.

Behold, I am coming quickly! Hold fast what you have, that no one may take your crown.

a. **Behold, I am coming quickly**: First, the church at Philadelphia must remember that Jesus is **coming quickly**, and they must prepare for His **coming**.

i. "The expression 'quickly' is to be understood as something which is sudden and unexpected, not necessarily immediate." (Walvoord)

b. **Hold fast what you have**: The church at Philadelphia must not depart from its solid foundation, as described in Revelation 3:8:

- Evangelistic opportunity (*I have set before you an open door*)
- Reliance on God (*You have a little strength*)
- Faithfulness to Jesus (*have kept My word, and have not denied My name*)

These things can and must continue among the church in Philadelphia, but it will only happen as they **hold fast what** they **have**.

c. **That no one may take your crown**: If they fail to **hold fast**, their **crown** might be *given* to another. The idea is not that it might be *stolen* by another, but *given*.

i. This is not a crown of royalty, given because of royal birth. This is a crown of victory. Jesus encourages His saints to finish their course with victory, to "play the second half" just as strongly as they "played the first half."

ii. "Never forget that the man most likely to steal your crown is *yourself*. 'Keep thy heart with all diligence, for out of it are the issues of life' (Proverbs 4:23). You are in no greater danger from anyone or anything than from yourself." (Havner)

6. (12) A promise of reward.

He who overcomes, I will make him a pillar in the temple of My God, and he shall go out no more. And I will write on him the name of My God and the name of the city of My God, the New Jerusalem, which comes down out of heaven from My God. And *I will write on him* My new name.

a. **He who overcomes, I will make him a pillar**: Overcomers are told that they will be as a **pillar in the temple of My God**. Pillars were pictures of strength, stability, and dignified beauty.

> i. The ancient city of Philadelphia suffered from frequent earthquakes. When a building collapsed in an earthquake often all that remained were the huge pillars. Jesus offers us this same strength, to remain standing in Him when everything around us crumbles.

> ii. The pillar holds up the building. The only thing supporting the pillar is the foundation. True pillars in the church support the church, and they look to Jesus as their support foundation.

b. **He shall go out no more**: The overcomer will have a place of permanence and stability with God, in contrast to an uncertain place in this world.

> i. "The citizens of Philadelphia lived an unsettled and tremulous life. Whenever the earthquake tremors came, and they came often, the people of Philadelphia fled from the city out into the open country, to escape the falling masonry and the flying stones which accompanied a severe earthquake shock. Then, when the earth was quiet again, they returned. In their fear the people of Philadelphia were always going out and coming in; they were always fleeing from the city and then returning to it." (Barclay)

c. **I will write on him the name of My God . . . I will write on him My new name**: The overcomer also receives many names - of God, the New Jerusalem, and the new name of Jesus. These names are marks of identification because they show who we belong to. They are marks of intimacy, because they show we are privileged to know Him in ways others are not.

> i. This works together well with the image of a **pillar**. In the ancient world, having a special inscribed pillar added to one of the temples sometimes honored a faithful city servant or distinguished priest. "Philadelphia honored its illustrious sons by putting their names on the pillars of its temples, so that all who came to worship might see and remember." (Barclay)

7. (13) A general exhortation to all who will hear.

He who has an ear, let him hear what the Spirit says to the churches.

a. **He who has an ear, let him hear**: We all want to hear the praise and encouragement Jesus gives to the church at Philadelphia. If we will be like this church, we must stay on their foundation, which was Jesus' name and Jesus' word. We must also depend on their source of strength which was Jesus, not themselves.

C. Jesus' letter to the church at Laodicea.

1. (14a) The character of the city of *Laodicea*.

And to the angel of the church of the Laodiceans write,

a. *Laodicea* was an important, wealthy city, with a significant Jewish population. Like other cities in the region, it was a center for Caesar worship and the worship of the healing god Asklepios. There was a famous temple of Asklepios in Laodicea, with a more famous medical school connected with the temple.

i. After an earthquake devastated the region in 60 A.D. Laodicea refused Imperial help to rebuild the city, successfully relying on their own resources. They didn't need outside help, they didn't ask for it, and they didn't want it. "Laodicea was too rich to accept help from anyone. Tacitus, the Roman historian, tells us: 'Laodicea arose from the ruins by the strength of her own resources, and with no help from us.' " (Barclay)

b. Laodicea was also a noted commercial center, and some of its goods were exported all over the world. "It is frequently noted that Laodicea prided itself on three things: financial wealth, an extensive textile industry, and a popular eye-salve which was exported around the world." (Mounce)

c. One of their problems was a poor water supply that made Laodicea vulnerable to attack through siege. If an enemy army surrounded the city, they had insufficient water supplies in the city, and the supplies coming into the city could be easily cut off. Therefore, the leaders of Laodicea were always accommodating to any potential enemy, and always wanted to negotiate and compromise instead of fight.

i. Their main water supply came on a six-mile aqueduct from the hot springs of Hierapolis. Because the water came from hot springs, it arrived unappetizingly lukewarm.

d. The church at Laodicea is mentioned by Paul - in a somewhat unfavorable light - in Colossians 2:1 and 4:16.

2. (14b) Jesus describes Himself to the church at Laodicea.

These things says the Amen, the Faithful and True Witness, the Beginning of the creation of God:

a. **These things says the Amen**: Jesus is **the Amen**, the "so be it," the "it is done." As 2 Corinthians 1:20 says, *For all the promises of God in Him are "Yes," and in Him "Amen."* Jesus is "the personification and the affirmation of the truth of God." (Barclay)

b. Jesus is **the Faithful and True Witness**, and this is a contrast to the Laodiceans, who will be shown to be neither faithful nor true.

c. Jesus is the **beginning of the creation of God**. The idea behind the word for **beginning** [the ancient Greek word *arche*] is that of a "ruler, source, or origin," not of first in a sequential order. This verse does *not* teach that Jesus was the first being created, but that He is the *ruler, source,* and *origin* of all creation. It has the idea of *first in prominence* more than *first in sequence.*

3. (15-16) What Jesus knows about the church of Laodicea.

I know your works, that you are neither cold nor hot. I could wish you were cold or hot. So then, because you are lukewarm, and neither cold nor hot, I will vomit you out of My mouth.

a. **You are neither cold nor hot**: This picture of lukewarmness would immediately strike the Christians of Laodicea because the water they drank every day was lukewarm. Jesus says "Just as the water you drink is disgustingly lukewarm, **you are lukewarm, and neither cold nor hot.**" In this spiritual sense, lukewarmness is a picture of *indifference* and *compromise*. It tries to play the middle, too hot to be cold and too cold to be hot. In trying to be both things, they end up being nothing - except to hear the words, "**I will vomit you out of My mouth.**"

i. Does Jesus mean to say that these Christians are intrinsically cold, but warmed up by their religious trappings? Or, that they are essentially hot, but cooled down by their apathy and self-reliance? Both are possible, but since He is talking to His church, there is an emphasis on the later.

ii. Has there been a greater curse upon the earth than *empty* religion? Is there any soul harder to reach than the one who has just enough of Jesus to think they have enough? The church of Laodicea exemplifies empty religion, and tax collectors and harlots were more open to Jesus than the scribes and Pharisees.

iii. Satan will have us any way he can get us, but he prizes a lukewarm religionist far above a cold-hearted sinner.

b. **I could wish that you were cold or hot**: What Jesus wants to change in us as much as anything is the deceptive playing of the middle, trying to please both the world and Jesus.

i. **I could wish that you were cold or hot** also points to another aspect of lukewarmness, as a picture of *uselessness*. "Hot water heals, cold water refreshes, but lukewarm water is useless for either purpose." (L. Morris) It's as if Jesus says, "If you were hot or cold I could do something with you. But because you are neither, I will do nothing." The lukewarm Christian has enough of Jesus to satisfy a craving for religion, but not enough for eternal life.

ii. The thief on the cross was cold towards Jesus and clearly saw his need. John was hot towards Jesus and enjoyed a relationship of love; but *Judas* was lukewarm, following Jesus enough to be considered a disciple, yet not giving his heart over to Jesus in fullness.

iii. Deep down, there is no one more miserable than the lukewarm Christian is. They have too much of the world to be happy in Jesus, but too much of Jesus to be happy in the world.

iv. But how could Jesus say, **I could wish that you were cold**? We know His deepest desire is that they be **hot**, with an on-fire love for Him (Revelation 3:19, where the word *zealous* is associated with this same word **hot**). Yet if they would not be **hot**, Jesus *prefers* **cold** rather than **lukewarm**. "So the Lord is saying, 'If instead of being lukewarm, you were so cold that should feel that coldness, then the very feeling of your need might drive you to the true warmth, but now in your lukewarmness, you have just enough to protect yourselves against a feeling of need.' " (Barnhouse)

c. **Lukewarm** prayers mock God. "O my brethren and sisters, have you ever really thought what an insult it is to God when we come before him with lukewarm prayers? There stands the heavenly mercy-seat; the road to it is sprinkled with the precious blood of Jesus, yet we come to it with hearts that are cold, or we approach it leaving our hearts behind us. We kneel in the attitude of prayer, yet we do not pray. We prattle out certain words, we express thoughts, which are not our real desires, we feign wants that we do not feel. Do we not thus degrade the mercy-seat? We make it, as it were, a common lounging-place, rather than an awful wrestling-place, once besprinkled with blood, and often to be besprinkled with the sweat of our fervent supplication." (Spurgeon)

d. **Lukewarm** lives turn people *away* from Jesus. "Now, lukewarm professor, what do worldlings see in you? They see a man, who says he is going to heaven, but who is only travelling at a snail's pace. He professes to believe that there is a hell, yet he has tearless eyes, and never seeks to snatch souls from going down into the pit. They see before them one who has to deal with eternal realities, yet he is but half awake; one who professes to have passed through a transformation so mysterious and wonderful that there must be, if it is true, a vast change in the outward life as the result of it; yet they see him as much like themselves as can be. He may be morally consistent in his general behavior, but they see no energy in his religious character." (Spurgeon)

i. "The careless worldling is lulled to sleep by the lukewarm professor, who, in this respect, acts the part of the syren to the sinner, playing sweet music in his ears, and even helping to lure him to the rocks where he will be destroyed. This is a solemn matter, beloved. In this way, great damage is done to the cause of truth; and God's name and God's honor are compromised by inconsistent professors. I pray you either to give up your profession, or to be true to it. If you really are God's people, then serve him with all your might; but if Baal be your god, then serve him. If the flesh be worth pleasing, then serve the flesh; but if God be Lord paramount, then cleave to him." (Spurgeon)

e. The name *Laodicea* means "rule of the people." This church well represents a church run by majority rule instead of God. "Its name designates it as the Church of mob rule, *the democratic Church*, in which everything is swayed and decided by popular opinion, clamour and voting." (Seiss)

i. This is reflected in Jesus' address to the church: *the church of the Laodiceans* (Revelation 3:14). For the other churches, it was *the church of Ephesus* (Revelation 2:1) or *the church in Smyrna* (Revelation 2:8) or *the church in Sardis* (Revelation 3:1). But here, it is *the church of the Laodiceans.*

ii. We might even say that lukewarmness is the natural tendency of our fallen natures. "Alas, this state of lukewarmness is so congenial with human nature that it is hard to fetch men from it. Cold makes us shiver, and great heat causes us pain, but a tepid bath is comfort itself. Such a temperature suits human nature. The world is always at peace with a lukewarm church, and such a church is always pleased with itself." (Spurgeon)

f. In his sermon *An Earnest Warning against Lukewarmness*, Spurgeon described the **lukewarm** church:

• They have prayer-meetings, but there are few present, for they like quiet evenings home

• When more attend the meetings they are still very dull, for they do their praying very deliberately and are afraid of being too excited

• They are content to have all things done decently and in order, but vigor and zeal are considered to be vulgar

• They may have schools, Bible-classes, preaching rooms, and all sorts of agencies; but they might as well be without them, for no energy is displayed and no good comes of them

• They have deacons and elders who are excellent pillars of the church, if the chief quality of pillars be to stand still, and exhibit no motion or emotion

- The pastor does not fly very far in preaching the everlasting Gospel, and he certainly has no flame of fire in his preaching

- The pastor may be a shining light of eloquence, but he certainly is not a burning light of grace, setting men's hearts on fire

- Everything is done in a half-hearted, listless, dead-and-alive way, as if it did not matter much whether it was done or not

- Things are respectably done, the rich families are not offended, the skeptical party is conciliated, and the good people are not quite alienated: things are made pleasant all around

- The right things are done, but as to doing them with all your might, and soul, and strength, a Laodicean church has no notion of what that means

- They are not so cold as to abandon their work, or to give up their meetings for prayer, or to reject the gospel

    i. "They are neither hot for the truth, nor hot for conversions, nor hot for holiness, they are not fiery enough to burn the stubble of sin, nor zealous enough to make Satan angry, nor fervent enough to make a living sacrifice of themselves upon the altar of their God. They are 'neither cold nor hot.' " (Spurgeon)

g. **I will vomit you out of My mouth**: How are churches in the mouth of Jesus?

- They are in His mouth because they spread His Word

- They are in His mouth because He prays for them constantly

    i. What a terrible thing - in either of these ways - to be expelled from the mouth of Jesus!

4. (17) What Jesus has *against* the church of Laodicea.

Because you say, "I am rich, have become wealthy, and have need of nothing"; and do not know that you are wretched, miserable, poor, blind, and naked;

a. **You say, "I am rich and have become wealthy, and have need of nothing."** The church at Laodicea lacked a sense spiritual poverty. They looked at their spiritual condition and said "**rich**." They looked again and said "**wealthy**." They looked a third time and said, "We **have need of nothing**." They are the opposite of *blessed are the poor in spirit* Jesus spoke of in Matthew 5:3.

    i. The Laodiceans put their trust in material prosperity, in outward luxury, and in physical health. They felt like they didn't need anything.

"The loss of a sense of need, as the drowsiness that besets a freezing man, is fatal." (Newell)

ii. "The cause of Christ has been hurt more by Sunday-morning bench-warmers who pretend to love Christ, who call Him Lord but do not His commands, than by all the publicans and sinners." (Havner)

b. **And do not know that you are wretched, miserable, poor, blind, and naked**: It wasn't that the church at Laodicea wasn't spiritually poor - they were, they were simply *blind* to it. Jesus looked at their spiritual condition and said, "**wretched**." He looked again and said, "**miserable**." A third time Jesus looked and said, "**poor**." He looked again and said, "**blind**." A final time Jesus looked and He saw that they were spiritually **naked**.

i. The city of Laodicea was famous for its wealth, but the Christians of the city were spiritually **wretched, miserable,** and **poor**. Laodicea was famous for its healing eye salve, but the Christians of the city were spiritually **blind**. Laodicea was famous for its fine clothing, but the Christians of the city were spiritually **naked**.

ii. The contrasts are shocking:

• The contrast between what they think they are and what they really are

• The contrast between what they see and what Jesus sees

• The contrast between the wealth and affluence of their city and their own spiritual bankruptcy

c. **You are**: This isn't just the *opinion* of Jesus. Spiritually speaking, they **are wretched, miserable, poor, blind, and naked**. What Jesus sees in them is more important than how they see themselves. The church in Smyrna thought they were poor when they were really rich (Revelation 2:9), but the church of the Laodiceans believe they are rich when they are really poor.

i. We might say that it all began with their spiritual blindness. If you are blind, you can't look at yourself and see that you are **wretched, miserable, poor . . . and naked**. Mental darkness is worse than a loss of sight; but a loss of spiritual vision is even worse.

ii. "The Laodiceans are typical of the modern world, which revels in that which the natural eye can see but is untouched by the gospel and does not see beyond the veil of the material to the unseen and real eternal spiritual riches." (Walvoord)

5. (18-20) What Jesus wants the church of Laodicea to do.

I counsel you to buy from Me gold refined in the fire, that you may be rich; and white garments, that you may be clothed, *that* the shame of your nakedness may not be revealed; and anoint your eyes with eye salve, that you may see. As many as I love, I rebuke and chasten. Therefore be zealous and repent. Behold, I stand at the door and knock. If anyone hears My voice and opens the door, I will come in to him and dine with him, and he with Me.

a. **I counsel you to buy from Me**: The change in the Laodiceans had to begin with understanding their spiritual poverty. As long as we believe we can meet the need for wealth, clothing, or sight ourselves, we can never receive them from Jesus. We must seek these things from Jesus *instead* of relying on them ourselves.

i. **Buy from Me gold refined in the fire**: If they will receive from Jesus His riches, His **gold** - beautifully **refined in the fire** - then they **may be rich**.

ii. **White garments, that you may be clothed**: If they will receive from Jesus the pure, righteous covering He gives, then they will **be clothed**, and no longer will **the shame of your nakedness . . . be revealed**. The merchants of Laodicea were famous for a glossy black wool they used to make beautiful garments. Jesus says, "I know the beautiful black that the world can clothe you in. But I have **white garments, that you may be clothed**."

iii. **Anoint your eyes with eye salve**: If they will receive from Jesus the healing of their spiritual sight, they will then be able to **see**.

b. **Buy from Me**: How can we **buy** these things from Jesus? We don't earn them through our good works. Instead, Jesus would say, "All this self-sufficiency must be expended in the labour of getting from Me (Jesus) these absolute necessaries." (Alford)

c. **As many as I love, I rebuke and chasten**: With such a sharp rebuke, has Jesus lost His love for this errant church? Not at all. Jesus' great love is expressed *in* His rebuke. "It is, in fact, God's final punishment to leave a man alone." (Barclay)

i. The word for **love** in **as many as I love** is not *agape*, but *phileo*. Jesus' heart to this church is, "Even though I **rebuke** you and **chasten** you, I am still your friend. I love you deeply as My friend."

ii. "Yet upon a church that has sunk so low as Laodicea, the risen Lord still showers His love." (Barnhouse)

iii. "The word here used for 'love' is a very choice one; it is one which signifies an intense personal affection." (Spurgeon)

d. Therefore be zealous and repent: He commands them to make a decision to repent, and to continue in *zeal.* "Turn your way," Jesus says. "Don't look to your own riches and resources, because they are really bankrupt. Turn around and look to Me."

> i. The ancient Greek word **zealous** comes from the same word as *hot* in Revelation 3:16. Though Jesus detests their lukewarmness, He would really have them be *hot* with zeal rather than cold.

> ii. "When you and I shall be stretched upon our dying beds, I think we shall have to regret, above everything else, our coldness of heart. Among the many sins . . . perhaps this will lie the heaviest upon our heart and conscience, 'I did not live as I ought to have done; I was not as earnest in my Lord's cause as I should have been.' Then will our cold sermons, like sheeted ghosts, march before our eyes in dread array. Then will our neglected days start up, each one seeming to wave its hair as though it were one of the seven furies, and to look right into our hearts, and make our very blood curdle in our veins." (Spurgeon)

> iii. We need to make *our life* following Jesus, not just a hobby or an occasional activity. This goes against the spirit of our age, which was long ago expressed by a famous Englishman when he read a sermon by G.W.E. Russell: "Things have come to a pretty pass when religion is allowed to invade the sphere of private life." (English statesman William Lamb [1779-1848])

> iv. Trapp, on the believer's repentance: "This is the rainbow, which if God seeth shining in our hearts, he will never drown our souls."

e. Behold, I stand at the door and knock: Jesus gives to this lukewarm church *The Great Invitation.* He knocks at the door, asking entry to come and **dine with** us, in the sense of sharing warm, intimate time. It only happens as we respond to His knock, but the promise is made to all: **If anyone hears my voice**.

> i. The idea of Jesus **at the door** applies to the sinner and to the saint just the same. Jesus wants to **come in to** us, and **dine with** us, in the sense of having a deep, intimate relationship.

> ii. **I stand at the door**: Sadly, Jesus stands on the outside, knocking to get in. If the church at Philadelphia was "The Church of the Open Door," then Laodicea has "The Church of the Shut Out Jesus."

> iii. **I stand at the door and knock . . . If anyone hears My voice and opens the door**: This statement of Jesus expresses a profound mystery. Why does Jesus **stand** outside the door? Why does He **knock**? Why does He wait until someone **opens** the door? Doesn't He have

every right to break down the door, or enter some other way on His own accord? But He doesn't. The sovereign, omnipotent Jesus has condescended to work out His eternal plan by wooing the cooperation of the human heart.

iv. "The occupant must open the door. That is, he must repent of his pride and self-sufficiency, his human wisdom, and his cowardly neutrality." (H. Morris)

v. "Christ *stands* - waits long, at the *door* of the sinner's heart; he *knocks* - uses judgments, mercies, reproofs, exhortations, to induce sinners to repent and turn to him; he lifts up his *voice* - calls loudly by his word, ministers, and Spirit." (Clarke)

vi. Jesus comes to the door as the lover in the Song of Solomon. This is similar to - or perhaps a quotation of - Song of Solomon 5:2: *It is the voice of my beloved! He knocks, saying, 'open for me, my sister, my love.'*

vii. The key to opening the door is to first **hear His voice**. When we give attention to what Jesus says, then we can be rescued from our own lukewarmness and enter into a "zealous" relationship with Him.

f. **I will come into him**: What a glorious promise! If we open the door, He **will come** in. He won't ring the bell and run away. He promises to **come** in, and then to **dine with** the believer.

i. When Jesus says **dine with him**, He speaks of a specific meal known as the *deipnon*. "The *deipnon* was the main meal of the day and was a leisurely affair, not a hurried snack." (L. Morris) This speaks of *fellowship*. This speaks of a *depth* to the relationship.

ii. "*Supper (deipnon)* was the main meal of the day. This was the meal at which a man sat and talked for long, for now there was time, for work was ended . . . it is not a mere courtesy visit, paid in the passing, which Jesus Christ offers to us. He desires to come in and to sit long with us, and to wait as long as we wish him to wait." (Barclay)

iii. *This* is where Jesus wants us, in the place of fellowship with Him. Everything He said to the Laodicean church up to this point must be seen in light of this loving desire for fellowship. "Rebuke and chastisement are no signs of rejection from Christ, but of His abiding and pleading love, even to the lukewarm and careless." (Alford)

g. **If anyone**: Notice that Jesus gives the call to *individuals*. He didn't say, "If any church," but **if anyone**. "We must not talk about setting the church right, we must pray for grace each one for himself, for the text does not say, 'If the church will open the door,' but 'If *any man* hear my voice and open the door.' It must be done by individuals: the church will only get right by each man getting right." (Spurgeon)

6. (21) A promise of reward.

To him who overcomes I will grant to sit with Me on My throne, as I also overcame and sat down with My Father on His throne.

a. **To him who overcomes**: Jesus' promise to the overcomer, even at Laodicea, shows that we *don't have to be* Christians who are compromising and lukewarm. If we are, we can change and become one of Jesus' overcomers.

b. **I will grant to sit with Me on My throne**: Those who overcome the battle against indifference, compromise, and self-reliance, receive a special reward. They enjoy a place with the enthroned Jesus (**as I also overcame and sat down with My Father on His throne**).

i. "This is the worst of the seven Churches, and yet the most eminent of all the promises are made to it, showing that the worst may repent, finally conquer, and attain even to the highest state of glory." (Clarke)

7. (22) A general exhortation to all who will hear.

He who has an ear, let him hear what the Spirit says to the churches.

a. **He who has an ear, let him hear**: Few want to identify themselves with the church of Laodicea. We would much rather identify ourselves with the church at Philadelphia.

b. **Let him hear what the Spirit says to the churches**: We *must* hear what the Holy Spirit says here, because He speaks **to the churches** - including us. May God deliver us from the self-reliant, compromising lukewarmness that marked the church of the Laodiceans!

Putting the Seven Churches of Revelation into Historical Perspective

Many have attempted to make sense of Revelation chapters 2 and 3 (the letters to the seven churches of Asia) by taking them as a unified whole. It is significant that Jesus chose these particular seven congregations to address, though there were other churches in the region that were not written to (such as the church at Collosse). Additionally, some have pointed to the *order* of the letters as evidence of their significance as a broad explanation of church history in the period between the Ascension and Jesus to His return.

It is also interesting to note that Paul addressed seven churches: Rome, Corinth, Galatia, Ephesus, Colosse, Phillipi, and Thessalonica (some also note with interest that Jesus gives seven "Kingdom Parables"). Early commentators on the Book of Revelation emphasized that as seven is a number of completion and fulfillment, so Jesus and Paul wrote to seven churches as an indication that they were in fact speaking to the complete church, not just these seven congregations. Speaking to seven churches means speaking to the church in perfection, *in completion and totality*. As one commentator puts it, "The churches of all time are comprehended in seven."

Here is what some say about each of these periods as they relate to church history:

Henry Morris, *The Revelation Record* (written in 1983)

"Although it is by no means the dominant theme, there is a sense also in which the seven churches seem to depict the respective stages of development and change of Christ's churches during the ensuing centuries. History has, indeed, shown such a general development through the years . . . He is not capricious in His selection. There is bound to be some significance in the *sequence* of the seven, as well as the total."

Following is a chart from page 66 of *The Revelation Record*:

Church	Period in Church History	Dates
Ephesus	Apostolic Age	Before 100 A.D.
Smyrna	Age of Persecution	100 to 313 A.D.
Pergamos	Imperial Church Age	313 to 590
Thyatira	Age of Papacy	590 to 1517
Sardis	Reformation Age	1517 to 1730
Philadelphia	Missionary Age	1730 to 1900
Laodicea	Age of Apostasy	1900 to ?

Joseph Seiss, *The Apocalypse* (written in 1900)

Ephesian: Warmth and love and labor for Christ; defection beginning with a gradual cooling of love, false professions and clergy/laity distinctions.

Smyrna: Sweet and precious martyrdom, but a progression of clergy and laity distinctions and Judaizing tendencies, with an increasing departure from the simplicity of the gospel.

Pergamite: True faith more and more disappearing; clericalism systematized, union with the world.

Thyatiran: Purple and glory for the corrupt priesthood; false prophets enthroned in a time when truth was exchanged for darkness (up to the Reformation).

Sardian: Separation and return to the rule of Christ; many great names, but also deadness, and lethargy (Protestant centuries).

Philadelphian: Closer adherence to Jesus' Word, more fraternity among Christians (modern evangelical movement of the 19th century).

Seiss does not give much of a description of the Laodicean church along this same pattern, because he felt that in his day (1900), it was yet to really emerge upon the scene.

Clarence Larkin, *The Greatest Book on Dispensational Truth in the World* (1918)

Ephesian: 70 to 170 A.D. - "The backslidden church."

Smyrna: 170 to 312 - "The persecuted church."

Pergamite: 312 to 606 - "The licentious church."

Thyatiran: 606 to 1520 - "A lax church."

Sardian: 1520 to 1750 - "A dead church."

Philadelphian: 1750 to 1900 - "A favored church."

Laodicean: 1900 to the end - "A lukewarm church."

Taylor Bunch, *The Seven Epistles of Christ* (1947)

Ephesian: "The universal church of the days of the apostles, or the first century of Christianity."

Smyrna: Second and third centuries, "the age of martyrdom, when pagan Roman emperors attempted to destroy Christianity with the violence of the sword."

Pergamite: Covering 250 years (from Emperor Constantine to Emperor Justinian the Great) "the church was exalted to royal power and kingly authority through a union, or marriage, with the state."

Thyatiran: 538 to 1520, the corrupt, political church of the Middle Ages.

Sardian: 1520 to the mid 1700's ("but doubtless embraces the entire history of Protestantism to the end of the gospel dispensation"); the church of the Reformation, and a partial work.

Philadelphian: From the mid 1700's to the present; the church of 18th and 19th century revivals, worldwide missions movements, and renewed expectation of Jesus' return.

Laodicean: Middle 1800's to the end of the Christian dispensation, "a sad comment on modern Christendom."

Chuck Smith, *What the World is Coming To* (1977)

Ephesian: The early church, up until the death of John.

Smyrna: 2nd to 4th centuries, Roman persecutions.

Pergamite: Beginning in 316, "development of church-state system under Constantine."

Thyatiran: The unrepentant, unfaithful church destined to go through the Great Tribulation.

Sardian: Dead Protestantism.

Philadelphian: The faithful church of the last days.

Laodicean: The apostate church of the last days.

Evaluating these Interpretations

This historical approach to the seven churches of Revelation is useful if these periods are seen as broad, imprecise descriptions of the church through history, allowing for generous periods of overlap. For example, it seems that the last four churches will persist until the coming of Jesus (see Revelation 2:25, 3:3, 3:11, and 3:20). If one accepts these seven letters as descriptive of the flow of church history, it does not require that we see them as exclusive, rigidly sequential ages.

It is good to remember that if these letters are a prophecy of the course of church history, this is their *secondary* significance. First and foremost, the letters were written to real, existing first-century congregations, and to "all who have an ear to hear." As Henry Morris says,

> "Since there is nothing directly said by Christ to require - or even to suggest - such an (prophetic) application, a literalistic approach to the study of Revelation cannot place much emphasis on it."

As well, we must remember that every age has had *some* characteristics of *all* seven churches. Though certain historical periods are marked by the conditions spoken of in these letters, we could never say that "only one letter" applies only to us or our age. Joseph Seiss speaks to this well:

> "There are Protestant Papists, and Papistical Protestants; sectarian anti-sectarians, and partyists who are not schismatics; holy ones in the midst of abounding defection and apostasy, and unholy ones in the midst of the most earnest and active faith; light in dark places, and darkness in the midst of light."

We need to hear what the Spirit says to the *churches* (in the plural sense), not just one church.

Revelation 4 - Before the Throne of God

A. The transition to the fourth chapter of the Book of Revelation.

1. Taking Revelation 1:19 as an outline of the book, chapter four begins the third section: *the things which shall take place after this*.

a. The phrase *after this* (*meta tauta* in ancient Greek) in Revelation 1:19 is repeated twice in Revelation 4:1. Certainly this is a marking point for beginning the third division of Revelation 1:19.

2. Chapter four begins a heavenly perspective, looking down on the earth.

a. The Bible has other important references to heaven, in passages such as Isaiah 6:1-8, Ezekiel 1, and in passages describing the Tabernacle, which symbolically describes heaven (Exodus 25-32 and 35-40).

b. In the description of heavenly things, John will use symbols. However, not *everything* is symbolic. As in the parables of Jesus, many of the details are merely descriptive and they are not necessarily intended to carry a special significance of their own.

i. Also, we should keep in mind the nature of symbolism: the symbol is always *less* than the *reality*. The reality of heaven is even greater than the description we have of it.

ii. "It is very little that we can know of the future state, but we may be quite sure that we know as much as is good for us. We ought to be as content with that which is not revealed as with that which is. If God wills us not to know, we ought to be satisfied not to know. Depend on it, he has told us all about heaven that is necessary to bring us there; and if he had revealed more, it would have served rather for the gratification of our curiosity than for the increase of our grace." (Spurgeon)

3. From Revelation 4 through 19 we have a section mainly concerned with God's judgment upon the world preceding Jesus' earthly reign, the period known as the "Messianic Woes" or the "Great Tribulation."

a. God's judgments are announced by a seven-sealed scroll, seven trumpets, seven signs, and seven bowls that pour out God's wrath.

b. Revelation four introduces us to the place judgment comes from: God's throne in heaven.

B. John enters heaven.

1. (1) John is called up into heaven.

After these things I looked, and behold, a door *standing* open in heaven. And the first voice which I heard *was* like a trumpet speaking with me, saying, "Come up here, and I will show you things which must take place after this."

a. **After these things**: Revelation chapters 2 and 3 spoke to the churches, and the *seven churches* comprehended all churches. After Jesus is finished speaking to the churches, **after these things**, John experienced the vision of Revelation 4.

b. **And the first voice which I heard**: The **first voice** that spoke to John in Revelation 1:10 speaks to him again here - the voice of Jesus. Jesus calls John up to heaven, through a **door standing open in heaven**.

i. **Like a trumpet**: The voice spoke loud and clear to John. It was like the trumpet that gathered the congregation of Israel together, or gathered an army for battle.

c. **Come up here, and I will show you things which must take place after this**: John will be shown things that concern the future (**which must take place after this**), not John's present day.

i. Some like to interpret what John saw up through Revelation 19 as fulfilled in what took place *before* John's day - notably, in the Roman invasion and destruction of Jerusalem. Jesus clearly tells John that He will **show** him **things which must take place after this**.

ii. Some like to interpret what John saw up through Revelation 19 as fulfilled in history *after* John's day but *before* our present day. But these events have yet to be fulfilled in any sort of literal sense; they can only be said to have been fulfilled by making them wildly symbolic. Therefore, we regard what Jesus **will show** John in the following chapters of Revelation as belonging to the future, and as proceeding the coming reign of Jesus on earth.

d. **Like a trumpet . . . Come up here**: Many see John's "going up" to heaven as a symbol of the rapture of the church. John is called up to heaven by a voice that sounds **like a trumpet**, just as the church will be as described in 1 Thessalonians 4:16-17.

i. The pattern is significant. Jesus is finished speaking to and dealing with the churches in Revelation chapters 2 and 3, and all churches are comprehended in the seven. Now, after dealing with the church, Jesus calls John up to heaven, "catching him away" with a voice that sounds **like a trumpet**. All this happens *before* the great wrath that will be described beginning at Revelation 6. As that great judgment on the earth unfolds, John - a representative of the church - is in heaven, looking down on earth.

ii. Significantly, the word "church" never occurs in the chapters describing this period of judgment on earth, no where in Revelation chapters 4 through 19.

2. (2a) John goes up, **in the Spirit**.

Immediately I was in the Spirit;

a. **Immediately I was in the Spirit**: John already said he was *in the Spirit* at Revelation 1:10. This is yet a different experience, as John comes to heaven and a heavenly perspective.

b. **In the Spirit**: Where was his body? Was John's body in heaven also, or was it just his spirit? This is impossible to know. Paul, when he had his heavenly experience, didn't know if he was "in the body" or not (2 Corinthians 12:1-4).

C. John's description of heaven.

1. (2b) The point of focus: **a throne set in heaven**.

And behold, a throne set in heaven, and *One* sat on the throne.

a. **And behold, a throne**: This **throne** is what first strikes John, and it is the centerpiece of this vision. John is fixated on the occupied **throne**, and everything else is described in relation to this **throne**.

i. The bottom line of atheism or materialism is that there *is no throne*, there is no seat of authority or power that the entire universe must answer to. The bottom line of humanism is that there is a throne, but *man* sits upon it.

ii. Essentially, man cannot live without the concept of *a throne*, a supreme ruler. So if man de-thrones God, he will inescapably place himself or some other man upon the throne, perhaps a political leader, as was the case with Lenin, Stalin, and Mao.

b. **And One sat on the throne**: The throne is not empty. There is some **One** who sits on this great heavenly throne. The throne is a powerful declaration of not merely God's *presence*, but of His *sovereign, rightful reign*, and His prerogative to judge.

i. We can't think rightly about much of anything until we settle in our mind that there is an occupied throne in heaven, and the God of the Bible rules from the throne. "While there may be many differing interpretations, the fundamental truths are self-evident. At the center of everything is an occupied throne." (Morgan)

2. (3) What John saw at the heavenly throne.

And He who sat there was like a jasper and a sardius stone in appearance; and *there was* a rainbow around the throne, in appearance like an emerald.

a. **And He who sat there was like**: As John describes the occupant of the throne, he does not describe a distinct figure. "There is here no description of the Divine Being, so as to point out any *similitude, shape,* or *dimensions*. The description rather aims to point out the surrounding *glory* and *effulgence* than the *person* of the almighty King." (Clarke)

b. **Like a jasper and a sardius stone in appearance**: Instead of describing a specific form or figure, John describes emanations of glistening light in two colors: white (**jasper** may mean "diamond") and red (**sardius**).

i. Perhaps these two colors are meant to communicate the glory of the empty tomb (white, Matthew 28:1-3) and the sacrificial love of Calvary (red, indicating blood). Or, perhaps they are linked with the first and last gems in the high priest's breastplate (Exodus 39:8-13).

c. **And there was a rainbow around the throne**: The throne is surrounded by a green-hued rainbow (**in appearance like an emerald**). The rainbow is a reminder of God's commitment to His covenant with man (Genesis 9:11-17).

i. Around this setting of all sovereignty, power, authority and glory - this setting of the throne of God - God has a *reminder* of His promise to never destroy the earth again with water, a promise that *directs* His sovereignty, so that it is not capricious or against His promises.

ii. A throne says, "I can do whatever I want, because I rule." A promise says, "I will fulfill this word to you, and I cannot do otherwise." **A rainbow around the throne** is a remarkable thing, showing that God will always limit Himself by His own promises.

iii. Trapp on the **rainbow**: "Which is *signum gratiae et foederis*, a sign of grace and the covenant of mercy, which is always fresh and green about Christ's throne of grace."

iv. The believer *glories* in the sovereignty of God, because he knows that God's sovereignty is *on his side*. It means that no good purpose of God relating to the believer will ever be left undone.

v. "Oh! Child of God! Thy heavenly Father in his sovereignty, *has a right to do with you, his child, as he pleases, but he will never let that sovereignty get out of the limit of the covenant.* As a sovereign, he might cast you away, but he has promised that he never will, and never will he. As a sovereign, he might leave you to perish, but he has said, 'I will not leave thee nor forsake thee.' As a sovereign, he might suffer you to be tempted beyond your strength, but he has promised that no temptation shall happen to you, but such as is common to man, and he will with the temptation make a way of escape." (Spurgeon)

3. (4) What John saw around the throne: the twenty-four elders.

Around the throne *were* twenty-four thrones, and on the thrones I saw twenty-four elders sitting, clothed in white robes; and they had crowns of gold on their heads.

a. **Around the throne were twenty-four thrones**: Before the elders catch John's eye, he noticed the **twenty-four thrones** they sat on. These twenty-four elders sit on lesser thrones, **around the throne**. Later we will hear their song of worship (Revelation 4:10-11).

b. **On the thrones I saw twenty-four elders sitting**: Who are these **twenty-four elders**? Commentators debate whether they are glorified human beings or angelic beings. Taking all things into consideration, the elders certainly seem to represent God's people.

i. **Elders** represent the people of God, especially in the Old Testament. The 24 courses of the priesthood represented all the priests (1 Chronicles 24), and the 12 tribes and the 12 apostles represent *all* the faithful.

ii. In Revelation 5:9-10, the twenty-four elders sing a song of praise to Jesus, and they cry out: *For You were slain, and have redeemed us to God by Your blood, out of every tribe and tongue and people and nation.* In that passage, the twenty-four elders are clearly speaking as representatives of all God's people, of the great company of the redeemed.

c. **Clothed in white robes; and they had crowns of gold on their heads**: The **white robes** and **crowns** of the elders seem to indicate that they are indeed human beings - in glory, of course.

i. Angels are sometimes presented in white robes or garments (Mark 16:5; John 20:12; Acts 1:10), but saints also have white robes (Revelation 6:11, 7:9, 13-14) as a picture of their imputed righteousness (Isaiah 61:10, Revelation 3:5-18). However, we never see angels *crowned* but believers will be (1 Corinthians 9:25; 2 Timothy 4:8; 1 Peter 5:4).

i. Therefore, redeemed, glorified man sits enthroned with Jesus. On lesser thrones, to be sure, but thrones none the less. We are *joint heirs with Christ* (Romans 8:17), and we will *reign with Him* (2 Timothy 2:12).

4. (5) Impressive and fearful sights at the throne of God.

And from the throne proceeded lightnings, thunderings, and voices. Seven lamps of fire *were* burning before the throne, which are the seven Spirits of God.

a. **And from the throne proceeded lightnings, thunderings, and voices**: The lightning, thunder, voices and fire are reminiscent of God's fearful presence at Mount Sinai (Exodus 19:16-19 and 20:18-19). They communicate the awe associated with the throne of God.

b. **Seven lamps of fire were burning before the throne**: The Holy Spirit (the **seven Spirits of God**, as referred to in Revelation 1:4 and Isaiah 11:2) is represented by seven burning **lamps**. In other passages He is represented as a dove (Matthew 3:16) or a flame of fire (Acts 2:3).

i. The lamps of fire are important because the Holy Spirit is not ordinarily visible. To become visible, He represents Himself in a physical form like a dove or a tongue of fire.

5. (6a) The sea of glass before the throne.

Before the throne *there was* a sea of glass, like crystal.

a. **A sea of glass**: Is this sea really made of **glass**, or does it just look like it? Commentators are divided on this point. For example, Robertson says, "appearance, not material" and Alford says, "material, not appearance." Whether it *looks* like glass or is actually *made of glass*, it is the *finest* **glass, like crystal**.

b. **A sea**: This body of water before the throne is reminiscent of the laver in the Tabernacle, and our *washing of the water of the word* (Ephesians 5:26).

i. "The word is to us a crystal glass, giving us a clear sight of God and of ourselves, 2 Corinthians 3:18; James 1:23." (Trapp)

6. (6b-8a) The four living creatures all around the throne.

And in the midst of the throne, and around the throne, *were* four living creatures full of eyes in front and in back. The first living creature *was* like a lion, the second living creature like a calf, the third living creature had a face like a man, and the fourth living creature *was* like a flying eagle. *The* four living creatures, each having six wings, were full of eyes around and within.

a. **Four living creatures full of eyes**: From comparison with Ezekiel 1:4-14 and 10:20-22, we understand these creatures to be *cherubim*, the spectacular angelic beings who surround the throne of God. Satan was once one of these high angelic beings, according to Ezekiel 28:14.

i. Cherubim were also prominent in design of the tabernacle, particularly in the Most Holy Place (Exodus 25:17-22 and 26:1-31). The Scriptures show us that the tabernacle is a model of the throne of God, in some manner (Exodus 25:8-9).

b. **Full of eyes in front and in back . . . full of eyes around and within**: Their multitude of eyes indicates these **living creatures** (not "beasts" as in the KJV) are not blind instruments or robots. They know and understand, and have greater insight and perception than any man.

i. These beings of incredible intelligence and understanding live their existence to worship God. All failure to truly worship is rooted in a lack of *seeing* and *understanding*.

ii. The way these super-intelligent beings worship God reminds us that *our worship must be intelligent*. "Our service must not be rash but reasonable, Romans 12:1, such as wherefore we can render a reason. God hates a blind sacrifice, a Samaritan's service, when men worship they know not what nor why, John 4:22." (Trapp)

iii. "The word *beast* is very improperly used here and elsewhere in this description. *Wiclif* first used it, and translators in general have followed him in this uncouth rendering." (Clarke)

c. **Like a lion . . . like a calf . . . a face like a man . . . like a flying eagle**: John describes four cherubim, each with a different **face**. From comparison with Ezekiel 1:6-10, we can see that each of the cherubim have *four faces*, and at the moment, John sees each one of the four different faces pointed in his direction. The significance of these four faces has been interpreted in many ways.

i. The four faces have been said to represent the elements, the cardinal virtues, the faculties and powers of the human soul, the patriarchal churches, the great apostles, the orders of churchmen, the principle angels, and so forth.

ii. Some commentators say these four creatures speak of the ensigns of the head tribes as Israel camped in four groups around the tabernacle in the wilderness. Numbers 2:3, 2:10, 2:18, and 2:25 mention this organization of the tribes under these four heads, but does not assign "mascots" to tribal banners. Seiss, Clarke, and Poole each mention this approach, and cite "Jewish writers" (Seiss), " the Talmudists" (Clarke), and "the learned Mede . . . from the Rabbins" (Poole). Poole explains: "That these were the four creatures whose portraitures were in the four ensigns of the Israelites as they were marshalled into four companies, allotting the men of three tribes to each company. Judah's standard had a lion in its colours, according to Jacob's prophecy of that tribe, Genesis 49:9, Ephraim had an ox, Reuben had a man, Dan an eagle. This the learned Mede proves from the Rabbins, who, though fabulous enough, yet in such a thing may be credited."

iii. The four different faces of the cherubim are often taken as symbols of Jesus as represented in each gospel. In classical church architecture, these four "characters" are repeated often as a motif that signifies both heaven and the four gospels.

iv. Most have seen Matthew as the "Lion" gospel, showing Jesus as the Lion of the Tribe of Judah. Mark is seen as the "Ox" gospel, showing Jesus as a humble servant, a worker. Luke is seen as the "Man" gospel, showing Jesus as the perfect man, the second Adam. John is seen as the "Eagle" gospel, showing Jesus as the man from heaven, the sky. Still, this approach also has other interpretations.

	Victorinus	Irenaeus	Augustine	Clarke	Tradition
Matthew	Man	Man	Lion	Man	Lion
Mark	Lion	Eagle	Man	Lion	Ox
Luke	Ox	Ox	Ox	Ox	Man
John	Eagle	Lion	Eagle	Eagle	Eagle

v. Perhaps it is safest to say that the four faces are important because they represent all of animate creation, in its utmost excellence. The lion is the mightiest of wild animals, the ox strongest of domesticated animals, the eagle king of all birds, and man is highest of all creation. "In *Shemoth Rabba*, sec. 23, fol. 122, 4, Rabbi Abin says: 'There are *four* which have principality in this world: among *intellectual creatures*, MAN; among *birds*, the EAGLE; among *cattle*, the OX; and among *wild beasts*, the LION: each of these has a kingdom and a certain magnificence, and they are placed *under the throne of glory*, Ezekiel 1:10, to show that no creature is to exalt itself in this world, and that the kingdom of God is over all.' These creatures may be considered the representatives of the whole creation." (Clarke)

vi. These cherubim are "Qualified with all necessary endowments, for the discharge of their duties, being bold as lions, painful as oxen, prudent as men, delighted in high flying as eagles." (Trapp)

vii. As well, it is significant to see that the Bible associates a *face* with the idea of *person* (1 Chronicles 12:8; 2 Chronicles 29:6; Isaiah 3:15,

13:8). Here we have singular beings with four faces. Apparently, there are beings that can be more than one person - as our God is One God in three Persons.

viii. Poole says that these four faces illustrate the different personalities God's ministers have: "By them is signified the various gifts with which God blesseth his ministers, giving to some more courage and fortitude, that they are like lions; to others more mildness and meekness, that they are like oxen or calves; others have more wisdom and prudence, which most adorn a man; others a more piercing insight into the mysteries of God's kindgom, rendering them like eagles."

D. John describes what happens at the throne of God.

1. (8b) The living creatures constantly worship God.

And they do not rest day or night, saying: "Holy, holy, holy, Lord God Almighty, Who was and is and is to come!"

a. **They do not rest day or night, saying, "Holy, holy, holy."** The cherubim constantly repeat the phrase **holy, holy, holy.** God's **holy** nature and character is declared, and emphasized with a three-time repetition.

i. "In Hebrew, the double repetition of a word adds emphasis, while the rare threefold repetition designates the superlative and calls attention to the infinite holiness of God." (Johnson)

ii. **They do not rest**: "They have no rest, and yet they have no unrest neither, the sweet content they take in their continual employment is fitter to be believed than possible to be discoursed." (Trapp)

b. **Lord God Almighty**: The cherubim declare that the **Lord God** is **Almighty.** As in Revelation 1:8, the ancient Greek word is *pantokrator*, with the idea of "the One who has His hand on everything."

c. **Who was and is and is to come**: This repeats another idea from Revelation 1:8, and refers to God's eternal Being. It translates the *thought* behind the meaning of the name "Yahweh."

2. (9-11) The twenty-four elders worship the enthroned God.

Whenever the living creatures give glory and honor and thanks to Him who sits on the throne, who lives forever and ever, the twenty-four elders fall down before Him who sits on the throne and worship Him who lives forever and ever, and cast their crowns before the throne, saying: "You are worthy, O Lord, to receive glory and honor and power; for You created all things, and by Your will they exist and were created."

a. Whenever the living creatures give glory . . . the twenty-four elders fall down before Him: The worship of the twenty-four elders is prompted by the cherubim. Since the cherubim worship God day and night, so do the elders.

> i. Knowing angels should worship God should prompt our worship also. Do we have any less to praise Him or thank Him for? "Do we sing as much as the birds do? Yet what have birds to sing about, compared with us? Do we sing as much as the angels do? Yet they were never redeemed by the blood of Christ. Birds of the air, shall you excel me? Angels, shall you exceed me? You have done so, but I intend to emulate you, and day by day, and night by night, pour forth my soul in sacred song." (Spurgeon, *Holy Song from Happy Saints*)

> ii. "If we would have our souls set as a pearl in the fair ring of heavenly courtiers that compass the Lamb's throne, let us praise God as they do." (Trapp)

b. The twenty-four elders fall down before Him who sits on the throne and worship Him: The twenty-four elders **worship** (which means to credit worth or worthiness to) God. The **elders** credit God for their own work and reward, and they do this as they **cast their crowns before the throne**. They recognize that the worth, the worthiness belongs to God, not to themselves.

> i. Casting the crowns simply acts out their declaration, **You are worthy, O Lord, to receive glory and honor and power**. If God is worthy of the **glory and honor and power**, then *He* should get the crown.

> ii. There is also an allusion made to a practice known in the Roman Empire. The Emperor of Rome ruled over many lesser kings, and these kings were at time commanded to come before the Emperor and lay their crowns down before him in homage. Then he would give them back, as a demonstration that their crowns, their right to rule, their victory, came from him. "This is an allusion to the custom of prostrations in the east, and to the homage of petty kings acknowledging the supremacy of the emperor." (Clarke)

> iii. The **crowns** mentioned in Revelation 4:10 are the *stephanos* **crowns**, the crowns of *victory*, not royalty. These are the crowns of achievement that a winning athlete would receive at the ancient Olympian Games. The **twenty-four elders** - representing all the redeemed of God - throw every achievement reward they have back to God, because they know and proclaim that He is **worthy . . . to receive glory and honor and power**.

iv. "Our text says they *all* cast their crowns before the throne. There are no divided opinions in heaven, no sects and parties, no schisms there. They are all in perfect harmony and sweet accord. What one does, all do. They cast their crowns, without exception, before the throne. Let us begin to practice that unanimity here. As fellow Christians, let us get rid of everything that would divide us from each other, or separate us from our Lord. I do not read that there was a single elder who envied his brother's crown, and said, 'Ah, I wish I were such an one as he is, and had his crown.' I do not read that one of them began to find fault with his brother's crown, and said, 'Ah, his jewels may be bright, but mine have a peculiar tint in them, and are of greater excellence.' I do not read ought of dissension; they were all unanimous in casting their crowns at Jesus' feet. They were all unanimous in glorifying God." (Spurgeon)

c. **For You created all things, and by Your will they exist and were created**: The twenty-four elders worship God because of His creative power and glory. The fact that God is Creator gives Him all right and every claim over everything - even as a potter has all rights and claims over the clay (Romans 9:21).

i. God's right over us as Creator is a fact that can be accepted and enjoyed, or rejected, leading to frustration. There is tremendous value in our recognizing our "creatureliness" before God.

ii. "God's power put forth in the creation and administration of the world is twice here mentioned; as that which can never be sufficiently admired and adored." (Trapp)

iii. We confess a fondness for the King James Version translation of Revelation 4:11: *Thou art worthy, O Lord, to receive glory and honour and power: for thou hast created all things, and for thy pleasure they are and were created.* The wonderful phrase *and for thy pleasure they are and were created* reminds us that we each exist to give glory and pleasure to God. Until we do that, we don't fulfill our created purpose.

d. Because they represent all the people of God, the worship, the crown, the robes, the heart of these twenty-four elders belongs to us also. "There is a throne in heaven that no one can occupy but you, and there is a crown in heaven that no other head can wear but yours, and there is a part in the eternal song that no voice can ever compass but yours, and there is a glory to God that would be wanting if you did not come to render it, and there is a part of infinite majesty and glory that would never be reflected unless you should be there to reflect it!" (Spurgeon)

i. But it also means that we should plan ahead for that great day. "If you and I should walk into some great cathedral where they were singing, and ask to be allowed to sing in the choir, they would ask whether we had ever learnt the tune, and they would not let us join unless we had. Nor can we expect that untrained voices should be admitted into the choirs above. Now, dear brothers and sisters, have you learnt to cast your crowns at the Savior's feet already?" (Spurgeon)

Revelation 5 - The Lion, the Lamb, and the Scroll

A. One worthy to take the scroll.

1. (1) The throne and the scroll.

And I saw in the right *hand* **of Him who sat on the throne a scroll written inside and on the back, sealed with seven seals.**

a. **I saw in the right hand of Him who sat on the throne a scroll:**
The focus of Revelation 4 was **the throne**. Here, John begins with reference to the throne, but now shifts his focus to the **scroll** held by the enthroned Lord.

b. **Written inside and on the back:** This means that this scroll is unusual. It wasn't common practice to write on both sides of the scroll. This means that whatever the information on this scroll, there is a lot of it - almost more than the scroll can contain.

i. Ancient scrolls were read *horizontally*, not *vertically*. The "rolls" of the scroll were on the left and the right, and the writing lay in narrow columns about three inches wide, written on a substance kind of like brown paper. The scroll was held in the left hand, and unrolled with the right, and as the reading went on, the previously read portion was re-rolled. On such a typical scroll, the Book of Revelation would fill a scroll 15 feet long.

c. **Sealed with seven seals:** When a roll was finished, it was fastened with strings and the strings were sealed with wax at the knots. This scroll is **sealed with seven seals**; there are seven strings around the scroll, each string sealed with wax.

i. These are not seven writings each separated by a seal; but seven seals all set upon one scroll. All the seals must be opened before the scroll can be read.

d. What is this scroll? What is written in it? Through the centuries, commentators suggest many different ideas. It's important to remember that whatever is on this scroll, no one except Jesus is worthy to open it (Revelation 5:3-4).

> i. Some think the scroll is the *Old Testament*, or the *Old and New Testaments together*, or fulfilled prophecy. But these ideas look back, not forward, and John speaks of things related to *things which must take place after this* (Revelation 4:1). Additionally, if the scroll is the Old or New Testament, who is unworthy to open *that* scroll?

> ii. Some think the scroll is God's claim of divorce against Israel, but there is little Scriptural evidence for this idea, and who is unworthy to open *that* scroll?

> iii. Some think the scroll is *God's sentence against the enemies of the church.* Perhaps this is true, but only in an indirect sense; but who is unworthy to open *that* scroll?

> iv. Some think the scroll is *the text of the Book of Revelation*, or the next few chapters. But this is rather unlikely considering how the idea of the scroll is communicated, and who would be unworthy to open *that* scroll?

> v. Some think the scroll is the *title deed to planet earth*. This is an attractive idea, especially because the coming time of tribulation will end with Jesus ruling on earth. But it is hard to demonstrate this with certainty. The best connection in this idea seems to be with Jeremiah 32:6-15, which describes Jewish title deeds as *sealed.* But there is no doubt that the *earth is the Lord's* (Psalm 24:1), though the *governments* of this world belong to Satan (Luke 4:5-8). If God has to get the title deed back, when did God ever "lose" the title deed to planet earth? In fact, God *holds* this scroll - it isn't lost. *But the scroll must be opened, it must be revealed.*

e. The best solution is to see the scroll as "God's will, his final settlement of the affairs of the universe." (Barclay) This is based on the idea that customarily, under Roman law, wills were sealed with seven seals, each from a witness to the validity of the will.

> i. "Roman law required a will to be sealed seven times as illustrated in the wills left by Augustus and Vespasian for their successors." (Walvoord)

> ii. "The book may mean the purposes and designs of God relative to his government of the world and the Church; but we, whose habitation is in the dust, know nothing of such things. We are, however, determined to *guess*." (Clarke)

iii. "The seven sealed book therefore is the comprehensive program of God culminating in the second coming of Christ." (Walvoord)

iv. "The book of the counsels, decrees, and purposes of God relating to his church, as to what more remarkable things should happen to it to the end of the world; which book was in the hand of the Father." (Poole)

v. The idea here is that God has a book in which the history of the universe is already written. He has *written* the history of the world in advance, He *holds* in His hand the history of the world in advance, and He *initiates* the consummation of all history. *Only God can hold this scroll.*

f. Remember the emphasis is not on the *content* of the scroll, but on its *seals* and the *One* who is worthy to take it.

2. (2-4) Who is worthy to open the scroll?

Then I saw a strong angel proclaiming with a loud voice, "Who is worthy to open the scroll and to loose its seals?" And no one in heaven or on the earth or under the earth was able to open the scroll, or to look at it. So I wept much, because no one was found worthy to open and read the scroll, or to look at it.

a. **A strong angel**: We don't know who this angel is. Many have suggested that it is Gabriel, but we don't know. Nonetheless, this angel issues a challenge to all creation: **Who is worthy to open the scroll and to loose its seals?** This is a challenge no creature can answer because no creature is worthy to open this particular scroll.

b. **No one in heaven or on the earth or under the earth was able to open the scroll, or to look at it**: John could not have said it any stronger. It is as if the **strong angel** looked through the entire universe to find someone worthy, and had not found anyone worthy to even **look at** the scroll.

i. There is no answer to the strong angel's challenge because the creation is utterly incapable of deciding or effecting its own destiny. Someone above the order of created beings must determine the course of history - only God can unfold this plan.

c. **So I wept much**: John's weeping is either because a previous promise to see the future may now be denied (Revelation 4:1), or more likely, because the consummation of history is now indefinitely postponed.

d. **No one was found worthy to open and read the scroll, or to look at it**: To look upon the scroll, one must have the right to open the scroll and possess it - and no creature **was found worthy**.

3. (5-7) The Lion of the tribe of Judah is worthy to open the scroll.

But one of the elders said to me, "Do not weep. Behold, the Lion of the tribe of Judah, the Root of David, has prevailed to open the scroll and to loose its seven seals." And I looked, and behold, in the midst of the throne and of the four living creatures, and in the midst of the elders, stood a Lamb as though it had been slain, having seven horns and seven eyes, which are the seven Spirits of God sent out into all the earth. Then He came and took the scroll out of the right hand of Him who sat on the throne.

a. **Behold, the Lion of the tribe of Judah**: One of the **elders** (not an angel) rescues John from his grief, showing him the one who **has prevailed to open the scroll**. This One is the great figure of Old Testament prophecy: **the Lion of the tribe of Judah, the Root of David**, Messiah of Israel and of the Gentiles.

i. The Messianic title **Lion of the tribe of Judah** comes from Genesis 49:9-10, Isaiah 31:4, and Hosea 11:10. The title **Root of David** comes from Isaiah 11:10 and is repeated in Revelation 22:16.

ii. Trapp says that a Lion is a fitting image of our Messiah, "1. For the excellency of his strength. 2. For his heroical spirit. 3. For his principality; the lion is the king of beasts. 4. For his vigilancy; the lion sleepeth with open eyes."

b. **And I looked, and behold . . . stood a Lamb**: Because of the elder's announcement, John expected to see a Lion, but sees a **Lamb** instead. John even uses the specific word for a little lamb; he "Signifies a *little* or *delicate* lamb." (Clarke)

i. The Lamb is presented in a way both sympathetic and powerful; He is living (**stood a Lamb**), but He still has the marks of previous sacrifice upon Him (**as though it had been slain**).

ii. When men want symbols of power they conjure up ferocious beasts and birds of prey such as those that represent nations and sports teams. But the representative of the kingdom of heaven is a **Lamb**, representing humility, gentleness, and sacrificial love.

iii. The **Lamb** looks **as though it had been slain**. It's hard to describe what John saw, but this **Lamb** had the marks of sacrifice on it. The coming judgment beginning in chapter six is dictated and administrated by the **Lamb** who already offered an escape from judgment by taking judgment upon Himself. The judgment comes upon a world that hates the **Lamb** and all He stands for, and rejects His offer of escape.

c. **As it had been slain**: The idea is that the sacrifice of Jesus is still *fresh* and *current* before God the Father. There is nothing "stale" or "outworn" in the work of Jesus on the cross. Thousands of years later, it is still "fresh" as the day He died on the cross.

> i. "This form of speech is put to show the continual recent virtue of Christ's death eternally effectual before God, as whereby once for all he hath purchased eternal redemption." (Trapp)

> ii. **As it had been slain**: "As if now *in the act of being offered*. This is very remarkable; so important is the sacrificial offering of Christ in the sight of God that he is still represented as being in the very act of pouring out his blood for the offences of man. This gives great advantage to faith; when any soul comes to the throne of grace, he finds a sacrifice there provided for him to offer to God. Thus all succeeding generations find they have the *continual* sacrifice ready, and the newly-shed blood to offer." (Clarke)

d. **Having seven horns and seven eyes, which are the seven Spirits of God sent out into all the earth**: Even though the marks of His sacrifice are evident, the Lamb is not presented as an object of pity. He also bears the marks of omnipotence (**seven horns**) and omniscience (**seven eyes**). What a figure! A slain Lamb, who has the marks of omniscience and omnipotence!

> i. Throughout the Scriptures, **eyes** suggest knowledge and wisdom, and **horns** suggest power. This **Lamb** has knowledge, wisdom, and power fulfilled perfectly: **seven horns and seven eyes**.

> ii. **Which are the seven Spirits of God sent out into all the earth**: The Holy Spirit is not only the *Spirit of God* (in the sense of being the "Spirit of the Father"), but also *the Spirit of Christ* (see Acts 16:7 and Romans 8:9).

> iii. The seven *eyes of the* LORD are a picture of omniscience drawn from the prophet Zechariah (Zechariah 4:10 and 3:9).

e. **Then He came and took the scroll**: No created being was found worthy to take the scroll, but the Lamb can take it. His rank, character and ability to take the scroll and open it (and thus dictate the destiny of creation) has been permanently demonstrated by His work on the cross.

B. Praise to the Worthy One.

1. (8-10) The song of the elders and the cherubim.

Now when He had taken the scroll, the four living creatures and the twenty-four elders fell down before the Lamb, each having a harp, and golden bowls full of incense, which are the prayers of the saints. And

they sang a new song, saying: "You are worthy to take the scroll, and to open its seals; for You were slain, and have redeemed us to God by Your blood out of every tribe and tongue and people and nation, and have made us kings and priests to our God; and we shall reign on the earth."

a. **The four living creatures and the twenty-four elders fell down before the Lamb**: When the Lamb takes the scroll, the response is immediate. High-ranking angels and redeemed man join to worship the Lamb.

b. **Each having a harp**: The **harp** is "Properly, a zithern or kind of guitar, played either with the hand, or with a pick." (Alford) Worship in heaven is accompanied by music. Of course, this is the passage that started the idea that we will all have harps in heaven.

c. **And golden bowls full of incense, which are the prayers of the saints**: With their **golden bowls full of incense**, the elders symbolically present the prayers of the saints. However, they are not interceding for the saints, functioning as mediators for God's people.

i. We are reminded that *there is one God and one Mediator between God and men, the Man Christ Jesus* (1 Timothy 2:5). These elders are not praying for the saints, and this in no way justifies the Roman Catholic practice of praying to the saints, asking them to pray for us.

ii. "It is also possible that these prayers represent the long-standing prayer of God's people, 'Your kingdom come.' " (Hocking)

iii. **Golden bowls full of incense**: In this we see how precious the prayers of the saints are to God. He regards them as a sweet smelling incense, as if set in precious **golden bowls**.

iv. The connection between prayer and incense is shown in Psalm 141:2: *Let my prayer be set before You as incense, the lifting up of my hands as the evening sacrifice.* Incense has a pleasing aroma, it ascends to heaven, and it needs *fire* before it is of any use.

d. **And they sang a new song**: The elders sing a **new song**, for mercies that are forever new.

i. "By a *new song* is either to be understood as an excellent song (for new songs were usually most valued,) or (which pleaseth me best) *new* as to the matter of it; for the servants of God under the Old Testament could not bless God for the actual redemption of man by the blood of Christ, but only rejoice in hope, embracing the promises seen afar off by the eye of faith." (Poole)

ii. "It is a new thing that the Son of God should become man. It is a new thing to ascend into the heavens with a body. It is a new thing to give remission of sins to men. It is a new thing for men to be sealed with the Holy Spirit. It is a new thing to receive the priesthood of sacred observance, and to look for a kingdom of unbounded promise." (Victorinus)

e. **You are worthy**: In the days of the Apostle John, Roman Emperors were celebrated upon their arrival with the Latin expression *vere dignus*, which is translated **You are worthy**. Here the true Ruler of the world is honored.

f. **For You were slain, and have redeemed us to God by Your blood out of every tribe and tongue and people and nation, and have made us kings and priests to our God; and we shall reign on the earth**: In the praise of Revelation 4:11, the emphasis is on God's work of *creation*. Here, the emphasis is on His work of *redemption*.

- The song honors the *price* of redemption: **for You were slain**

- The song honors the *worker* of redemption: **have redeemed us**

- The song honors the *destination* of redemption: **have redeemed us to God**

- The song honors the *payment* of redemption: **by Your blood**

- The song honors the *scope* of redemption: **every tribe and tongue and people and nation**

- The song honors the *length* of redemption: **have made us kings and priests to our God**

- The song honors the *result* of redemption: **and we shall reign on the earth**

g. **Kings and priests to our God**: Believers are **kings** because of their royal birth and their destiny to reign with Jesus. They are **priests** because they need no mediator other than Jesus Himself.

i. "When a fellow comes forward in all sorts of curious garments, and says he is a priest, the poorest child of God may say, 'Stand away, and don't interfere with my office: I am a priest; I know not what you may be. You surely must be a priest of Baal, for the only mention of the word vestments in Scripture is in connection with the temple of Baal.' The priesthood belongs to all the saints." (Spurgeon)

2. (11-12) Countless angels join in, declaring the worthiness of the Lamb because of the redemption He accomplished.

Then I looked, and I heard the voice of many angels around the throne, the living creatures, and the elders; and the number of them was ten thousand times ten thousand, and thousands of thousands, saying with

a loud voice: "Worthy is the Lamb who was slain to receive power and riches and wisdom, and strength and honor and glory and blessing!"

a. **I heard the voice of many angels around the throne**: The angels and the elders fell down before the Lamb together (Revelation 5:8). But it seems that only the elders sang the song of the redeemed (Revelation 5:9-10), because in no place does the Bible tell us of the redemption of angels. But now, **the voice of many angels around the throne** rises up with the praise of the Great Redeemer.

i. In Revelation 4:9-10, the angels prompt the elders into worship. Here, the elders seem to prompt the angels. It is a wonderful cycle in heaven, with the angels and elders encouraging each other to more and more praise.

b. **The number of them was ten thousand times ten thousand, and thousands of thousands**: This is an innumerable company of angels.

c. **Worthy is the Lamb who was slain**: In their song, the angels do not offer praise for their redemption. This is because angels are not (to the best of our knowledge) *subjects* of this redemption but they are careful observers of it, and are therefore able to praise God because of it (1 Peter 1:12 and Ephesians 3:10).

i. The angels can clearly see the greatness of God's work in redeeming fallen men, so in response they credit **power and riches and wisdom, and strength and honor and glory and blessing** to the Lamb. In the same way, we can praise God for the way He works in the lives of other people.

3. (13-14) All creation praises the Father and the Lamb.

And every creature which is in heaven and on the earth and under the earth and such as are in the sea, and all that are in them, I heard saying: "Blessing and honor and glory and power *be* to Him who sits on the throne, and to the Lamb, forever and ever!" Then the four living creatures said, "Amen!" And the twenty-four elders fell down and worshiped Him who lives forever and ever.

a. **Every creature**: John couldn't be any more complete in his description. Truly, this is *every creature* - **in heaven and on the earth and under the earth and such as are in the sea, and all that are in them.**

b. **Blessing and honor and glory and power be to Him who sits on the throne, and to the Lamb**: This combined worship of the Father and the Lamb is strong testimony to the deity of Jesus. "There cannot be the slightest doubt that the Lamb is to be reckoned with God and as God." (L. Morris)

i. "Now if Jesus Christ were not properly GOD this would be *idolatry*, as it would be giving to the *creature* what belongs to the *Creator*." (Clarke)

ii. "Depend upon it, my hearer, you never will go to heaven unless you are prepared to worship Jesus Christ as God. They are all doing it there: you will have to come to it, and if you entertain the notion that he is a mere man, or that he is anything less than God, I am afraid you will have to begin at the beginning and learn what true religion means. You have a poor foundation to rest upon. I could not trust my soul with a mere man, or believe in an atonement made by a mere man: I must see God himself putting his hand to so gigantic a work." (Spurgeon)

c. **Fell down and worshipped Him**: The ancient Greek word for **worshipped** is literally "to prostrate" or "to lay before another in complete submission." The scene may be that the elders **fell down** to their knees, then laid themselves before **Him who lives forever and ever** as an expression of their total submission and worship.

i. "This is the eastern method of *adoration*: first, the person worshipping fell down on his knees; and then, bowing down touched the earth with his forehead. This latter act was *prostration*." (Clarke)

d. **Forever and ever . . . worshipped Him who lives forever and ever**: The living God reigns eternally. The Caesars come and go, including those who persecute God's people. But the Lord God **lives forever and ever** and is *ever* worthy of our praise.

Revelation 6 - The First Six Seals

A. The first four seals of the scroll bring four horsemen.

1. (1-2) The white horse brings a man of conquest.

Now I saw when the Lamb opened one of the seals; and I heard one of the four living creatures saying with a voice like thunder, "Come and see." And I looked, and behold, a white horse. He who sat on it had a bow; and a crown was given to him, and he went out conquering and to conquer.

a. **I saw when the Lamb opened one of the seals**: From the previous chapter, we understand this scroll is the history and destiny of mankind and creation, and only Jesus - **the Lamb** - has the right to loose the seals on this scroll of the culmination of history.

i. If the scroll details the culmination of history, then these things must happen *before* the scroll is opened. This is not the fulfillment of history itself, but the *preparation* for it. The actual culmination will be detailed in Revelation 19.

ii. "It is worthy of remark that the opening of the seals is not merely a declaration of what God will do, but is the exhibition of a purpose then accomplished; for whenever the seal is opened, the sentence appears to be *executed*." (Clarke)

b. **And I heard one of the four living creatures saying with a voice like thunder, "Come and see."** Each seal is associated with a living creature (*zoa*, one of the cherubim of Ezekiel 1 and 10) who calls out "**come**" (or, it could be translated "go forth") to each horseman.

c. **Behold, a white horse**: Some - perhaps they take their interpretive clues more from cowboy movies than from the Bible - believe the rider on the **white horse** is Jesus. Jesus does return on a **white horse** in Revelation 19:11-16. But this is a satanic dictator who imitates Jesus.

i. He rules (**a crown was given**); he rules with **a bow**, not a sword; and he exercises dominion over the earth (**went out conquering and to conquer**). But the *results* of his rule, as described in the following verses, show this is not the reign of Jesus.

ii. "The whole context and character of these seals absolutely forbid our thinking of this rider being the Lord Jesus, as so many affirm. *His* reign shall not bring war, famine, and strife in its train." (Jennings)

iii. Here we reach an interpretive crossroads of the Book of Revelation. You can tell much about how a person understands this book and God's prophetic plan by seeing how they understand this first rider. Those who think Revelation is mostly a book of *history* believe that this rider is Jesus, the apostles, or the Roman emperors. Those who believe that this is a *prophetic* passage, yet to be fulfilled, often account this rider to be the antichrist.

d. **He went out conquering and to conquer**: This final satanic dictator over men will be the more terrible than all previous dictators were. He will rule over men as a false Messiah, and lead man in organized rebellion against God, in the pattern of Nimrod, his first predecessor. He is the one often called the antichrist.

i. The idea of a satanic dictator over men goes back all the way to Nimrod, the ruler over Babel in Genesis 10:8-14, where it says he was a *mighty hunter before the LORD*. This has the sense that he was a mighty hunter of *men*, and that this was offensive to the face of God.

e. Today's political and social scene is certainly set for the emergence of such a political leader. All that waits is for the Lord to allow it in His timing after He takes His church from this earth.

i. *And now you know what is restraining, that he may be revealed in his own time. For the mystery of lawlessness is already at work; only He who now restrains will do so until He is taken out of the way.* (2 Thessalonians 2:6-7)

ii. Significantly, the *first* seal opened brings this dictator to prominence. We understand that the seventieth week of Daniel 9 begins when this dictator will *confirm a covenant with* [the] *many*, referring to the Jewish people.

iii. Many wonder if these four horsemen of Revelation 6 are connected with the seventieth week of Daniel and the great tribulation itself, or with the course of history up until that time. This initial emergence of the antichrist, connected with what we know about this leader from Daniel 9 shows that these four horsemen are connected with Daniel's seventieth week and the great tribulation.

2. (3-4) The red horse brings war and conflict.

When He opened the second seal, I heard the second living creature saying, "Come and see." Another horse, fiery red, went out. And it was granted to the one who sat on it to take peace from the earth, and that *people* should kill one another; and there was given to him a great sword.

a. **Another horse, fiery red, went out. And it was granted to the one who sat on it to take peace from the earth**: This rider doesn't need to *bring* war and destruction. All he needs to do is *take* **peace from the earth**. Once this **peace** - God's gift to man - is taken, men rush in with war and destruction.

i. Peace between men and nations is a gift from God. It is not the *natural* state of relations between men.

b. **And it was granted**: This authority is **granted** to the horseman. This is, directly or indirectly, the judgment of God.

c. **That people should kill one another**: We live in the age of war and conflict. Since World War II, there have been more than 150 wars of some kind in the world, and at any given time there may be some three dozen armed conflicts taking thousands of lives yearly. The nations of the world often spend more than $1 trillion on military expenditures a year.

3. (5-6) The black horse brings scarcity and inequity.

When He opened the third seal, I heard the third living creature say, "Come and see." So I looked, and behold, a black horse, and he who sat on it had a pair of scales in his hand. And I heard a voice in the midst of the four living creatures saying, "A quart of wheat for a denarius, and three quarts of barley for a denarius; and do not harm the oil and the wine."

a. **A black horse, and he who sat on it had a pair of scales in his hand**: The scales symbolize the need to carefully measure and ration food. This speaks of a time of *scarcity*.

b. **A quart of wheat for a denarius, and three quarts of barley for a denarius**: These prices are about twelve times higher than normal. It means that it would cost a day's wage to buy the ingredients for a loaf of bread. This describes "a time of famine when life will be reduced to the barest necessities." (Walvoord)

i. We often see great famine in the world today, yet fewer people suffer from hunger today than 100 years ago. However, understanding the ecological balance, it would not take much to plunge many into the kind of scarcity and inequity mentioned here.

c. **Do not harm the oil and the wine**: Yet, the nicer things will be available for those who can afford them. There will still be **the oil and the wine** that should not be harmed.

4. (7-8) The pale horse brings death.

When He opened the fourth seal, I heard the voice of the fourth living creature saying, "Come and see." So I looked, and behold, a pale horse. And the name of him who sat on it was Death, and Hades followed with him. And power was given to them over a fourth of the earth, to kill with sword, with hunger, with death, and by the beasts of the earth.

a. **A pale horse. And the name of him who sat on it was Death**: This last rider shows that there will be a tremendous death toll from the dictatorship, war, famine and other calamities described by the previous three horsemen.

i. Our century has seen hundreds of millions killed by dictators, war, and famine. Yet this will pale in comparison to the death toll coming in the wake of this ultimate dictator. No wonder Jesus said of this time *For then there will be great tribulation, such as has not been since the beginning of the world until this time, no, nor ever shall be.* (Matthew 24:21)

b. **Power was given to them over a fourth of the earth, to kill**: Power is **given** to the horseman, and **given** by God. Though all hell is breaking loose on the earth, God is very much in control. He still holds the scroll and opens the seals.

B. The fifth and sixth seals of the scroll are opened.

1. (9-11) The fifth seal brings forth the cry of the martyrs.

When He opened the fifth seal, I saw under the altar the souls of those who had been slain for the word of God and for the testimony which they held. And they cried with a loud voice, saying, "How long, O Lord, holy and true, until You judge and avenge our blood on those who dwell on the earth?" Then a white robe was given to each of them; and it was said to them that they should rest a little while longer, until both *the number of* their fellow servants and their brethren, who would be killed as they *were*, was completed.

a. **I saw under the altar the souls of those who had been slain for the word of God**: That these souls are *under the altar* emphasizes that their life blood was poured out as an offering to God. The idea is drawn from Leviticus 4:7: *And he shall pour the remaining blood at the base of the altar of the burnt offering.*

b. **Who had been slain for the word of God**: It is probably best to see this as the cry of *all* martyrs for God's truth, not merely believers persecuted by the coming world leader, the first horseman of Revelation 6:1-2.

c. **And they cried with a loud voice**: These souls in heaven cry out for vengeance (**until You judge and avenge our blood**). We usually don't think of God's people crying out for vengeance, but they make their cry to God, and leave the matter with Him.

> i. When God's people are persecuted, He will set it right. It isn't wrong for God's people to ask Him to do what He promised to do. So the blood of Abel cried out from the ground for vengeance (Genesis 4:10), as did the blood of unavenged murders in the land of Israel (Numbers 35:33).

d. **It was said to them that they should rest a little while longer**: These saints are instructed to *wait*. How long do they wait? **Until both the number of their fellow servants and their brethren, who would be killed as they were, was completed**. This may mean that they should wait until *all* God's appointed martyrs are killed.

> i. Or, because the words **the number of** are supplied by the translators, not the text, it may mean that they wait until the *character* of the remaining martyrs on earth is perfected and complete. It is the way that you *live* that makes you a martyr, not the way that you *die*.

2. (12-17) The opening of the sixth seal brings cosmic disruption.

I looked when He opened the sixth seal, and behold, there was a great earthquake; and the sun became black as sackcloth of hair, and the moon became like blood. And the stars of heaven fell to the earth, as a fig tree drops its late figs when it is shaken by a mighty wind. Then the sky receded as a scroll when it is rolled up, and every mountain and island was moved out of its place. And the kings of the earth, the great men, the rich men, the commanders, the mighty men, every slave and every free man, hid themselves in the caves and in the rocks of the mountains, and said to the mountains and rocks, "Fall on us and hide us from the face of Him who sits on the throne and from the wrath of the Lamb! For the great day of His wrath has come, and who is able to stand?"

> a. **A great earthquake; and the sun became black as sackcloth of hair, and the moon became like blood. And the stars of heaven fell to the earth**: In the Bible, celestial disturbances are often connected with the coming of the Messiah. Isaiah, Jeremiah, Ezekiel, Joel, Zephaniah and Jesus Himself all describe such things.

i. A passage from Zephaniah is an example: *The great day of the* LORD *is near; it is near and hastens quickly. The noise of the day of the* LORD *is bitter; there the mighty men shall cry out. That day is a day of wrath, a day of trouble and distress, a day of devastation and desolation, a day of darkness and gloominess, a day of clouds and thick darkness, a day of trumpet and alarm against the fortified cities and against the high towers.* (Zephaniah 1:14-16)

ii. Or, as in Joel 2:10-11: *The sun and moon grow dark, and stars diminish their brightness . . . for the day of the* LORD *is great and terrible; who can endure it?*

iii. Those who regard these events as *history* have to spiritualize them. One example is Adam Clarke, who says this **great earthquake** is "A most stupendous change in the civil and religious constitution of the world. If it refer to Constantine the Great, the change that was made by his conversion to Christianity might be very properly represented under the emblem of an *earthquake.*"

b. **The sun became black as sackcloth of hair, and the moon became like blood. And the stars of heaven fell to the earth**: It is best to regard these pictures as *real*, but *poetic*. John isn't using technically precise scientific language, but he simply describes what he saw.

c. **And the kings of the earth, the great men, the rich men, the commanders, the mighty men, every slave and every free man, hid themselves**: All people are equally brought low by God's wrath. The judgment is all the more profound because it is the **wrath of the Lamb**.

i. "It is the wrath of love, the wrath of sacrificial love which, having done the absolute utmost for us and our salvation, tells us as nothing else could the certainty with which evil awaits its doom at the hand of God." (Torrance)

d. **Hide us from the face of Him who sits on the throne**: They hide not only from the terror of the judgments, but **from the face of Him who sits on the throne**. "What sinners dread most is not death, but the revealed presence of God." (Swete)

C. Observations: How do the seals fit in God's prophetic plan?

1. There are many different opinions, but it seems best to say that the seals, trumpets, and bowls that will be described later are not strictly sequential events. Chronologically, the trumpets do not follow the seals and the bowls do not follow the trumpets.

a. The first six seals are "a summary of the judgments distributed over the whole book; a brief summary of what will occur in 'the day of the Lord,' up the time of His actual Apocalypse or Unveiling in chapter 19." (Bullinger)

b. That span begins with the revelation of the Antichrist (the first seal) and it concludes with the revealing of the *face of Him who sits on the throne* (the seventh seal).

2. Do the seals represent conditions *immediately before* the end, or more *general conditions* prevailing over a more extended period, up until the return of Jesus?

a. There is a sense in which we can say that the they represent *both* - dictators, war, famine, death and persecution have been familiar throughout all history, but not to the *magnitude* and *severity* with which they will be present in the Great Tribulation.

b. "The wars and famines predicted in the second and third seals are not unfamiliar events in the history of the world, but never before since the time of Noah has a judgment so devastating been consummated as to destroy one-fourth of the earth's population at one stroke." (Walvoord)

c. As far as the seals are concerned, they will be an *intense amplification* of "business as usual." God will give mankind over to his fallen nature - *and more!*

i. This is not the case with some of the trumpet and bowl judgments of later chapters. They are completely unique manifestations of God's judgment.

3. The sixth seal concludes with a valid question: *Who is able to stand?* Only the believer can stand before this great judgment, the one who is justified by grace through faith in Jesus Christ.

a. *Therefore, having been justified by faith, we have peace with God through our Lord Jesus Christ, through whom also we have access by faith into this grace in which we stand.* (Romans 5:1-2)

b. *I declare to you the gospel which I preached to you, which you also received and in which you stand.* (1 Corinthians 15:1)

c. *Testifying that this is the true grace of God in which you stand.* (1 Peter 5:12)

d. The believer can stand in the face of this great wrath of God because Jesus already bore the wrath the believer deserved.

Revelation 7 - The 144,000 and the Great Multitude

A. The 144,000.

1. (1-3) Holding back judgment until the servants of God are sealed.

After these things I saw four angels standing at the four corners of the earth, holding the four winds of the earth, that the wind should not blow on the earth, on the sea, or on any tree. Then I saw another angel ascending from the east, having the seal of the living God. And he cried with a loud voice to the four angels to whom it was granted to harm the earth and the sea, saying, "Do not harm the earth, the sea, or the trees till we have sealed the servants of our God on their foreheads."

a. **Four angels standing at the four corners of the earth**: The phrase **four corners of the earth** is an ancient (and sometimes modern) equivalent to the idea of "the four points of the compass." The idea is that these angels effect the entire earth.

b. **Holding the four winds of the earth**: These **winds** are a destructive force of God's judgment, as they often are in the Old Testament.

i. Hosea 13:15 gives an example: *Though he is fruitful among his brethren, an east wind shall come; the wind of the Lord shall come from the wilderness. Then his spring will become dry, and his fountain shall be dried up.*

ii. The **four winds of the earth** may refer back to the four horsemen of Revelation 6:1-8, after the pattern of Zechariah 6:1-8. In that passage, four chariots with horses of the same colors of Revelation 6:1-8 go out to all the earth, and are called *the four spirits of heaven. Spirits* in that passage translates the Hebrew word *ruach*, which can also be translated *winds*.

c. **Another angel ascending from the east, having the seal of the living God**: Another angel has a **seal**, and he seals the people of God. In the ancient world, such seals were familiar. A king or a property owner could use a seal to show ownership or authenticity.

d. **Do not harm the earth, the sea, or the trees till we have sealed the servants of our God on their foreheads**: These servants of God will receive a protective seal on their forehead, containing God's name in some manner (Revelation 14:1).

> i. In Ezekiel 9, a similar protective seal is given to the righteous before Jerusalem is judged. The seal is the Hebrew letter *tau* ("t," as in the shape of a small cross).

e. **The servants of our God**: We are not told what exactly their service is, but the 144,000 are sealed for a specific and unique purpose. However, the general idea of being sealed is not limited to them.

> i. Jesus was sealed; *God the Father has set His seal on Him.* (John 6:27)

> ii. We are sealed with the Holy Spirit as a down payment of our eventual total redemption. Paul wrote: *God, who also has sealed us and given us the Spirit in our hearts as a guarantee.* (2 Corinthians 1:21-22)

> iii. This sealing of the Holy Spirit belongs to every believer when they are saved: *having believed, you were sealed with the Holy Spirit of promise.* (Ephesians 1:13)

> iv. The sealing of the Holy Spirit is meant to be both a *comfort* and a *challenge* to us. We are comforted in that it assures us that we belong to Him. We are *challenged* by it to depart from all evil and identify ourselves with the One we belong to: *Nevertheless the solid foundation of God stands, having this seal: "The Lord knows those who are His," and, "Let everyone who names the name of Christ depart from iniquity."* (2 Timothy 2:19) *And do not grieve the Holy Spirit of God, by whom you were sealed for the day of redemption.* (Ephesians 4:30)

2. (4-8) The number of those sealed.

And I heard the number of those who were sealed. One hundred *and* forty-four thousand of all the tribes of the children of Israel *were* sealed: of the tribe of Judah twelve thousand *were* sealed; of the tribe of Reuben twelve thousand *were* sealed; of the tribe of Gad twelve thousand *were* sealed; of the tribe of Asher twelve thousand *were* sealed; of the tribe of Naphtali twelve thousand *were* sealed; of the tribe of Manasseh twelve thousand *were* sealed; of the tribe of Simeon twelve thousand *were* sealed; of the tribe of Levi twelve thousand *were* sealed; of the tribe of Issachar twelve thousand *were* sealed; of the tribe of Zebulun twelve thousand *were* sealed; of the tribe of Joseph twelve thousand *were* sealed; of the tribe of Benjamin twelve thousand *were* sealed.

a. **One hundred and forty-four thousand of all the tribes of the children of Israel were sealed**: This is their *general* identification. They are of **all the tribes of the children of Israel**. Ethnically, they are Jewish, and there are 144,000 of these chosen ones.

b. **Of the tribe of Judah twelve thousand were sealed**: This is their *specific* identification. The 144,000 are divided among the 12 tribes of Israel. Though only God may know their tribal ancestry, there are 12,000 from each tribe.

c. The omission of the tribe of Dan: Why is Dan left out? Some think it is because Dan is the tribe of the Antichrist, based on Daniel 11:37 and Jeremiah 8:16. This may or may not be the case, but without doubt, Dan was the tribe which introduced idolatry into the nation of Israel (Genesis 49:17; Judges 18:30).

i. There is a wonderful redemption for the tribe of Dan. Dan is the *first* tribe listed in Ezekiel's millennial role call of the tribes (Ezekiel 48).

d. The slighting of the tribe of Ephraim: This tribe is referred to, but only indirectly. The **tribe of Joseph** is mentioned, but Joseph was represented by two tribes: Ephraim and Manasseh. Since the **tribe of Manasseh** is mentioned, by elimination, the **tribe of Joseph** must mean the tribe of Ephraim - who is listed, but not by name.

i. Why is Ephraim slighted? Perhaps it is because the tribe of Ephraim was also associated with great idolatry (Hosea 4:17).

e. It is often claimed that this list must be purely symbolic because it is "irregular," but what is a "regular" listing of the tribes?

i. There are not less than 20 different ways of listing the tribes of Israel in the Old Testament, including one that omits the tribe of Dan (1 Chronicles 4-7).

ii. Just because a list is *different* doesn't mean it is fanciful symbolism. It is proper to regard each of these lists as legitimate, and to consider that each specific variation serves a purpose, meaning to emphasize something.

3. Who are these 144,000?

a. Many different groups have claimed to be the 144,000. For example, the Jehovah's Witnesses said their entire group was, until they surpassed 144,000 in number. Now they say that the 144,000 are only a select group of Witnesses who go to heaven.

i. Most scholars either regard the 144,000 as the *church* or as *converted Jews*, who are still identified as Israelites in some manner.

ii. It is an important issue. If they are a symbol of the church, then the church is definitely *in* the Great Tribulation, but sealed for survival *through* the Great Tribulation.

b. Some facts about the 144,000 from Revelation 7 and Revelation 14 give us insight regarding their identity.

i. They are called *the children of Israel* (Revelation 7:4).

ii. Their tribal affiliation is specific (Revelation 7:4-8).

iii. They seem to be protected and triumphant through the period of God's wrath, meeting with Jesus at Mount Zion at His return (Revelation 14:1).

iv. They are celibate (Revelation 14:4).

v. They are the beginning of a greater harvest (Revelation 14:4).

vi. They are marked by integrity and faithfulness (Revelation 14:5).

c. Taken together, these facts make it difficult to say that the 144,000 are a symbolic picture of the church.

i. *Israel* is a term never specifically applied to the church in the New Testament, and never by any Christian until 160 A.D.

ii. Their tribal affiliation is emphatic and known to God. Even if God only knows it, there is absolutely no reason to regard their tribal affiliation as symbolic, not literal.

iii. It is difficult to imagine the entire church surviving through the tribulation without martyrdom and remaining celibate through the period, something that was never required for the church as a whole (1 Corinthians 7:1-6).

iv. If the 144,000 are a symbol of the entire church, what *greater harvest* are they the beginning of?

d. It is best to see the 144,000 as specifically chosen Jewish believers in Jesus, protectively sealed throughout the tribulation as a sign.

i. They are the beginning harvest of the salvation of Israel (Romans 11:1, Romans 11:26, Matthew 23:37-39).

ii. "They are not a part of the Church proper; for their repentance comes too late for that. They are a superaddition to the Church - a supplementary body - near and precious to Christ, but made up after the proper Church has finished its course." (Seiss)

B. The Great Multitude.

1. (9-10) More worship at the throne of God.

After these things I looked, and behold, a great multitude which no one could number, of all nations, tribes, peoples, and tongues, standing before the throne and before the Lamb, clothed with white robes, with palm branches in their hands, and crying out with a loud voice, saying, "Salvation *belongs* to our God who sits on the throne, and to the Lamb!"

a. **A great multitude which no one could number, of all nations, tribes, peoples, and tongues**: The diversity here is evidence that the Great Commission will be fulfilled before the end, even as Jesus promised (Matthew 24:14).

> i. Because John knew they came from different **nations, tribes, peoples, and tongues**, we know that there will be *differences* among people in heaven, just as there is on earth. We will not all be the same. We will be individuals.

> ii. "I suppose as he looked at them he could tell where they come from. There is individuality in heaven, depend upon it. Every seed will have its own body. There will sit down in heaven not three unknown patriarchs, but Abraham - you will know him; Isaac, you will know him; and Jacob, you will know him. There will be in heaven not a company of persons, all struck off alike so that you cannot tell who is who; but they will be out of every nation, and kindred, and people, and tongue." (Spurgeon)

b. **Standing before the throne and before the Lamb**: Again, John sees everything in heaven in reference to the *throne* of God. "This is a peculiar subject of their joy: that God has a throne, that he sits upon it, and that he ruleth over all things, and all things do his bidding. The central thought of heaven, then, is divine sovereignty." (Spurgeon)

c. **Clothed with white robes**: These **robes** remind us not only of the covering righteousness of Jesus, but also of *priestly service*. "They are *arrayed for holy service*, and arrayed at once, for they wear white robes fitted for their priestly service." (Spurgeon)

d. The **palm branches** remind us of Jesus' triumphal entry into Jerusalem (John 12:12-16), where Jesus was also praised as Savior and King. The word *Hosanna* means "save now!"

> i. **Palm branches** were emblems of victory. It shows this **great multitude** celebrates a great victory. "The palm, the ensign of triumph, indicates most certainly a conflict and conquest. As on earth palm would not be given if not won, we may conclude that the Lord would not have distributed the prize unless there had been a preceding warfare and victory . . . From the very fact that the glorified carry palms, we may infer that they did not come from beds of sloth, or gardens

of pleasure, or palaces of peace, but that they endured hardness, and were men trained for war." (Spurgeon)

e. Salvation belongs to our God who sits on the throne, and to the Lamb! Having an emblem of righteousness (**white robes**), they worship God for **salvation**. They recognize that *God* is the source of salvation, and no one else. Salvation isn't something we earn, it is something God gives.

> i. Sometimes believers on earth take their salvation almost for granted. This isn't true of this great multitude in heaven.

2. (11-12) All heavenly creatures join in worship.

All the angels stood around the throne and the elders and the four living creatures, and fell on their faces before the throne and worshiped God, saying: "Amen! Blessing and glory and wisdom, thanksgiving and honor and power and might, *be* to our God forever and ever. Amen."

> a. **All the angels . . . the elders and the four living creatures . . . worshiped God**: As the great multitude worships God, the others in heaven are compelled to join their voices in praise. All created beings around the throne join in.

> b. **Blessing and glory and wisdom, thanksgiving and honor and power and might**: As these other created beings hear the worship the great multitude brings to God, *they* see more clearly the power and wisdom and majesty of God. They can worship God all the more by seeing the salvation He brought to the great multitude.

3. (13-14) The identity of the great multitude.

Then one of the elders answered, saying to me, "Who are these arrayed in white robes, and where did they come from?" And I said to him, "Sir, you know." So he said to me, "These are the ones who come out of the great tribulation, and washed their robes and made them white in the blood of the Lamb."

> a. **Then one of the elders answered**: It was important that John knew the identity of this great multitude. But he didn't know that he should ask, so **one of the elders** prompts him to ask.

> b. **These are the ones who come out of the great tribulation**: This vast multitude, from every tribe and tongue and nation, are those rescued for God's kingdom in the period of **the great tribulation**.

> > i. They have had trouble on the earth during **the great tribulation**. In the ancient Greek grammar of this passage, "**the**" is emphatic. This was a time of **great tribulation** *for this multitude*. This leads many to

believe that most, if not all, of these are *martyrs* from **the great tribulation**.

ii. The presence of so many tribulation saints is a powerful statement of God's grace and mercy. Even in this time of judgment and wrath on the earth, many are saved.

iii. Because the great multitude are mentioned right after the 144,000, many think they are - at least in part - due to the work of those 144,000 servants of God. Perhaps the 144,000 are evangelists who help reap this huge harvest for the kingdom during **the great tribulation**.

c. **Washed their robes and made them white in the blood of the Lamb**: Those saved in the great tribulation are saved just like everybody else, by **the blood of the Lamb**. Even if they are martyred, their martyrdom does not save them. Only the work of Jesus can cleanse and save.

i. "They have washed their robes and made them white in the blood of the Lamb. Not one of them became white through his tears of repentance, not one through the shedding of the blood of bulls or of goats. They all wanted a vicarious sacrifice, and for none of them was any sacrifice effectual, except the death of Jesus Christ the Lord. They washed their robes nowhere but in the blood of the Lamb." (Spurgeon)

ii. **White by blood** is an interesting phrase; we don't think of things being made white by blood! But the blood of Jesus cleanses us: *Though your sins are like scarlet, they shall be as white as snow; though they are red like crimson, they shall be as wool.* (Isaiah 1:18)

4. (15-17) What this great multitude does, and how it is blessed.

Therefore they are before the throne of God, and serve Him day and night in His temple. And He who sits on the throne will dwell among them. They shall neither hunger anymore nor thirst anymore; the sun shall not strike them, nor any heat; for the Lamb who is in the midst of the throne will shepherd them and lead them to living fountains of waters. And God will wipe away every tear from their eyes.

a. **They are before the throne of God**: In heaven, the redeemed enjoy the immediate presence of God. They can come right into the throne room and be with God. There are no barriers, no waiting lists.

i. These saints knew affliction on earth, and they triumphed over it. But it wasn't their affliction that saved them. It was Jesus and their relationship of faith with Him. "Affliction of itself does not sanctify anybody, but the reverse. I believe in sanctified afflictions, but not in sanctifying afflictions." (Spurgeon)

b. **And serve Him day and night**: In heaven, the redeemed **serve** God. We don't know exactly how, but they do. "Heaven is not only a place of rest from earthly toil but also a place of privileged service." (Walvoord)

c. **He who sits on the throne will dwell among them**: In heaven, God **will dwell** with His people. This is the ultimate fulfillment of King David's great desire in Psalm 27:4: *One thing I have desired of the LORD, that will I seek: that I may dwell in the house of the LORD all the days of my life, to behold the beauty of the LORD, and to inquire in His temple.*

d. **The Lamb who is in the midst of the throne will shepherd them**: In heaven, the redeemed will know the loving care and nurture of their Savior. He will protect them from every affliction (**they shall neither hunger anymore nor thirst anymore; the sun shall not strike them, nor any heat**). He will also provide for their every need (**lead them to living fountains of waters**).

> i. Doesn't Jesus **shepherd** us now? Isn't He close to us and caring for us now? Yes, but in heaven it will be so much more. "The true Christian life, when we live near to God, is the rough draft of the life of full communion above. We have seen the artist make with his pencil, or with his charcoal, a bare outline of his picture. It is nothing more, but still one could guess what the finished picture will be from the sketch before you." (Spurgeon)

e. **God will wipe away every tear from their eyes**: In heaven, the redeemed will know no more sorrow or pain. The hurt and the struggle of this earthly life are gone, and tears are a thing of the past, because **God will wipe away every tear**.

> i. What tender love! We think of a mother's loving hand, brushing away the tears from her child's face. God loves us with that kind of nurturing care.

> ii. We also understand from this that **every tear** will only be wiped away in *heaven*. On this earth, we have our share of pain and tears to endure and bring to God. He shows His love *now* with sweet consolation and strength for our tears; but *one day* - in heaven, not now - He will wipe them away forever.

> iii. This passage *does not* have the idea that in heaven, we will weep over our wasted life or unconfessed sin, but God will still wipe those tears away. That idea may be a powerful, guilt-inducing motivator, but it has nothing to do with the meaning of this verse. "The point is that the grief and tears of the past, speaking of their trials in the tribulation, will be over when they get to heaven . . . God will wipe away all tears resulting from their suffering on earth." (Walvoord)

iv. Many wonder, "How can there be no sorrow in heaven if we have relatives or loved ones who perish in hell? Won't we be sorry for them?" Spurgeon answers well: "Now, how is this? If you will tell me, I shall be glad, for I cannot tell you. I do not believe that there will be one atom less tenderness, that there will be one fraction less of amiability, and love, and sympathy - I believe there will be more - but that they will be in some way so refined and purified, that while compassion for suffering is there, detestation of sin shall be there to balance it, and a state of complete equilibrium shall be attained. Perfect acquiescence in the divine will is probably the secret of it; but it is not my business to guess; I do not know what handkerchief the Lord will use, but I know that he will wipe all tears away from their faces, and these tears among them."

Revelation 8 - The First Four Trumpets

A. The seventh seal is loosed.

1. (1) Silence in heaven.

When He opened the seventh seal, there was silence in heaven for about half an hour.

> a. **When He opened the seventh seal**: The sealed scroll was introduced in Revelation 5, and the seals were opened one by one up to the sixth seal in Revelation 6. We waited for the last seal to be opened and the contents of the scroll to be revealed - but then were given a pause with Revelation 7 and the revealing of the 144,000 and the great multitude out of the great tribulation. Now the idea of a pause between the sixth and **the seventh seal** is emphasized by this **silence in heaven for about half an hour**.

> > i. This **silence** is striking; some have seen it as "breathing space," or, that the angels are silent so the prayers of the saints can be heard, perhaps even the cry of the martyrs of Revelation 6:9-11.

> > ii. More likely, this **silence in heaven** demonstrates a sober, awestruck silence at the judgments to come, now that the seals are off and the scroll can be opened.

> b. **Silence in heaven for about half an hour**: A half-hour silence is not long, but things seem long or short in their context. If a preacher were to stop his sermon and remain silent for ten minutes, it would seem like an eternity. Since heaven is a place of constant praise and worship to God (Revelation 4:8-11), **silence** for **about half an hour** is a long time.

2. (2) Seven angels with seven trumpets.

And I saw the seven angels who stand before God, and to them were given seven trumpets.

a. **The seven angels who stand before God**: According to Jewish tradition, there are seven angels who stand in God's presence. Apparently, based on this verse, that traditional idea was accurate.

b. **And to them were given seven trumpets**: In the Old Testament, **trumpets** sounded the alarm for war and threw the enemy into a panic, or they called an assembly of God's people. These **seven trumpets** will sound as God's battle-alarm during the great tribulation.

3. (3-6) The other angel with the golden censer.

Then another angel, having a golden censer, came and stood at the altar. He was given much incense, that he should offer *it* with the prayers of all the saints upon the golden altar which was before the throne. And the smoke of the incense, with the prayers of the saints, ascended before God from the angel's hand. Then the angel took the censer, filled it with fire from the altar, and threw *it* to the earth. And there were noises, thunderings, lightnings, and an earthquake. So the seven angels who had the seven trumpets prepared themselves to sound.

a. **Then another angel**: Some see this **angel** as Jesus, functioning as a mediator and because of Old Testament references to Jesus as "the Angel of the LORD." Others say it can only be a mere angelic being because the specific ancient Greek word for **another** means "another of the same kind."

b. **A golden censer . . . the smoke of the incense, with the prayers of the saints, ascended before God**: Prayer and incense are often associated in the Bible. The idea is that just as incense is precious, pleasant, and drifts to heaven, so do our prayers. So here, before anything *happens* at the opening of the seventh seal, the prayers of God's people come before the Lord God.

i. Significantly, the prayers of God's people set in motion the coming consummation of history. "More potent, more powerful than all the dark and mighty powers let loose in the world, more powerful than anything else, is the power of prayer set ablaze by the fire of God and cast upon the earth." (Torrance)

ii. 2 Peter 3:10-12 indicates that there is a sense in which we can *hasten* the Lord's coming by our holy conduct and godly lives. But here we see that we can also hasten the Lord's coming through prayer, even as Daniel asked for a speedy fulfillment of prophecy regarding captive Israel (Daniel 9), we can and should also pray *Even so, come, Lord Jesus!* (Revelation 22:20)

iii. "It is not said that the angel presents these prayers. He presents the incense, and the *prayers ascend* WITH *it*. The *ascending* of the *incense* shows that the prayers and offering were accepted." (Clarke)

c. **Then the angel took the censer, filled it with fire from the altar, and threw it to the earth**: As God's people pray for the resolution of all things, their prayers are touched by the **fire from the altar** in heaven, and then "thrown" back down to earth. All things will not be resolved on this earth until judgment comes, and when the prayers of God's people "come back" to earth, they bring the groundswell of judgment (**noises, thunderings, lightnings, and an earthquake**).

d. **So the seven angels who had the seven trumpets prepared themselves to sound**: We waited for the seven seals to be opened and saw them loosed one by one. But when the seventh seal was finally loosed, the end did not immediately come. It set in motion **seven trumpets** that would **sound** upon the earth.

i. How do the seals and the trumpets relate to each other? Some people believe they are *poetic and repetitive*, and John describes the same events with different words and details in both the seal and trumpet judgments. "This is typical of John's method. He goes over the ground again and again, each time teaching us something new. There is more to the End than we can readily take in. Every series of visions brings out new facets of it." (L. Morris)

ii. How do the seals and the trumpets related to each other? Some people believe they are *sequential*, and that the seventh seal contains the seven trumpets, and the seventh trumpet contains the seven bowls of judgment. Yet there are problems with a sequential approach. For example, are the people of Revelation 6:15-17 mistaken about Jesus' return? They don't seem to be. But if the trumpets simply follow in sequence to the seals, then it is a striking display of God's mercy in stretching out the end and allowing repentance.

iii. Since John brings a report from eternity, it is difficult to assign a chronological and sequential element to these judgments. It is most important to emphasize that they are *real*, even if their sequence is hard to pin down with certainty.

B. The first four trumpets.

1. (7) The first trumpet brings a plague on vegetation.

The first angel sounded: And hail and fire followed, mingled with blood, and they were thrown to the earth. And a third of the trees were burned up, and all green grass was burned up.

a. **Hail and fire followed, mingled with blood: Blood** may indicate the *color* or the *result* of the phenomenon described here. We don't know if the **hail and fire** was red in color or if it brought forth red blood, but one way or another this should be understood straightforwardly, without escaping into a creative symbolism.

i. "Many eminent men suppose that the irruption of the barbarous nations of the Roman empire is here intended. It is easy to find coincidences when fancy runs riot." (Clarke)

ii. "The truth is, if *earth, trees,* and *grass* do not mean earth, trees, and grass, no man can tell what they mean. Letting go the literal signification of the record, we launch out upon an endless sea of sheer conjecture." (Seiss)

b. **A third of the trees were burned up, and all green grass was burned up**: Because of this **hail and fire**, **trees** and **grass** are destroyed - one-third of the vegetation of the planet is **burned up** during the great tribulation.

i. *How* will this happen? Many wonder if it will happen through phenomenon we know today, like nuclear war, fallout, pollution, meteors, and so forth. These ideas are interesting and possible, but they should never obscure the essential truth: *God* brings judgment. He isn't a passive bystander. This is not "nature" taking its course.

ii. God may use whatever *method* He desires to bring judgment, but people on earth *know* these events are from God, and do not think them to be merely natural disasters (Revelation 16:9, and 16:11, Revelation 19:19).

2. (8-9) The second trumpet brings a plague on the sea.

Then the second angel sounded: And *something* like a great mountain burning with fire was thrown into the sea, and a third of the sea became blood. And a third of the living creatures in the sea died, and a third of the ships were destroyed.

a. **Something like a great mountain**: John carefully says that this is not an actual mountain (note the use of *like*), but it is a blazing mass as large as a **mountain**.

b. **A third of the sea became blood**: This disaster is a cataclysm, perhaps a meteor that crashes into the sea and results in great oceanic upheaval with residual pollution. Researchers today say that this sort of phenomenon has happened many times in the history of the earth, sometimes resulting in great ecological upheaval and disaster. Here, the result is that **a third of the living creatures in the sea died, and a third of the ships**

were destroyed. The **blood** may be either the *cause* or the *effect* of the widespread death in the oceans of the world.

> c. **The sea** may be a specific reference to the Mediterranean and not a reference to all oceans. In the world of the Apostle John, the Mediterranean Sea *was* the sea and they really had little knowledge of other oceans.

c. It is common to take this **great mountain** as a symbol for a nation that will be judged. It is true that mountains are sometimes used as figures of governments or nations (Jeremiah 51:25, 51:27, 51:30). But in this context, the symbol doesn't make sense. What does it mean that the **great mountain** is burning with fire? What does it mean that it **was thrown into the sea?** What does the **sea** symbolize? Who are the **living creatures in the sea?** What are the **ships** on the sea? What is their destruction a symbol of? All these questions make us say that the best solution is to see this as some literal mass of land with probably a meteor or asteroid falling into the sea and bringing ecological disaster.

3. (10-11) The third trumpet brings a plague on fresh waters.

Then the third angel sounded: And a great star fell from heaven, burning like a torch, and it fell on a third of the rivers and on the springs of water. The name of the star is Wormwood. A third of the waters became wormwood, and many men died from the water, because it was made bitter.

> a. **A great star fell from heaven, burning like a torch**: We may easily associate this with a comet or meteor crashing into the earth and bringing ecological disaster. But God may have something else in mind also.
>
> > i. "Some say the star means *Attila* and his Huns; others, Genseric with his Vandals falling on the city of Rome; others, Eleazer, the son of Annus, spurning the emperor's victims, and exciting the fury of the Zealots; others, Arius, infecting the pure Christian doctrine with his heresy, [and so on and so on]. It certainly cannot mean *all these*; and probably *none* of them. Let the reader judge." (Clarke)
>
> b. **The name of the star is Wormwood: Wormwood** is a very bitter substance, and proverbial for bitterness and sadness.
>
> c. **A third of the rivers . . . a third of the waters**: The *proportion* of ecological disaster stays the same. In each one of the trumpets, **a third** of an ecological system is destroyed in judgment.

4. (12-13) The fourth trumpet brings a plague on the heavens, and darkness on the earth.

Then the fourth angel sounded: And a third of the sun was struck, a third of the moon, and a third of the stars, so that a third of them were darkened. A third of the day did not shine, and likewise the night. And I looked, and I heard an angel flying through the midst of heaven, saying with a loud voice, "Woe, woe, woe to the inhabitants of the earth, because of the remaining blasts of the trumpet of the three angels who are about to sound!"

a. **A third of the day did not shine, and likewise the night**: This does not describe a one-third lessening of light, but one-third of the day and night are plunged into absolute darkness. As Jesus said: *the sun will be darkened, and the moon will not give its light* (Matthew 24:29).

b. **Woe, woe, woe to the inhabitants of the earth, because of the remaining blasts of the trumpet**: The angel's woes are well founded, because one-third of the earth's population will die in the next three trumpets.

i. The ancient Greek words for *angel* and *eagle* are very close in spelling. Some ancient versions say that it is an *eagle* **flying through the midst of heaven**, making this cry.

5. Observations on the first four trumpets.

a. These first four trumpets reveal the severity of God's judgment. He attacks all the ordinary means of subsistence, such as food and water; and He attacks all the ordinary means of comfort, and knowledge, such as light and the regular rhythm of days.

i. Man has come to see these aspects of the created order as impersonal, perpetual forces. During the great tribulation, God proclaims His Lordship through their agonizing disruption.

ii. We know the great humility that comes upon men in the midst of something like an earthquake, because they know that "nature" is not as reliable as they had thought. With these four trumpets, that effect will be multiplied greatly.

b. The first four trumpets also reveal the *mercy* of God's judgment; these are partial judgments striking only one-third, and are meant to warn and lead a rebellious world to repentance before the final curtain. For now, God *spares* more than He *smites*.

Revelation 9 - The Fifth and Sixth Trumpets

A. The fifth trumpet brings demonic *locusts* from the bottomless pit.

1. (1) A star fallen from heaven.

Then the fifth angel sounded: And I saw a star fallen from heaven to the earth. To him was given the key to the bottomless pit.

a. **Then the fifth angel sounded**: This is the fifth angel sounding a trumpet. There were seven seals, followed - thematically if not chronologically - by seven trumpets. In their arranged order, they are similar.

i. The first four seals and trumpets presented judgments directed against the earth. In the first four seals, these were the "four horsemen" bringing tyranny, war, famine, and death on the earth. In the first four trumpets, these were the ecological destruction of the vegetation, seas, fresh waters, and sky.

ii. The last three seals focused upon heaven: the cry of the martyrs, cosmic disturbances, and the heavenly prelude to the seven trumpets. The last three trumpets will speak of hell, in terms of the demonic.

b. **I saw a star fallen from heaven**: The text clearly shows us that this star is a *person* (**to him**), not a literal star. The verb tense (**fallen**) indicates that he already had fallen.

i. But who is this **star**? Suggestions have included Nero, a fallen angel, an evil spirit, Satan, the Word of God, a good angel, or even Jesus Himself.

ii. In the context, this **star** is best seen as an angel; whether he is a good or bad angel depends on his relation to the *angel of the bottomless pit* in Revelation 9:11. If the angel of Revelation 9:1 is the same as the angel of Revelation 9:11, it is an evil angel - perhaps Satan himself. If it is a different angel, it may be a good angel sent by God to open up this **bottomless pit** for the purposes of judgment.

c. **To him was given the key to the bottomless pit**: That this **star** is **fallen** makes us associate him with Satan, or another high-ranking evil angelic being. But the fact that he is **given the key to the bottomless pit** makes us *not* want to associate him with Satan. The idea that Satan is the "master of hell" is foreign to the rest of the Scriptures. He will be hell's victim, not ruler.

i. At the same time, we notice that the **key** is **given** to this being, and that it is **given** at a specific time and for a specific purpose that furthers God's plan. This angel - evil or good - serves God's purpose, even if he does not intend to.

d. Where is the **bottomless pit**? The most straightforward answer is that it is in the center of the earth, because there, one might say that all is "top" and nothing is "bottom." However, some think that the "bottomlessness" of the pit is symbolic.

i. The *abyssos* is a prison for certain demons (Luke 8:31, 2 Peter 2:4, and Jude 6). This is probably the same place as this **bottomless pit**. More generally, this place is considered the realm of the dead, the same as Hades (Romans 10:7).

e. Revelation 9:1 is a good example of how the Book of Revelation is wrongly spiritualized in its interpretation. Some commentators say that the **star** is the word of God, the **pit** is human nature, and the lesson is that if the gospel is rejected, horrors are unleashed. But this is far from the plain meaning of Revelation 9:1.

2. (2-6) Locusts from the bottomless pit.

And he opened the bottomless pit, and smoke arose out of the pit like the smoke of a great furnace. So the sun and the air were darkened because of the smoke of the pit. Then out of the smoke locusts came upon the earth. And to them was given power, as the scorpions of the earth have power. They were commanded not to harm the grass of the earth, or any green thing, or any tree, but only those men who do not have the seal of God on their foreheads. And they were not given *authority* to kill them, but to torment them *for* five months. Their torment *was* like the torment of a scorpion when it strikes a man. In those days men will seek death and will not find it; they will desire to die, and death will flee from them.

a. **Out of the smoke locusts came upon the earth**: These are obviously not "natural" locusts. They avoid plants and attack men like scorpions attack. They are "A visual representation of the hordes of demons loosed upon the earth." (Walvoord)

i. The idea is simply that as part of the judgment of the great tribulation, God will allow demonic hordes, previously imprisoned, to descend upon the earth like a swarm of destructive **locusts**. They are not, as some have suggested, heretics, Muslims, Turks, Saracens, Jesuits, monks, or Protestants!

b. Those who have the **seal of God on their foreheads** (the 144,000 and perhaps more) are protected, but *none* other are. This is an inescapable judgment of God.

c. **They were not given authority to kill them, but to torment them for five months**: Their purpose and period is expressly governed by God, and the purpose of all this is to bring repentance (Revelation 9:20-21).

d. **In those days men will seek death and will not find it; they will desire to die, and death will flee from them**: Death will offer no escape from this prolonged torture. Their **power** is described like the power of **scorpions**, and the bite of a scorpion, though extremely painful, is rarely fatal.

i. **They will desire to die**: The tormented ones want to die, as Paul did in Philippians 1:21-23, but for a completely different reason and result than Paul. For Paul, death led to eternal blessing, but for these tormented ones, death is a leap from the frying pan of present torment into eternal fire.

ii. The idea of "death as an escape" is a demonic deception. The infamous murderers of Littleton, Colorado made chilling home movies before their killing spree. Eric Harris and Dylan Klebold left behind a videotaped document spelling out their motivation. In the last segment of tape, shot the morning of the murders, Harris & Klebold are dressed and say they are ready for "our little Judgement Day." Then Klebold, looking tense, says goodbye to his parents. He concludes, "I didn't like life too much. Just know I am going to a better place than here." What tragic deception to think - on the day you will commit terrible murders - that you will go "to a better place." There was no escape in death for Eric Harris and Dylan Klebold. *Now* is the time of repentance, to escape from sin, and to be restored.

3. (7-10) The appearance of these locusts.

The shape of the locusts was like horses prepared for battle. On their heads were crowns of something like gold, and their faces *were* like the faces of men. They had hair like women's hair, and their teeth were like lions' *teeth*. And they had breastplates like breastplates of iron, and the sound of their wings *was* like the sound of chariots with many horses

running into battle. They had tails like scorpions, and there were stings in their tails. Their power *was* **to hurt men five months.**

a. **The shape of the locusts was like horses prepared for battle**: Many attempts have been made to show that this is an accurate (though poetic) description of natural locusts. But this approach misses the obvious demonic connection.

i. Why would God call them **locusts** if they are not literal locusts, but demonic spirits who swarm and destroy like locusts? Among other reasons, because locusts are agents of God's judgment. This is a consistent Old Testament figure in passages like Exodus 10:4-14, Deuteronomy 28:38, 1 Kings 8:37, 2 Chronicles 7:13, Joel 1:4, and Amos 4:9.

b. **Like horses . . . like gold . . . like the faces of men . . . like women's hair . . . like lion's teeth**: The repetition of **like** indicates something other than a literal description is intended. The total impact of this picture is one of unnatural and awesome cruelty.

i. Suggestions that these locusts actually describe something such as the "helicopter gunships of the Antichrist" are interesting, but purely speculative, and don't fit *all* the details.

ii. "There seems to be no alternative to concluding that God, satisfying the age-long desire of those wicked spirits to possess bodies of their own, has created bodies for them, bodies appropriate in demonic appearance to the character of the demonic inhabitants." (H. Morris)

iii. "There can be no specific answer to the question of exactly who or what is symbolized by the plague of locusts. All we can know for sure is that in the period immediately before the end the wicked will be subjected to a time of unprecedented demonic torment. Exactly how this will take place will remain unknown until disclosed by history itself." (Mounce)

4. (11) The leader of these locusts.

And they had as king over them the angel of the bottomless pit, whose name in Hebrew *is* **Abaddon, but in Greek he has the name Apollyon.**

a. **And they had as king over them**: This is another indication that these creatures are not literal locusts. The Bible tells us that literal locusts have no king, and these do. Proverbs 30:27 says, *The locusts have no king, yet they all advance in ranks.*

b. **Whose name in Hebrew is Abaddon**: Their king is given a name. **Abaddon** and **Apollyon** both have the same thought of *destruction* or *torment* (perdition).

c. **The angel of the bottomless pit**: Since this is the king of these locusts, and since he has the name **Abaddon** or **Apollyon**, this is obviously Satan himself or another high-ranking leader of demons.

5. (12) The worst is yet to come.

One woe is past. Behold, still two more woes are coming after these things.

B. The sixth trumpet: an army of destruction.

1. (13) A voice from the altar.

Then the sixth angel sounded: And I heard a voice from the four horns of the golden altar which is before God,

a. **I heard a voice from the four horns of the golden altar**: In the tabernacle and temple of Israel, **the golden altar** was the altar of incense, which was a representation of the prayers of God's people.

b. The **four horns of the golden altar** stood at each corner. Atoning blood was applied to the horns. From these **horns**, John hears a **voice**. In this, John recalls a persistent theme: the prayers of God's people play a large role in the end-times drama.

2. (14-15) The angels and their mission.

Saying to the sixth angel who had the trumpet, "Release the four angels who are bound at the great river Euphrates." So the four angels, who had been prepared for the hour and day and month and year, were released to kill a third of mankind.

a. **Release the four angels who are bound at the great river Euphrates**: These four angels have no *necessary* connection with the four angels of Revelation 7:1. They may be the same **four angels** or they may not be. Whoever they are, they are **prepared for the hour and day and month and year** of the unleashing of this judgment.

i. **Were released**: "Most of Satan's angels are yet free - being the principalities against which we wrestle, but some terrible offenders of high rank have been bound." (Newell)

ii. This assumes these are "bad" angels; they may or may not be, but they probably are evil angels. No matter what, they are servants of the divine purpose.

b. **Were released to kill a third of mankind**: The demonic locusts described earlier in the chapter were restricted to tormenting mankind. But these **four angels** have the authority to kill on a massive scale.

i. These angels have a specific sphere of activity (**a third of man-kind**), and are only activated in God's timing. They execute God's will in God's timing.

c. **The great river Euphrates**: Why are these angels of judgment con-nected with the Euphrates River? The Euphrates was a landmark of an-cient Babylon. It was the frontier of Israel's land as fully promised by God (Genesis 15:17-21). It was also the boundary of the old Roman Empire, which will be revived under the Antichrist.

ii. The Euphrates is also associated with the first sin (Genesis 2:10-14), the first murder (Genesis 4:16), the first organized revolt against God (Genesis 11:1-9), the first war confederation (Genesis 14:1), and the first dictatorship (Genesis 10:8-10).

3. (16-19) Description of the army led by these angels.

Now the number of the army of the horsemen *was* two hundred mil-lion; I heard the number of them. And thus I saw the horses in the vision: those who sat on them had breastplates of fiery red, hyacinth blue, and sulfur yellow; and the heads of the horses *were* like the heads of lions; and out of their mouths came fire, smoke, and brimstone. By these three *plagues* a third of mankind was killed; by the fire and the smoke and the brimstone which came out of their mouths. For their power is in their mouth and in their tails; for their tails *are* like ser-pents, having heads; and with them they do harm.

a. **The number of the army of the horsemen was two hundred mil-lion**: Is this number literal or symbolic? "It is possible that the number is not to be taken literally, but simply suggests an army that is impossible to count and is greater than anything mankind has ever seen." (Hocking)

b. **Breastplates of fiery red, hyacinth blue, and sulfur yellow; and the heads of the horses were like the heads of lions; and out of their mouths came fire, smoke, and brimstone**: They are given a weird, gro-tesque description. This is a powerful picture of horror, destruction and demonic association.

c. Does this speak of a natural or a supernatural army? Is this an army of men or an army of demons?

i. If this describes a natural army of men, then the weird description may speak of modern, mechanized warfare. It may be John simply describes modern machinery in the only terms he can, and the result is this weird, grotesque, terrifying account.

ii. But, a human army this size has never been seen. The total size of all armies - on both sides - at the height of the Second World War was only 70 million. In 1965 China claimed to have an army and militia of 200 million, but this claim was doubted by many. Even if such an army was assembled, and marched towards the west, it is hard (but not impossible) to see such an army killing a billion or more people - **a third of mankind**.

iii. Therefore, perhaps the safest interpretation is to see this as a literal 200 million strong army, but a demonic army invading earth. This continues the idea of the demonic army like locusts described earlier in the chapter.

4. (20-21) The response of man.

But the rest of mankind, who were not killed by these plagues, did not repent of the works of their hands, that they should not worship demons, and idols of gold, silver, brass, stone, and wood, which can neither see nor hear nor walk. And they did not repent of their murders or their sorceries or their sexual immorality or their thefts.

a. **But the rest of mankind, who were not killed by these plagues, did not repent**: In general, mankind shows no repentance, despite the presence of some pretty overwhelming "signs and wonders."

b. **That they should not worship demons, and idols**: Instead, man continues with his idol worship in a "business as usual" sort of way. They continue in their worship of demons, whether their worship is witting or unwitting.

i. It is amazing to see how quickly things return to "normal" after some calamity such as an earthquake. We are so quick to forget God's lessons, even the lessons that come in judgment.

c. **And they did not repent of their murders or their sorceries or their sexual immorality or their thefts**: This list of sins is a striking accusation against our present age. Certainly, our modern world is characterized by **murders, sorceries** (associated with the taking of drugs), **sexual immorality** and **thefts**.

Revelation 10 - No More Delay

A. The mighty angel.

1. (1) A mighty angel comes down from heaven.

I saw still another mighty angel coming down from heaven, clothed with a cloud. And a rainbow *was* on his head, his face *was* like the sun, and his feet like pillars of fire.

a. **I saw still another mighty angel**: Revelation 9 left off with the sounding of the sixth of seven trumpets, which usher in the end of all things. Now, instead of the seventh trumpet, we have another interlude until Revelation 11:15.

i. These interludes serve a dramatic purpose, but also show mercy in allowing more opportunity for repentance. It is as if God brings things to the brink, then pulls back a little to grant mankind more time to repent.

b. **Another mighty angel coming down from heaven**: Many have identified this **mighty angel**, this messenger, as Jesus because some of the imagery also applies to Him. Revelation 1:15-16 also describes Jesus with *His countenance . . . like the sun shining in its strength.*

i. But, angels are never clearly identified with Jesus in Revelation or in the New Testament, though He is clearly associated with the "Angel of the LORD" in the Old Testament. A better identification is with Michael because there are also similarities to this **mighty angel** and to Michael as he is described in Daniel 12:1 and 12:6-7.

c. **A rainbow was on his head**: Not only is the rainbow a reminder of God's promise to man, but it is also a natural result when the **sun** shines through a **cloud**.

d. Whoever his exact identity, "clearly this angel has come from the very presence of God" (Barclay), and he has great might and authority.

2. (2-3) The angel cries out, and seven thunders utter their voices.

He had a little book open in his hand. And he set his right foot on the sea and *his* left *foot* on the land, and cried with a loud voice, as *when* a lion roars. When he cried out, seven thunders uttered their voices.

a. **He had a little book open in his hand**: Is this **little book** the same as the scroll no one except Jesus could open in Revelation 5:1-7? If one takes the *mighty angel* to be Jesus, then it very well could be. But John does use different words to describe the *scroll* of Revelation 5:1 and the **little book** written of here. It is probably best to see them as *different*, yet probably closely related. The **little book** is perhaps an "abridged version" of the disposition of all things, the portion that John himself will see and write about.

i. "The contents of the little book are nowhere revealed in Revelation, but they seem to represent in this vision the written authority given to the angel to fulfill his mission." (Walvoord)

ii. Clarke on the **little book**: "Meaning probably some *design* of God long concealed, but now about to be made manifest. But who knows what it means?"

b. **He set his right foot on the sea and his left foot on the land**: The angel's stance projects his authority over both land and sea. His authority is either direct (if the *mighty angel* is Jesus), or indirect (if this is indeed an angelic being as a messenger of God).

i. His stance "indicates complete authority over the entire earthly situation." (Walvoord)

ii. He has his feet on both land and sea "to show that he had the command of each, and that his power was universal, all things being under his feet." (Clarke)

c. **When he cried out, seven thunders uttered their voices**: This relates the same idea of the thunderous voice of God as described in Psalm 29, seven times repeating the phrase *the voice of the LORD*.

i. *The voice of the LORD is over the waters; the God of glory thunders; the LORD is over many waters. The voice of the LORD is powerful; the voice of the LORD is full of majesty. The voice of the LORD breaks the cedars, yes, the LORD splinters the cedars of Lebanon. He makes them also skip like a calf, Lebanon and Sirion like a young wild ox. The voice of the LORD divides the flames of fire. The voice of the LORD shakes the wilderness; the LORD shakes the Wilderness of Kadesh. The voice of the LORD makes the deer give birth, and strips the forests bare; and in His temple everyone says, "Glory!"* (Psalm 29:3-9)

3. (4) John is commanded not to write what the thunders said.

Now when the seven thunders uttered their voices, I was about to write; but I heard a voice from heaven saying to me, "Seal up the things which the seven thunders uttered, and do not write them."

a. **I was about to write . . . do not write them**: Of course, this irritates many commentators and sets speculation running wild. What did they say that John must not tell us?

b. If John is not permitted to tell us what they said, why should he even record the incident? One result of it should be to let us know there are secrets in the prophetic scenario, mysteries that should keep our exposition and prediction humble.

i. "This illustrates the principle that while God has revealed much, there are secrets which God has not seen fit to reveal to man at this time." (Walvoord)

ii. "Let us not proceed as though all has been revealed." (L. Morris)

4. (5-7) No more delay.

The angel whom I saw standing on the sea and on the land raised up his hand to heaven and swore by Him who lives forever and ever, who created heaven and the things that are in it, the earth and the things that are in it, and the sea and the things that are in it, that there should be delay no longer, but in the days of the sounding of the seventh angel, when he is about to sound, the mystery of God would be finished, as He declared to His servants the prophets.

a. **Raised up his hand to heaven and swore by Him who lives forever and ever**: The *mighty angel* gives a solemn oath declaring that the end is irrevocably set in motion, **that there should be delay no longer**. There is absolutely no turning back.

b. **The mystery of God would be finished**: What mystery? One important aspect of this mystery is that it has been **declared to His servants the prophets**.

i. Remember that in Biblical vocabulary, a **mystery** isn't something no one knows. A **mystery** is something no one *could* know unless it was revealed to him. If you could know it by intuition or personal investigation, it isn't a mystery, because mysteries must be *revealed*. Therefore, something can be *known* and still be a **mystery** in the Biblical sense.

c. It's hard to say what this precise **mystery of God** is, because the phrase - or its equivalent - is used for a many different aspects of God's plan.

- The ultimate conversion of the Jewish people is called a mystery (Romans 11:25)

- God's purpose for the church is called a mystery (Ephesians 3:3-11)

- The bringing in of the fullness of the Gentiles is called a mystery (Romans 11:25)

- The living presence of Jesus in the believer is called the mystery of God (Colossians 1:27-2:3)

- The gospel itself is called the mystery of Christ (Colossians 4:3)

d. In this context, **the mystery of God** probably refers to the unfolding of His resolution of all things, the finishing of His plan of the ages.

i. "The mystery of God which is declared as subject to fulfillment is unfolded therefore in the Old Testament in the many passages which speak of the establishment of the kingdom of God on earth." (Walvoord)

ii. Possibly, the mystery also regards the great question "Why does God allow Satan and man to rebel and go their own way?" The idea may be that this question, this unanswered **mystery**, is coming to an end under rule of Jesus. God is beginning the end, the resolution of all things, the gathering together (resolution, summing up) of all things in one in Jesus (Ephesians 1:10).

iii. God freely acknowledges that life today is full of mysteries; but it will not always be so. A day will come when all questions of this age will be answered.

B. John is commissioned to preach.

1. (8-9) Curious instructions.

Then the voice which I heard from heaven spoke to me again and said, "Go, take the little book which is open in the hand of the angel who stands on the sea and on the earth." So I went to the angel and said to him, "Give me the little book." And he said to me, "Take and eat it; and it will make your stomach bitter, but it will be as sweet as honey in your mouth."

a. **Take and eat it**: John is commanded to **take the little book** from the *mighty angel* and actually **eat it**.

b. Because John is invited to **take the little book**, some take this to say that God never forces His revelation on anyone, and we always must be willing to take what He has offered. That may often be the case, but it would be news to Paul on the road to Damascus.

2. (10-11) A book both sweet and bitter.

Then I took the little book out of the angel's hand and ate it, and it was as sweet as honey in my mouth. But when I had eaten it, my stomach became bitter. And he said to me, "You must prophesy again about many peoples, nations, tongues, and kings."

a. **I took the little book out of the angel's hand and ate it**: In Ezekiel 3:1-3, the prophet was also commanded to eat a scroll, the revelation of God to Israel. "This figure of eating the book is familiar, and suggests the feeding of the soul on the Word of God." (Morgan)

i. John can only proclaim the Word of God if he has taken it in; "Such an action symbolized the reception of the Word of God into the innermost being as a necessary prerequisite to proclaim it with confidence." (Johnson)

b. **It was as sweet as honey in my mouth. But when I had eaten it, my stomach became bitter**: This **little book** is initially sweet to the taste, but becomes bitter in John's stomach. "Every revelation of God's purposes . . . is 'bitter-sweet,' disclosing judgment as well as mercy." (Swete)

i. "When he came to think upon it, it was either so mysterious that he could not comprehend it, or the matter of it was so sad that it gave him great trouble." (Poole)

ii. Any effective communicator of God's Word has experienced both the sweetness and bitterness that is associated with His Word.

iii. Those who believe the church is raptured *after* the great tribulation argue that the scroll is bitter because the lot of the faithful is bitter in the last days. Mounce is an example of this approach: "The sweet scroll which turns bitter is a message for the church. Before the final triumph believers are going to pass through a formidable ordeal."

c. **You must prophesy again about many peoples, nations, tongues, and kings**: Whatever the content of the scroll, it is connected to John's command to prophesy to *all* men. This is not a message just focused to the church.

i. John's prophecy speaks of the fate of the *entire world*, not just one nation, empire or emperor, such as the Roman Empire.

Revelation 11 - The Two Witnesses

A. The temple of God.

1. (1) John is instructed to measure the temple, the altar and its worshippers.

Then I was given a reed like a measuring rod. And the angel stood, saying, "Rise and measure the temple of God, the altar, and those who worship there."

a. **A reed like a measuring rod**: In Ezekiel 40-43, there is an extended passage where a temple is measured. The temple in Ezekiel is the temple of the millennial earth, but this temple seems to be before that temple. The temple in Ezekiel is measured extensively, including the outer courts (Ezekiel 40:17-19).

i. There are a few other Biblical examples of measuring. In Zechariah chapter 2, a man measures Jerusalem, a scene that evidently shows God's coming judgment on the city. In Revelation chapter 21, the New Jerusalem is measured.

b. **Rise and measure the temple of God**: Sometimes in the Old Testament, the idea of measuring communicates ownership, protection, and preservation. When Habakkuk prophesies, *He stood and measured the earth* (Habakkuk 3:6), the idea is that the Lord owns the earth and can do with it as He pleases. When this temple is measured, it shows that God knows its every dimension, and He is in charge.

i. *God is in charge.* This is one of the glorious, mighty themes of the Book of Revelation. Revelation 11:17 again uses the title *Almighty* for God. The Greek word for *Almighty* is *pantokrater*, and it describes "the one who has his hand on everything." Nine out of the ten times this word is used in the New Testament, it is used in Revelation. This temple will be the scene of great horror and great glory, but God is in charge of it all!

c. **The temple of God**: The identity of this temple is an important matter of interpretation. Many see this temple as a symbol of the church.

 i. Paul describes the church as a temple: *Now, therefore, you are no longer strangers and foreigners, but fellow citizens with the saints and members of the household of God, having been built on the foundation of the apostles and prophets, Jesus Christ Himself being the chief cornerstone, in whom the whole building, being joined together, grows into a holy temple in the Lord.* (Ephesians 2:19-21)

 ii. Peter describes the church as a temple: *You also, as living stones, are being built up a spiritual house.* (1 Peter 2:5)

 iii. However, if this temple in Revelation 11 is a symbolic representation of the church, why should it be measured? What is the significance of the courts and the altar - and if the church itself is the temple, who are the worshippers (**those who worship there**)? There is too much specific detail here for this to be using the generalized picture of the church as a temple unto God.

d. It is more likely that this is the temple that must be on the earth for the fulfillment of what Daniel, Jesus, and Paul said about the *abomination of desolation.*

 i. The prophet Daniel told us the Antichrist will break his covenant with the Jews and bring sacrifice and offerings to an end; the Antichrist will defile the temple by setting something abominable there (Daniel 9:27, 11:31, and 12:11).

 ii. Jesus said to look for an abomination standing in the holy place, which would be the pivotal sign that the season of God's wrath was upon the earth (Matthew 24:15-16 and 24:21).

 iii. Paul told us that the Antichrist would sit in the temple as God (2 Thessalonians 2:3-4).

 iv. The concept of the *abomination of desolation* is often spiritualized with explaining it as idolatrous worship established in the hearts of God's people (His "temple"). But in what sense can people be called *God's* temple if they worship the Antichrist - an emissary of Satan himself? Certainly this isn't the most plain or straightforward interpretation. The simplest explanation of all these passages is to see a real Jewish temple in Jerusalem, yet to be built – but coming soon.

e. In point of fact, today there are Jews *very* interested in rebuilding the temple and resuming sacrifice, and are making preparations to do that exact thing even now.

 i. Today you can visit the Temple Institute in the Jewish Quarter of the old city in Jerusalem. There, a group of Jews absolutely dedicated to rebuilding the temple attempt to educate the public and raise aware-ness for a new temple. They are trying to replicate everything they can for a new temple, down to the specific pots and pans used in sacrifice.

ii. Israel is a nation again, and efforts to rebuild the temple are for real. The main Jewish group leading the charge to rebuild the temple is an organization called *Faithful of the Temple Mount*, who say they will con-tinue their efforts to re-establish the Jewish temple on the Mount. One leader in the group said, "We shall continue our struggle until the Israeli flag is flying from the Dome of the Rock." In Israel, there are students being trained for the priesthood, learning how to conduct animal sacrifices in the rebuilt temple.

iii. It is important to understand that most Jews - religious or secular - do not care one bit about building a temple. And if there were one rebuilt, sacrifice would be difficult in a day of aggressive animal rights activists! Yet, there is a small, strong, highly dedicated group who live to see a rebuilt temple – a temple that will fulfill prophecy.

iv. Rightly, Christians get excited when they see efforts to rebuild the temple. At the same time, we should understand that the basic im-pulse behind rebuilding the temple is not of God at all – the desire to have a place to sacrifice for sin. Christians believe that all sacrifice for sin was finished at the cross, and any further sacrifice for sin is an offense to God, because it denies the finished work of Jesus on the cross.

v. Orthodox Jews consider that the Messiah will rebuild the temple; however, the man they may initially embrace as their Messiah may in fact be the Antichrist: *I have come in My Father's name, and you do not receive Me; if another comes in his own name, him you will receive.* (John 5:43)

2. (2) The outer court of the temple.

But leave out the court which is outside the temple, and do not measure it, for it has been given to the Gentiles. And they will tread the holy city underfoot *for* forty-two months.

a. The outer court need not be measured because it has been **given to the Gentiles**. Perhaps this is because the outer courts of this rebuilt temple include the Islamic Dome of the Rock shrine, which currently stands on the temple mount and is a point of great contention between Jews and Muslims.

i. When the Romans conquered Jerusalem in 70 A.D. they destroyed the city so completely that the foundations of the old temple are not easily found. Most have long assumed that the Dome of the Rock shrine stands on the place of the old temple. But new research gives some evidence that the temple may have stood to the north where the Dome of the Rock shrine is today, and that if the temple were to be rebuilt at its old place, the Dome of the Rock shrine would be in its outer courts. If this is the case (and the research is by no means settled), then it would explain why the angel told John **leave out the court which is outside the temple, and do not measure it, for it has been given to the Gentiles.**

b. The **holy city** (Jerusalem) will be **tread underfoot** for a period of **forty-two months**, which equals 1260 days (three and one-half years). This "trampling" by Gentiles probably takes place in the last half of the final seven year period described by Daniel 11:26-27 - when the Antichrist pours out his fury on the people of Israel (as described in Revelation 12:13-17 and Matthew 24:15-28).

c. Greek scholar A.T. Robertson says that to **tread underfoot** means "to trample with contempt."

B. The two witnesses.

1. (3-6) The ministry of the two witnesses.

"And I will give *power* to my two witnesses, and they will prophesy one thousand two hundred and sixty days, clothed in sackcloth." These are the two olive trees and the two lampstands standing before the God of the earth. And if anyone wants to harm them, fire proceeds from their mouth and devours their enemies. And if anyone wants to harm them, he must be killed in this manner. These have power to shut heaven, so that no rain falls in the days of their prophecy; and they have power over waters to turn them to blood, and to strike the earth with all plagues, as often as they desire.

a. **My two witnesses**: This introduces two of the more interesting characters of Revelation, the **two witnesses**. The character of their ministry is prophetic (**they will prophesy**); they preach and demonstrate repentance (**clothed in sackcloth**), and they have an effective ministry (**I will give power**).

i. The **two witnesses** indeed minister with **power**. "Such power, in fact, that they are able to witness for 1,260 days in spite of the antagonism of the world." (Walvoord)

b. **These are the two olive trees and the two lampstands**: The witnesses have an unique, continual empowering from the Holy Spirit, as shown in Zechariah's olive trees and oil lamps picture (Zechariah 4:2-3 and 4:14).

i. The passage from Zechariah had its first application to two men in Zechariah's day: Joshua and Zerubbabel. "Just as these two witnesses were raised up to be lampstands or witnesses for God and were empowered by olive oil representing the power of the Holy Spirit, so the two witnesses of Revelation 11 will likewise execute their prophetic office." (Walvoord)

ii. In the picture from Zechariah, oil lamps are filled directly from olive trees which "pipe" oil right to the lamps. This is a picture of continual, abundant supply. If we will be **witnesses**, we must first have something to *witness* – our own personal encounter with Jesus Christ. Then, we must have the *power of the Holy Spirit* to bring forth the story of what we have witnessed effectively.

iii. "In this book of the Revelation the Holy Ghost borrows all the elegancies and flowers in the story of the Old Testament, thereby to set out the story of the New in succeeding ages." (Trapp)

c. **And if anyone wants to harm them, fire proceeds from their mouth and devours their enemies**: The two witnesses have special protection from God, similar to Elijah's in 2 Kings 1.

d. **These have power to shut heaven . . . they have power over waters to turn them to blood, and to strike the earth with all plagues, as often as they desire**: The two witnesses have the power to bring both drought and plague, similar to the power Elijah (James 5:17-18) and Moses (Exodus 7-12) had.

e. In the ancient Greek grammar, all the nouns used to speak of the two witnesses in this passage are in the masculine gender. The two witnesses are definitely two men.

2. (7-10) The death of the two witnesses.

When they finish their testimony, the beast that ascends out of the bottomless pit will make war against them, overcome them, and kill them. And their dead bodies *will lie* in the street of the great city which spiritually is called Sodom and Egypt, where also our Lord was crucified. Then *those* from the peoples, tribes, tongues, and nations will see their dead bodies three-and-a-half days, and not allow their dead bodies to be put into graves. And those who dwell on the earth will rejoice over them, make merry, and send gifts to one another, because these two prophets tormented those who dwell on the earth.

a. The two witnesses are killed by the **beast that ascends out of the bottomless pit** (first introduced in Revelation 9:11, and who is most likely

Satan himself) but their ministry is *not* cut short. They fully accomplish their task (**when they finish their testimony**).

> i. Praise God, we cannot be taken off of this earth until we **finish** our **testimony**. The devil does not have power over our lives. We are witnesses of the Lord, and He will protect us until our testimony is finished.

> ii. This passage illustrates the difference between being a *witness* and giving *testimony*. *Witness* is not something we do; it is something we are. Giving *testimony* is what a witness does.

b. **And their dead bodies will lie in the street of the great city which spiritually is called Sodom and Egypt, where also our Lord was crucified**: The two witnesses are killed in the city of Jerusalem, which is described in three illustrative terms.

- As **Sodom**, speaking of immorality

- As **Egypt**, speaking of oppression and slavery

- As **the great city**, a term often applied to "Babylon," the headquarters of Antichrist (Revelation 16:19, 17:18, 18:10, 18:16, 18:18, 18:19, 18:21)

> i. If, during the first three and one-half years, Jerusalem's leadership is in league with the Antichrist, it is easy to see how these titles apply. Any city in love with the Antichrist, or entering into a covenant with him, could be called **Sodom, Egypt**, and Babylon.

c. **Those who dwell on the earth will rejoice over them, make merry, and send gifts to one another**: The earth sees and rejoices over the deaths of the two witnesses. The fact that this is seen by all **people, tribes, tongues, and nations** is perhaps an oblique prophecy of modern mass media.

> i. It is amazing – and not far-fetched at all – to think of a live, worldwide broadcast on CNN, "Live from Jerusalem," and seeing the amazing scene described here taking place.

> ii. The idea is also that the world treats these two witnesses in a humiliating manner. "To have his dead body lie in view of all was the worst humiliation a person could suffer from his enemies." (Johnson)

> iii. **Make merry, and send gifts to one another**: Donald Grey Barnhouse tells of a Christmas card with Revelation 11:10 on its cover - a terrible misquoting of the Scriptures!

d. **Because these two prophets tormented those who dwell on the earth**: The preaching of these two witnesses and their call to repentance was a torment for many, because they could not stand to hear the truth while they loved their lie.

3. (11-14) The reviving of the two witnesses.

Now after the three-and-a-half days the breath of life from God entered them, and they stood on their feet, and great fear fell on those who saw them. And they heard a loud voice from heaven saying to them, "Come up here." And they ascended to heaven in a cloud, and their enemies saw them. In the same hour there was a great earthquake, and a tenth of the city fell. In the earthquake seven thousand people were killed, and the rest were afraid and gave glory to the God of heaven. The second woe is past. Behold, the third woe is coming quickly.

a. **They stood on their feet, and great fear fell on those who saw them**: As this happens before the eyes of the watching world, the enemies of these two witnesses are horrified and astonished.

b. **Come up here**: The earth is not worthy of these two witnesses, so God simply calls them home, and **they ascended to heaven in a cloud.**

c. **In the same hour there was a great earthquake**: An earthquake brings judgment, and moves many to give glory to God. But it remains to be seen if this will become true repentance unto salvation.

4. The identity of the two witnesses.

a. Many interpreters see them as symbolic of the entire church in the tribulation period or as symbols of the law and the prophets. But how can so many *specific details* in their ministry be reconciled with such a symbolic interpretation?

b. The most plain and straightforward interpretation sees them as two real individuals, not symbolic representations.

  i. Unfortunately, the list is not short of modern nuts who think *they* are one of the two witnesses. I think that if you added them all together, there would be about 144,000 of them!

c. Who they are must not be terribly important, or we would have been told exactly who they are!

  i. Generally, if the two witnesses are identified with any two individuals from the past, the leading candidates are Elijah, Moses, or Enoch. Or, perhaps these are merely two believers ministering in the *spirit and power* of these great men, even as John the Baptist went forth in the *spirit and power of Elijah* (Luke 1:17 and Matthew 7:12-13).

  ii. Some think Enoch is one of the witnesses because:

  • He was carried up to heaven by God (Genesis 5:25)

iii. Some think Elijah is one of the witnesses because:

- His ministry seems like one of these two witnesses (2 Kings 1 and James 5:17-18)

- He was carried up to heaven (2 Kings 2:11)

- Enemies of Elijah were destroyed by fire (2 Kings 1)

- It is specifically prophesied that Elijah will return before the end of the age (Malachi 4:5-6)

- Elijah had a unique "conference" with Jesus at the Mount of Transfiguration (Matthew 17:1-6)

iv. Some think Moses is one of the witnesses because:

- His ministry seems like one of these witnesses (Exodus 7:20-21)

- God seems to have a special purpose for the body of Moses that Satan wanted to defeat (Jude 9)

- The enemies of Moses were destroyed by fire (Numbers 16:35)

- Moses had a unique "conference" with Jesus at the Mount of Transfiguration (Matthew 17:1-6)

v. Some believe the two witnesses must be Enoch and Elijah, because neither of them died a natural death and were instead carried to heaven, and Hebrews 9:27 says that it is appointed for men to die once - so Enoch and Elijah must return to die on the earth. This is a misunderstanding of Hebrews 9:27, which is a principle rather than an absolute, immutable law. For example, Lazarus and others were raised from the dead and apparently died *twice* - yet this does not disprove Hebrews 9:27. The entire church on earth at the time of the rapture will not die, but be carried to heaven. Hebrews 9:27 stands as a principle, and there are a few notable exceptions which ultimately serve to prove the rule, not deny it. There may be good reasons for considering Enoch and Elijah as the two witnesses, but the principle of Hebrews 9:27 is not among those good reasons.

C. The seventh trumpet.

1. (15) The seventh trumpet finally sounds.

Then the seventh angel sounded: And there were loud voices in heaven, saying, "The kingdoms of this world have become *the kingdoms* of our Lord and of His Christ, and He shall reign forever and ever!"

a. **Then the seventh angel sounded**: The seventh seal brought forth a profound silence (Revelation 8:1); the seventh trumpet initiates joy at the inevitable resolution. There can't be a more glorious proclamation than this: **The kingdoms of this world have become the kingdoms of our Lord and of His Christ, and He shall reign forever and ever!**

b. **Have become the kingdoms of our Lord**: In the ancient Greek grammar, the verb tense of **have become** indicates an absolute certainty about Jesus' coming and reign, even *before* the fact is accomplished.

c. How can there be such joy, when the King is not reigning completely yet? At the headquarters at a successful political campaign on election night, there is joy, even though it will be a while until their candidate is actually installed into office. The joy anticipates a certain result.

2. (16-18) The twenty-four elders worship God.

And the twenty-four elders who sat before God on their thrones fell on their faces and worshiped God, saying: "We give You thanks, O Lord God Almighty, the One who is and who was and who is to come, because You have taken Your great power and reigned. The nations were angry, and Your wrath has come, and the time of the dead, that they should be judged, and that You should reward Your servants the prophets and the saints, and those who fear Your name, small and great, and should destroy those who destroy the earth."

a. **We give You thanks**: This thanksgiving isn't to thank God that He has *already* done this; but that the hour has come for it to take place, and that these things are permanently set in motion.

b. "In their praise, impending events are set forth, to be more fully described later." (Morgan) Now comes the fitting time for judgment, reward, and destruction.

c. **The nations were angry, and Your wrath has come**: God's punishment fits the crime; there is nothing arbitrary about it. The nations are **angry** with God and He responds with **wrath**; those that **destroy** the earth are themselves destroyed.

d. **The nations were angry**: They are angry because God comes to rule. The world wants *anything* but the reign of God. As it says in a parable of Jesus, *We will not have this man to reign over us* (Luke 19:14).

i. "Religion is decent, but surrender to God is intolerable to the nations of this world." (Newell)

3. (19) The temple in heaven is opened.

Then the temple of God was opened in heaven, and the ark of His covenant was seen in His temple. And there were lightnings, noises, thunderings, an earthquake, and great hail.

a. **The ark of His covenant was seen in His temple**: The **ark** refers to God's throne, the place where the previously mentioned resolution will come from.

b. It is called the **ark of His** *covenant* - in the Old Testament, this was the earthly representation of God's throne - to emphasize God's faithfulness.

> i. The ark of the covenant is "The symbol of God's faithfulness in bestowing grace on His people, and inflicting vengeance on His people's enemies." (Alford)

c. **And there were lightnings, noises, thunderings, an earthquake, and great hail**: The great and awesome phenomenon at the opening of the temple and the revelation of the ark show that the presence of the Lord is there; it is reminiscent of God's manifested presence at Mount Sinai (Exodus 19:16-19).

Revelation 12 - The Woman, the Child, and the Dragon

A. The woman.

1. (1) The woman is described in celestial images.

Now a great sign appeared in heaven: a woman clothed with the sun, with the moon under her feet, and on her head a garland of twelve stars.

a. **Now a great sign appeared**: This is the first of seven signs that John relates, and is described as a **great sign** (*mega semeion*). In Revelation chapters 12, 13, and 14 the main figures of the Great Tribulation are described, and this **great sign** introduces the first of the seven:

- The woman, representing Israel

- The dragon, representing Satan

- The man-child, referring to Jesus

- The angel Michael, head of the angelic host

- The offspring of the woman, representing Gentiles who come to faith in the Tribulation

- The beast out of the sea, representing the antichrist

- The beast out of the earth, representing the false prophet who promotes the antichrist

b. **A woman clothed with the sun**: Because John plainly says this is a **sign**, we don't expect this woman to appear literally on the earth. God will use this sign to communicate something to John and to us. Women often represent religious systems in Revelation.

- *Jezebel* is associated with a religious system promoting false teaching (Revelation 2:20)

- The *Great Harlot* is associated with false religion (Revelation 17:2)

- The *Bride* is associated with the church (Revelation 19:7-8)

c. The **woman clothed with the sun** in this passage has been associated with many different religious ideas. Roman Catholics claim this woman is Mary, pictured as the "Queen of Heaven." Mary Baker Eddy said she was this woman.

> i. It is common in Roman Catholic art to represent Mary as standing on a crescent moon with **twelve stars** around her head.

d. Scripturally, this **woman clothed with the sun** should be identified with Israel, according to Joseph's dream (Genesis 37:9-11). In that dream, the sun represents Jacob, the moon represents Joseph's mother Rachel, and the eleven stars are the sons of Israel which bow down to Joseph. In this sign with **twelve stars**, Joseph is now "among" the other tribes of Israel.

> i. In other Old Testament passages, Israel (or Zion or Jerusalem) is often represented as a woman (Isaiah 54:1-6, Jeremiah 3:20, Ezekiel 16:8-14, and Hosea 2:19-20).

2. (2) The woman gives birth.

Then being with child, she cried out in labor and in pain to give birth.

> a. **Being with child**: Later in the chapter, it is clear that this child born of Israel is Jesus (*She bore a male Child who was to rule all nations with a rod of iron*, Revelation 12:5).

> b. **She cried out in labor and in pain to give birth**: The **pain** described refers to the travail of Israel at the time of Jesus' birth (under Roman occupation and oppression).

B. The dragon.

1. (3) A fearful, powerful dragon appears.

And another sign appeared in heaven: behold, a great, fiery red dragon having seven heads and ten horns, and seven diadems on his heads.

> a. **Another sign appeared in heaven**: Again, we are reminded that this is a **sign**. The creature here is not literally a **great, fiery red dragon**, but the dragon represents his nature and character.

> > i. His description "symbolically suggests his fierce power and murderous nature . . . a picture of the fullness of evil in all its hideous strength." (Johnson)

> b. **Seven diadems on his heads**: This dragon has great power (**seven heads and ten horns**) and claims royal authority (**seven diadems**). The

crowns represent his presumptive claims of royal authority against the true King. *He* wants to be considered a king.

> i. "From the similar description given in 13:1 and the parallel references in Daniel 7:7-8, 2, it is clear that the revived Roman Empire is in view . . . The seven heads and ten horns refer to the original ten kingdoms of which three were subdued by the little horn of Daniel 7:8, who is to be identified with the world ruler of the great tribulation who reigns over the revived Roman Empire." (Walvoord)

2. (4) The dragon looks to the earth.

His tail drew a third of the stars of heaven and threw them to the earth. And the dragon stood before the woman who was ready to give birth, to devour her Child as soon as it was born.

> a. **His tail drew a third of the stars of heaven**: Many believe this describes one-third of the angelic host in league with Satan (*his angels* of Revelation 12:9). This army of angelic beings in league with Satan makes up the world of demonic spirits.

> > i. "God never made an evil being; but He made angels, principalities, and powers capacitated for mighty joys and distinctions in His glorious domain, yet with free will, implied in the very creation of moral beings, which they could exercise for their everlasting weal or woe. Many have remained steadfast, to wit, 'Michael and his angels.' But some abode not in the truth, but revolted against the rule of Heaven, and became unchanging enemies of God and His Kingdom." (Seiss)

> b. **To devour her Child as soon as it was born**: The attempt to **devour her Child** was initially fulfilled by Herod's attempts to kill Jesus as a child (Matthew 2:16-18). It was also fulfilled throughout Jesus' life as Satan attacked Him (John 8:58 and Mark 4:35-41).

C. The child.

1. (5) Jesus' ministry is described by its earthly beginning and end.

She bore a male Child who was to rule all nations with a rod of iron. And her Child was caught up to God and His throne.

> a. **A male Child who was to rule all nations with a rod of iron**: Clearly, this refers to Jesus Christ, the Messiah. He rules the world with a **rod of iron** (Psalm 2 and Revelation 19:15).

> b. **She bore a male Child** refers to Jesus' birth. **Rule all nations with a rod of iron** refers to the triumphant return of Jesus. By stating the "bookends" of Jesus' earthly work, John alludes to all that stands in between.

i. "After a conflict with the Prince of this world, who came and tried Him, but found nothing in Him, the Son of the woman was taken up to heaven and sat on the right hand of God. Words can hardly be plainer than these." (Alford)

c. This **male Child** is obviously Jesus. This means that the *woman* of Revelation 12:1 cannot be the church, because Jesus "gives birth" to the church, not the other way around. The *woman* must therefore either be Mary or Israel, the only two "women" who could have "given birth" to Jesus. The rest of Revelation 12 will demonstrate that this woman is Israel, not Mary.

2. (6) The woman in the wilderness.

Then the woman fled into the wilderness, where she has a place prepared by God, that they should feed her there one thousand two hundred and sixty days.

a. **Then the woman fled into the wilderness**: Persecuted by the dragon, the woman is protected by God in a **prepared** place for **one thousand two hundred and sixty days**

i. This helps us to understand with certainty that the *woman* is Israel and not Mary. How could Mary possibly flee into the wilderness in this way?

b. **One thousand two hundred and sixty days**: This reference to a three and one-half year period connects these events with the final seven years of the Daniel 9 prophecy. Since Revelation 12:5 describes the ascension of Jesus, and Revelation 12:6 describes yet-to-occur events in the 70th week of Daniel, between these two verses lies hundreds of years (our current period). This obvious "near-far" break in time is typical of prophecy. Daniel's seventy week prophecy has such a break (Daniel 9:24-27).

c. **Into the wilderness, where she has a place prepared by God**: Some believe this **place** in the **wilderness** is the rock city of Petra, south of the Dead Sea. Reportedly, Christian businessmen have stocked the place with food and evangelistic tracts written in Hebrew.

d. **Prepared in the wilderness**: **Prepared** uses the same ancient Greek word Jesus used in *I go to prepare a place for you* (John 14:2-3). This demonstrates that God's careful planning works on earth as well as in heaven.

D. Conflict in heaven.

1. (7-8) War between Michael and the dragon.

And war broke out in heaven: Michael and his angels fought with the dragon; and the dragon and his angels fought, but they did not prevail, nor was a place found for them in heaven any longer.

a. **War broke out in heaven**: At the mid-point of the great tribulation, God will turn the tide against Satan - first in heaven, then on earth. A battle will take place that will deny Satan access to heaven.

b. **Michael and his angels**: Some individuals and groups (such as the Seventh Day Adventists and Jehovah's Witnesses) insist on saying that **Michael** is actually Jesus. This is wrong on every count.

i. Some say Michael must be Jesus, because he has **his angels**. But if Satan - a fallen angelic being - has **his angels** (Revelation 12:7), can't Michael - an unfallen angelic being - have **his angels**?

ii. Some say Michael must be Jesus, because his name means *One like God*. But if this were a title of Jesus, it could argue *against* His deity, not for it - because it would say that Jesus is *like* God, but *not* God. "There is also an unquestionable Godlikeness in all holy beings, which must be very exalted in those preeminent among the ministers of the throne." (Seiss)

iii. Some say Michael must be Jesus, because he is called *the archangel* (Jude 9), which means leader or prince among the angels, and they say that only Jesus is the leader of the angels. But we know from Daniel 10:13, 10:20 and 10:21 that Michael is one angelic *prince* among others. Also, Paul refers to *an archangel* in 1 Thessalonians 4:16 in a way that presupposes other archangels.

iv. Some say that Michael must be Jesus, because Paul says that at the rapture, the Lord will call His people with *the voice of an archangel* (1 Thessalonians 4:16). But Jesus can use an angel to call out for His people without being that angel, just as much as God can use a trumpet to sound out a call without being the trumpet.

v. Jude 9 says that Michael would not rebuke or accuse Satan on His own authority, but only say "The Lord rebuke you." This shows that Michael isn't Jesus, because Jesus often rebuked Satan and demons in His own authority (Matthew 17:18, Mark 1:25, 9:25, Luke 4:8, 4:35).

vi. "Michael is not to be identified with Christ, any more than any other of the great angels in this Book. Such identification here would confuse hopelessly the actors in this heavenly scene." (Alford)

c. **Michael and his angels fought with the dragon; and the dragon and his angels fought**: This is a dramatic scene of battle between good angels and bad angels.

i. *Who* fights in this battle? This is truly a battle between equals. The **dragon** represents Satan (Revelation 12:9), and Satan is not the counterpart of God - God has no counterpart. If anyone, Satan is the counterpart of Michael, who seems to be the chief angel opposite this chief of fallen angels.

ii. *Why* is the battle fought? In a previous scene of conflict between Michael and Satan (Jude 9), Satan wanted to prevent the resurrection and glorification of Moses, because he knew God had plans for the resurrected and glorified Moses (Luke 9:30-31). Here is another occasion where Satan wants to get in the way of God's plan for the end-times.

iii. *When* is this battle fought? This battle occurs at the mid-point of the seven-year period, as described by Daniel. *At that time Michael shall stand up, the great prince who stands watch over the sons of your people; and there shall be a time of trouble, such as never was since there was a nation, even to that time. And at that time your people shall be delivered.* (Daniel 12:1)

iv. *How* is this battle fought? We know this is a real fight; but is it a material or a spiritual battle? Our battle with Satan and his demons is *spiritual*, fought on the battleground of truth and deception, of fear and faith (Ephesians 6:12). In regard to material attacks against the believer, Satan and his demons were disarmed at the cross (Colossians 2:15). But it is possible that among angels, there is a *material* battle to be fought in a way we can only imagine. In his classic work *Paradise Lost*, the great poet Milton imagined this battle:

> Michael bid sound
> Th' archangel trumpet: through the vast of heaven
> It sounded, and the faithful armies run
> Hosanna to the Highest: nor stood at gaze
> The adverse legions, nor less hideous joined
> The horrid shock: now storming fury rose,
> And clamour such as heard in heaven till now
> Was never; arms on armour clashing brayed
> Horrible discord, and the madding wheels
> Of brazen chariots raged; dire was the noise
> Of conflict; overhead the dismal hiss
> Of fiery darts in flaming volleys flew,
> And flying vaulted either host with fire:
> So under fiery cope together rushed
> Both battles main, with ruinous assault
> And inextinguishable rage; all heaven
> Resounded, and had earth been then, all earth
> Had to her centre shook.

d. **Nor was a place found for them in heaven any longer:** This shows us that up until this happens (at the mid-point of Daniel's 70th week), Satan *does* have access to heaven, where he accuses God's people before the throne (Job 1:6-12, Revelation 12:10).

i. It troubles some to think that Satan has access to heaven, because of the mistaken teaching that God can allow nothing unholy in His presence. But the Bible clearly says that while Satan appears on earth (Luke 4:1-13), and describes him as *the prince of the power of the air* (Ephesians 2:2), it also says that Satan has access to heaven, where he accuses God's people before the throne (Job 1:6-12).

2. (9) Satan and his angels are cast out of heaven.

So the great dragon was cast out, that serpent of old, called the Devil and Satan, who deceives the whole world; he was cast to the earth, and his angels were cast out with him.

a. **So the great dragon was cast out**: This single verse uses many different titles for our spiritual enemy, including **Dragon, serpent of old, the Devil, Satan**, and he **who deceives the whole world**. These titles describe Satan as vicious, an accuser, an adversary, and a deceiver.

i. Walvoord on **the Devil**: "The title 'Devil' is from the Greek *diabolos*, from the verb *diaballo*, which has the meaning of 'defaming' or 'slandering.' He is the master accuser of the brethren."

b. **He was cast to the earth**: The Bible describes four different falls of Satan. Revelation 12:9 describes the second of these four falls.

- From glorified to profane (Ezekiel 28:14-16)
- From having access to heaven (Job 1:12, 1 Kings 22:21, Zechariah 3:1) to restriction to the earth (Revelation 12)
- From the earth to bondage in the bottomless pit for 1,000 years (Revelation 20)
- From the pit to the lake of fire (Revelation 20)

c. In Luke 10:18, Jesus said *"I saw Satan fall like lightning from heaven."* This refers either to the first fall of Satan (from glorified to profane), or it is a prophetic look ahead to the second fall at the mid-point of the seven year tribulation period.

d. **His angels were cast out with him**: This indicates that demonic spirits are indeed fallen angels, those who joined with Satan in His rebellion against God. These are **"his angels."**

i. These **angels** are also the same as the *third of the stars of heaven* described in Revelation 12:4. Since Satan only drew a *third of the stars of heaven*, it means that two-thirds of the angels remained faithful to God. It's comforting to know that faithful angels outnumber fallen angels two to one.

3. (10-12) A joyful declaration in heaven.

Then I heard a loud voice saying in heaven, "Now salvation, and strength, and the kingdom of our God, and the power of His Christ have come, for the accuser of our brethren, who accused them before our God day and night, has been cast down. And they overcame him by the blood of the Lamb and by the word of their testimony, and they did not love their lives to the death. Therefore rejoice, O heavens, and you who dwell in them! Woe to the inhabitants of the earth and the sea! For the devil has come down to you, having great wrath, because he knows that he has a short time."

a. Whoever is behind this **loud voice**, it is some representative of redeemed humanity - not an angel or God - because the voice speaks of the **accuser of *our* brethren**.

b. **The accuser of our brethren, who accused them before our God day and night, has been cast down**: Satan's work of accusing only ends here, when he is cast out from his access to heaven. Today, we have (and *need*) an intercessor and advocate (Hebrews 7:25, and 1 John 2:1).

c. **And they overcame him by the blood of the Lamb and by the word of their testimony, and they did not love their lives to the death**: This tells us three keys to the saint's victory over Satan.

d. **They overcame him by the blood of the Lamb**: The **blood** overcomes Satan's accusations. Those accusations mean nothing against us because Jesus has already paid the penalty our sins deserved. We may be even *worse* than Satan's accusations, but we are still made righteous by the work of Jesus on the cross (Ephesians 1:7, Colossians 1:14, and Hebrews 9:14).

i. Although, it is important to say that we should not regard the blood of Jesus in a superstitious manner. It is not a magical potion, nor is it the literal blood of Jesus, literally applied that saves or cleanses us. If that were so, then His Roman executioners, splattered with His blood, would have been automatically saved, and the actual number of molecules of Jesus' literal blood would limit the number of people who could be saved. The **blood** speaks to us of the real, physical death of Jesus Christ in our place, on our behalf, before God. *That literal death in our place, and the literal judgment He bore on our behalf, is what saves us.*

ii. **By the blood** emphasizes the *death* of Jesus. He did not only suffer, He *died*. **Of the Lamb** emphasizes the *substitutionary work* of His death, because the Passover **Lamb** died as a *substitute* for others.

iii. The blood of Jesus heals our troubled conscience, because we know that by His death our sin is atoned for (Hebrews 9:14). But to *only* use the blood of Jesus in that way is selfish. We should be like "these saints used the doctrine of atonement not as a pillow to rest their weariness, but as a weapon to subdue their sin." (Spurgeon)

iv. How does **the blood of the Lamb** conquer Satan in the life of the believer? How does the death of Jesus on the cross as our substitute bring us victory?

v. It works first because *His victory is our victory.* "First, you are to regard Satan this day as being already literally and truly overcome through the death of the Lord Jesus. Satan is already a vanquished enemy. By faith grasp your Lord's victory as your own, since he triumphed in your nature and on your behalf . . . Come, my soul, thou hast conquered Satan by thy Lord's victory. Wilt thou not be brave enough to fight a vanquished foe, and trample down the enemy whom thy Lord has already thrust down? Thou needest not be afraid, but say, 'Thanks be to God which giveth us the victory through our Lord Jesus Christ.' " (Spurgeon)

vi. It works because the work of Jesus on the cross for us is the ultimate demonstration of God's love (Romans 5:8), and a constant remembrance of **the blood of the Lamb** assures us that every fear Satan whispers into our mind is a lie.

vii. It works because the death of Jesus on the cross as our substitute reveals the true nature of sin, and this makes us want to avoid sin. "Satan makes sin seem pleasurable, but the cross reveals its bitterness. If Jesus died because of sin, men begin to see that sin must be a murderous thing." (Spurgeon)

viii. It works because the death of Jesus on the cross as our substitute purchases us as God's personal property, and this makes us want to live unto God. "If anything can make a man holy it is a firm faith in the atoning sacrifice. When a man knows that Jesus died for him, he feels that he is not his own, but bought with a price, and therefore he must live unto him that died for him and rose again." (Spurgeon)

ix. Therefore, we *use the blood of the Lamb* in spiritual warfare - *not* as a Christian "abracadabra," as if chanting "The blood of Jesus, the blood of Jesus" could keep Satan away like garlic is said to keep away vampires. Rather, our *understanding*, our *apprehension*, our *focus* - may I say our *obsession* with the death of Jesus on the cross as our substitute wins the battle.

x. "The precious blood of Jesus is not meant for us merely to admire and exhibit. We must not be content to talk about it, and extol it, and do nothing with it; but we are to use it in the great crusade against unholiness and unrighteousness, till it is said of us, 'They overcame him by the blood of the Lamb.' This precious blood is to be used for overcoming, and consequently for holy warfare. We dishonor it if we do not use it to that end . . . The dog of hell knows the dread name which makes him lie down: we must confront him with the authority, and specially with the atonement of the Lamb of God." (Spurgeon)

e. **They overcame him . . . by the word of their testimony**: The **word of their testimony** overcomes Satan's deception. Knowing and remembering the work of God *in their life* protects them against Satan's deceptions. As faithful witnesses, they have a testimony to bear - and because they know what they have seen and heard and experienced from God, they cannot be deceived by Satan's lies telling them it isn't true (as the testimony of the man born blind in John 9:25).

f. **They overcame him . . . they did not love their lives to the death**: Loving not **their lives** overcomes Satan's violence. If they do not cling to their own earthly lives, then there really is no threat Satan can bring against them. If they believe *to live is Christ, and to die is gain* (Philippians 1:21), then how can Satan's violence against them be effective?

  i. The ancient Greek word for **love** here is *agape*, which speaks of a self-sacrificing, decision-based love. It is up to each one of us to *choose*: Will we **love** our **lives to the death**? Will our physical lives be the most precious thing to us, or will we find our life by losing it for Jesus? (Mark 8:35)

g. **Therefore rejoice, O heavens, and you who dwell in them!** Heaven rejoices at the eviction of Satan. But heaven's gain is the earth's loss: **Woe to the inhabitants of the earth and sea!**

h. **He knows that he has a short time**: Satan's power is real and terrifying, but not because he is triumphant, but because he knows he is beaten and has a **short time** left. He is like a wounded, cornered animal that fights ferociously.

  i. Why doesn't he just give up? Don't forget that Satan is utterly depraved, and probably "insane" - he may have deceived even himself into thinking that he has a chance. A better question is "Why don't we give up?" Our rebellion against God makes even less sense than Satan's rebellion does.

E. Conflict on the earth.

  1. (13-16) Satan attacks the woman, and God protects her.

Now when the dragon saw that he had been cast to the earth, he perse- cuted the woman who gave birth to the male *Child*. But the woman was given two wings of a great eagle, that she might fly into the wilderness to her place, where she is nourished for a time and times and half a time, from the presence of the serpent. So the serpent spewed water out of his mouth like a flood after the woman, that he might cause her to be carried away by the flood. But the earth helped the woman, and the earth opened its mouth and swallowed up the flood which the dragon had spewed out of his mouth.

    a. **He persecuted the woman who gave birth to the male Child**: Some teach that the woman is a symbol representing all the people of God, including faithful Israel and the church. They use this to advance the idea that the church is here during the tribulation period. But if the woman represents *all* the people of God (the church and faithful Israel), then who are *the rest of her offspring* described in Revelation 12:17? It is better to see her as Israel in general or Messianic Jews in particular.

        i. *Why* does Satan attack the Jewish people? This is a question for all history, not only for the Great Tribulation. The reason is because from the time of Abraham, Israel has had a critical role in God's plan of redemption. First, it was in bringing forth the Redeemer. Then, it was in the fulfillment of His plan, because Jesus promised that the Jewish people would exist and welcome Him when He returns in glory to this world (Matthew 23:39). If Satan succeeds in destroying the Jew- ish people, then God's eternal plan is thwarted.

        ii. "The persecution of Israel is part of the satanic program to thwart and hinder the work of God . . . Israel is hated by Satan not because of any of its own characteristics but because she is the chosen of God and essential to the overall purpose of God for time and eter- nity." (Walvoord)

    b. **But the woman was given two wings of a great eagle, that she might fly into the wilderness to her place**: *Eagle's Wings* are an emblem from the Exodus deliverance (Exodus 19:4), another way of connecting these people with Israel.

        i. Some have wondered if the reference to the **two wings of a great eagle** do not in fact describe a great military transport plane used to evacuate people in an emergency situation.

    c. **Where she is nourished for a time and times and half a time**: This is another reference to a three and one-half year period, indicating that these events - this dramatic persecution of Israel - takes place during the 70th week of Daniel 9.

d. **So the serpent spewed water out of his mouth like a flood after the woman**: The fury poured out against Israel after the abomination of desolation (marking the half-way point of the 70th week of Daniel) was spoken of by Jesus in Matthew 24:15-22, and spoken of in distinctly *Jewish* terms (*housetop . . . pray that your flight may not be in winter or on the Sabbath*). This passage in Revelation describes the fury that Jesus told them to flee.

e. **The earth opened its mouth and swallowed up the flood which the dragon had spewed out of his mouth**: This passage also describes God's ultimate protection of Israel from the fury of Satan and his antichrist in the great tribulation.

    i. As it says in Isaiah 59:19, *When the enemy comes in like a flood, the Spirit of the* LORD *will lift up a standard against him.*

2. (17) The wrath of the dragon is focused against God's people.

And the dragon was enraged with the woman, and he went to make war with the rest of her offspring, who keep the commandments of God and have the testimony of Jesus Christ.

a. **The dragon was enraged with the woman, and he went to make war with the rest of her offspring**: This may refers to Israel (**the woman**) and Gentiles who come to faith in Jesus during the Great Tribulation (**the rest of her offspring**). These two groups are particular targets of Satan and his antichrist's persecution in the last days.

b. This either begins or continues the fierce persecution of all those who would not submit to and worship this great Satanic dictator. The martyrs of this period were shown in Revelation 6:9-11 and Revelation 7:9-17.

    i. "It is precisely when Satan has lost the battle for the souls of saints in heaven that he begins the fruitless persecution of their bodies." (Farrer)

Revelation 13 - The Two Beasts

A. The beast rising from the sea.

1. (1) John's vision of a beast rising from the sea.

Then I stood on the sand of the sea. And I saw a beast rising up out of the sea, having seven heads and ten horns, and on his horns ten crowns, and on his heads a blasphemous name.

a. **Then I stood on the sand of the sea**: In Revelation 12, John's vision mainly had in *heaven* in view. Now the scene of his vision shifts to the earth, and in his vision he **stood on the sand of the sea**.

i. Many people today love **the sea**, but as a whole Jewish people in Biblical times regarded the sea as a wild, untamed, frightening place. While ancient Israel under Solomon had a navy, Hiram the King of Tyre supplied the sailors (1 Kings 9:26-27).

ii. Because ancient Israel was wary of **the sea**, it was a figure of evil and chaos that seemed to resist God, though the resistance was unsuccessful:

For God is my King from of old, working salvation in the midst of the earth. You divided the sea by Your strength; You broke the heads of the sea serpents in the waters. (Psalm 74:12-13)

O LORD God of hosts, who is mighty like You, O LORD? Your faithfulness also surrounds You. You rule the raging of the sea; when its waves rise, You still them. (Psalm 89:8-9)

But the wicked are like the troubled sea, when it cannot rest, whose waters cast up mire and dirt. (Isaiah 57:20)

b. **And I saw a beast rising up out of the sea**: From the place identified with evil and chaos and resisting God, a **beast** comes forth. The ancient Greek word translated **beast** here has the idea of a wild, dangerous animal. Because John calls him a **beast** and not a *dragon* (as in Revelation

12:3), this creature represents someone distinct from Satan who was represented by the dragon (Revelation 12:9).

c. **Having seven heads and ten horns**: Though this **beast** is distinct from the dragon of Revelation 12, he is still closely identified with him. He is not the dragon, but he is *like* him, because the dragon also had **seven heads and ten horns** (Revelation 11:3).

> i. Any creature with **seven heads** would be hard to kill, because if you wounded one head, six would still remain. In Biblical imagery **horns** express strength and power. A bull with two horns is a powerful creature, but a **beast** with **ten horns** has that much more power - just like the dragon of Revelation 12:3.

> ii. This likeness to Satan is just one of the things that identifies this **beast** with the one popularly known as the *Antichrist*. The word *Antichrist* only appears in the Bible five times in four verses (1 John 2:18, 2:22, 4:3, and 2 John 7). 1 John 2:18 is a good example: *Little children, it is the last hour; and as you have heard that the Antichrist is coming.* With this, John refers to an individual who has captured the imagination of many people, some who don't even know the Bible. But many are ignorant about this person called *the Antichrist*, except what they have learned from movies like *The Omen*.

> iii. We can begin by understanding what the title *Antichrist* means. The prefix *anti* can mean "the opposite of" or "instead of." The Antichrist is the "opposite Jesus"; he is the "instead of" Jesus. Most people have focused on the idea of the "opposite Jesus." This has made them think that the Antichrist will appear as a supremely evil person, that as much as Jesus went around doing good, he will go around doing bad. As much as Jesus' character and personality was beautiful and attractive, the Antichrist's character and personality will be ugly and repulsive. As much as Jesus spoke only truth, the Antichrist will speak only lies. This emphasizes the idea of the "opposite Jesus" too much. The Antichrist will instead be more of an "instead of Jesus." He will look wonderful, be charming and successful. He will be the ultimate winner, and appear as an angel of light. In this sense the Antichrist will be a satanic messiah, *instead of* the true Messiah Jesus Christ.

> iv. In 1 John 2:18, John also speaks of *the Antichrist and many antichrists*. There is a "spirit" of antichrist, and this "spirit" of antichrist will one day find its ultimate fulfillment in *the Antichrist*, who will lead humanity in an end-times rebellion against God. In other words, though the world still waits to see the ultimate revelation of the Antichrist, there are little "previews" of this man and his mission to come. These are the *antichrists* with a little "a."

v. Though we commonly call this coming world leader the Antichrist, the Bible gives him many names or titles. He is known as:

- The *little horn* of Daniel 7:8

- The *king of fierce countenance* of Daniel 8:23

- *The Prince that shall come* of Daniel 9:26

- The *willful king* of Daniel 11:36-45

- The one who comes *in his own name* of John 5:43, whom Israel will receive as a messiah

- *The son of perdition, the man of sin, the lawless one* of 2 Thessalonians 2:3

d. **And on his horns ten crowns**: This is something *different* about the **beast** compared to the dragon of Revelation 12:3, who had *seven diadems on his heads*. The seven crowns of the dragon expressed his strength and power, because seven is a number associated with strength and completeness. The **ten crowns** of the **beast** express his rule over a group of ten nations.

i. Most commentators think that the **ten horns** are distributed among the seven heads, but David Hocking sees all **ten horns** upon one of the heads. The figure of **ten horns** also associates this **beast** with the beast of Daniel 7:7, which represent the final world empire of the Antichrist, which the Messiah will ultimately conquer: *After this I saw in the night visions, and behold, a fourth beast, dreadful and terrible, exceedingly strong. It had huge iron teeth; it was devouring, breaking in pieces, and trampling the residue with its feet. It was different from all the beasts that were before it, and it had ten horns.* (Daniel 7:7)

ii. In Daniel's vision, the *ten horns* specifically represented *ten kingdoms* that this final world dictator has authority over (Daniel 7:24). In John's vision the **ten crowns** on the **ten horns** emphasize this idea.

iii. The visions of Daniel 7 and Daniel 2 also connect the governments represented by the **ten crowns** with the ancient Roman Empire. In those visions, Daniel saw three successive world empires, each succeeded by a fourth - which in the context of the visions is plainly the Roman Empire. In the days of that fourth empire the Messiah will come, destroy all earthly rule and reign over the earth. Since we do not see the reign of Jesus on earth in the way Daniel prophesied, we can see that the Roman Empire will "resume" in some way, expressed by this collection of **ten crowns**.

e. **And on his heads a blasphemous name**: The seven heads of the **beast** each advertise blasphemy against God. This speaks of more than the beast's message; it speaks of his character. He is a blasphemer, who speaks against God (as in Daniel 7:25).

2. (2) The description of the beast of the sea again connects it to images from Daniel 7.

Now the beast which I saw was like a leopard, his feet were like *the feet of* a bear, and his mouth like the mouth of a lion. The dragon gave him his power, his throne, and great authority.

a. **Like a leopard . . . a bear . . . a lion:** In this vision, God used images from Daniel's vision of Daniel 7 to communicate the identity and nature of this **beast** to John. Daniel 7 uses four animals *(beasts)* to describe the course of human government from Daniel's time until the ultimate reign of Jesus on this earth.

i. The first three animals are a **lion** (in Daniel, a picture of the Babylonian Empire), a **bear** (a picture of Medo-Persian Empire), and a **leopard** (a picture of the Greek Empire). The fourth animal was a dreadful, indescribable beast which shared the most terrifying characteristics of the previous beasts, yet represents the final world empire under the leadership of a Satanic dictator (Daniel 7:7-8).

ii. John presents this **beast** as the extension of the fourth beast of Daniel 7, connecting his empire with the characteristics of the great empires of the past. This final world empire will have the catlike vigilance of a **leopard**, the slow and crushing power of a **bear**, and the authority and ferociousness of a **lion**.

iii. Since the beasts of Daniel 7 represented empires more than specific men, some have thought that the **beast** of Revelation 13 is not a person, but a government or a cultural system. Many believe the beast is a broad picture of totalitarian governments, especially the totalitarian states of the 20th century. For example, Mounce writes: "The beast has always been, and will always be, in a final intensified manifestation, the deification of secular authority" (Mounce). But others see the **beast** as a person, specifically the Antichrist - the final Satanic dictator who leads the world in rebellion against God. Some (like David Hocking) combine the approaches and say that the beast is a modern, world totalitarian government, *but* the one head that has ten horns is specifically the Antichrist - the leader of this beast of a final satanic dictatorship. But with any empire, especially brief empires, the government is almost totally identified with the ruler. When we think of Germany in the 1930s and 1940s, the figures of Hitler as an individual and Nazi Germany as a state are virtually the same.

b. All the indications in Revelation 13 are that the **beast** is a man, though he is closely identified with his world-dominating government.

i. "The Beast is worshipped as a god; but people never worship an empire as such; neither do they make a succession of emperors into an object of religious devotion. The paying of divine homage to kings has been a common thing in the world's history, but it has always been rendered to individuals." (Seiss)

ii. An image is set up of the beast, and the whole world is commanded to worship it. How can one set up an image of an empire or a government? This hasn't been done in the past, but men have often bowed down to an image of a political ruler.

iii. "This Beast also has a proper name - a name expressive of a particular number, and that number 'a number of *a man*,' which cannot be conceived except on the idea of an individual person." (Seiss)

iv. "This beast is finally damned. He goes to perdition, into the lake of fire, where he continues to exist and suffer, after passing from this earthly scene (Revelation 17:11; 20:10), which cannot be true of systems of government." (Seiss)

v. The antichrist is also called *the son of perdition* (2 Thessalonians 2:3), as was Judas (John 17:12). Judas was a man, not a system or a government, so it follows that the antichrist will also be a man.

vi. With all this in mind, we agree with Seiss: "We would therefore greatly err from the Scriptures, as well as from the unanimous conviction and teaching of the early Church, were we to fail to recognize this Beast as *a real person*, though one in whom the political power of the world is finally concentrated and represented."

c. **The dragon gave him his power, his throne, and great authority**: This world leader is really empowered and supported by Satan. Through this man, Satan will express his own desire and authority. In this, the **beast** takes the offer that Jesus refused (Matthew 4:8-10).

i. The **beast** is not an ordinary man. He is called *the beast that ascends out of the bottomless pit* (Revelation 11:7, 17:8), and ordinary men do not come from there. "One who hails from that place must either be a dead man brought up again from the dead, or some evil spirit which takes possession of a living man . . . In either case, the Beast, as a person, is an extraordinary and supernatural being." (Seiss)

ii. It may be that Satan himself takes possession of this man, and this is what makes him exceptional. This was the case with Judas, who was possessed by Satan (John 13:27).

3. (3) The beast and his wound.

And *I saw* one of his heads as if it had been mortally wounded, and his deadly wound was healed. And all the world marveled and followed the beast.

a. **One of his heads as if it had been mortally wounded**: This is a *head* wound, a *mortal* wound, not a superficial injury. Perhaps it is an expression of God's judgment against the beast.

b. **And his deadly wound was healed**: The recovery of the beast increases his fame and authority (**all the world marveled and followed the beast**). Twice later (Revelation 13:12 and 13:14) this recovery is mentioned in connection to the world's worship and devotion to the beast.

i. Some who see the beast not as a man but as a government see this as the revival of the Roman Empire, fulfilling Daniel 7. In this perspective, the Roman Empire has been "dead" but will again be "revived," and the world will marvel. Yet the most natural way to understand John's words in Revelation 13 make us believe that he speaks of a man who will be **mortally wounded** and then **healed**. The man will lead a revived Roman Empire, and his personality will dominate it - yet he and the empire are not exactly the same.

c. **Wounded . . . healed**: This is truly an *Anti*christ, who even imitates Jesus in His death and resurrection. The world will believe this, and it will add tremendously to his fame and power.

4. (4) The authority and popularity of the beast.

So they worshiped the dragon who gave authority to the beast; and they worshiped the beast, saying, "Who *is* like the beast? Who is able to make war with him?"

a. **So they worshiped the dragon who gave authority to the beast**: As people worship this beast and bow down before his government, it may be that they do not know they are bowing down to Satan himself; but it is worship of Satan none the less. They clearly worship both the **beast** and the **dragon**, but their worship of the dragon may be unknowing.

i. Though Satan worship becomes more and more popular each year, it is still only a tiny fraction of people who openly worship Satan. But this is because more people expect Satan to appear with ugliness and horror. This is wrong, *for Satan himself transforms himself into an angel of light. Therefore it is no great thing if his ministers also transform themselves into ministers of righteousness, whose end will be according to their works.* (2 Corinthians 11:14-15)

b. **Who is like the beast? Who is able to make war with him?** The world will be amazed at the power of the beast, and will believe he is so mighty that he cannot be conquered. For a time, the beast will look like a tremendous winner. When he blasphemes Jesus and persecutes God's people, they will appear to be complete losers - for a short time.

> i. They worship the beast, and the dragon behind the beast, simply because of the beast's might. "Worship of the devil and the devil's agent is justified purely on the ground of brute force." (Robertson)

5. (5-6) The beast's blasphemies.

And he was given a mouth speaking great things and blasphemies, and he was given authority to continue for forty-two months. Then he opened his mouth in blasphemy against God, to blaspheme His name, His tabernacle, and those who dwell in heaven.

a. **Speaking great things and blasphemies**: "Blasphemer" may be a more accurate title than "Antichrist" for this end-times dictator. This beast is a man who speaks against God and everything God stands for (**His name, His tabernacle, and those who dwell in heaven**).

> i. Some Roman Emperors blasphemed God this way; but they did not fulfill these prophecies, even if they did prefigure their fulfillment.

b. **And he was given authority to continue for forty-two months**: The beast continues without restraint by God for a period of **forty-two months** - the familiar three and one-half years. The duration of the period shows that the beast has full reign for the first half of the final seven years, and that during the whole time he is still under God's authority.

c. Why does the beast **blaspheme . . . those who dwell in heaven?** This means he speaks against those who were taken in the rapture, and are therefore out of his reach.

6. (7-8) The beast makes war against the saints.

It was granted to him to make war with the saints and to overcome them. And authority was given him over every tribe, tongue, and nation. All who dwell on the earth will worship him, whose names have not been written in the Book of Life of the Lamb slain from the foundation of the world.

a. **It was granted to him to make war with the saints**: Revelation 12 described the broad phenomenon of Satanic persecution during the tribulation period. Here, the main instrument of that persecution is revealed: the government of the beast will persecute and kill all those who do not bow in worship to the beast.

b. **To overcome them: Overcome** does not mean that the beast can overcome the faith of the saints, but that he can destroy their physical lives, and by all appearances defeat the cause of God's people on this earth.

i. Who are these **saints** who are **overcome** by the beast? Various views of the timing of the rapture will determine who these persecuted ones are. Those who believe in a pre-tribulation rapture believe that these saints are God's people who come to Christ after the church has been raptured. Those who believe in a post-tribulation rapture believe that these saints are God's people who are on the earth before the final rapture, including what we think of today as the "church."

ii. Jesus said of the church, that *the gates of Hades shall not prevail against it* (Matthew 16:18). If this group of saints (a term not exclusively applied to the New Testament church) is overcome by Satan, perhaps they are not the same New Testament *church* that Jesus spoke of.

c. **All who dwell on the earth will worship him**: This final world dictator will demand and receive worship from the whole **earth**. But those who **worship him** pay the price: they are **whose names have not been written in the Book of Life**.

i. *How* will **all who dwell on the earth . . . worship him**? It will probably be after the pattern of the worship demanded by the Roman Emperors in the days of the early church. There were times in the early church when all residents in the empire were required to burn a pinch of incense before a statue of Caesar and say, "Caesar is Lord." Christians refused to do this and were persecuted because of it. The Romans saw it as an act of *political* allegiance, but the Christians rightly saw it as an act of religious worship. After the great and terrible totalitarian rulers of the 20th Century (Lenin, Stalin, Hitler, Mao), it isn't hard to imagine a dominating world leader demanding such a declaration of allegiance, tantamount to worship.

ii. The **Book of Life** contains the names of all God's redeemed (Revelation 20:15). The idea is that worshipping the beast and having your name in the **Book of Life** are mutually exclusive.

d. **The Lamb slain from the foundation of the world**: This deeply meaningful title for Jesus reminds us that God's plan of redemption was set in place before He even created the beings who would be redeemed. God wasn't "surprised" by the fall of Adam or any other evidence of the fallen nature of man. God isn't making it up as He goes along. It is all going according to plan.

- God the Son had a relationship of love and fellowship with God the Father *before the foundation of the world* (John 17:24)

- The work of Jesus was ordained *before the foundation of the world* (1 Peter 1:20)

- God chose His redeemed *before the foundation of the world* (Ephesians 1:4)

- Names are written in the Book of Life *before the foundation of the world* (Revelation 17:8)

- The kingdom of heaven was prepared for the redeemed *before the foundation of the world* (Matthew 25:34)

7. (9-10) A warning to all.

If anyone has an ear, let him hear. He who leads into captivity shall go into captivity; he who kills with the sword must be killed with the sword. Here is the patience and the faith of the saints.

a. **He who has an ear, let him hear**: This introduces a solemn word of warning, meant to capture the attention of all who hear.

b. **He who leads into captivity shall go into captivity**: This means that the functionaries of the beast are not without guilt. Though these things are prophesied and part of God's predetermined plan, it does not lessen in the slightest way man's personal responsibility. If you work for the beast and lead others **into captivity**, you certainly **shall go into captivity** yourself. God will measure unto you what you have measured to others.

i. This may have a secondary or additional meaning: there is no hope in fighting against the Antichrist. The only way of victory is steadfast faith and endurance in Jesus.

c. **Here is the patience and the faith of the saints**: Though they are viciously attacked by the Antichrist and his followers, the **saints** of God must keep steadfast **faith** in the ultimate justice of God. He will reward their persecutors with persecution of His own.

B. The beast rising from the land.

1. (11) John's initial description of this second beast.

Then I saw another beast coming up out of the earth, and he had two horns like a lamb and spoke like a dragon.

a. **Then I saw another beast**: This creature represents someone *like* the beast rising from the sea, because the same word **beast** is used to describe them both. At the same time, this **beast** is different.

i. They are different in origin, because one comes *out of the sea*, the other **out of the earth**.

ii. They are different in rank, because the second is subordinate to the first (*causes the earth . . . to worship the first beast*, Revelation 13:12)

iii. They are different in appearance, because the second has a mild, "lamb-like" appearance.

b. **And he had two horns like a lamb**: The **two horns** may express the fact that this beast has authority in two realms, such as religious and political authority. Or, he may have **two horns** simply because that's how many horns lambs have (**two horns like a lamb**).

c. **Spoke like a dragon**: Despite his lamb-like appearance, the message of the second beast is the same as the message of the first beast.

i. This second beast is called *the false prophet* (Revelation 16:13, 19:20, 20:10), as someone distinct from the first beast (the Antichrist) and the dragon (Satan).

ii. With the dragon, the beast rising from the sea, and the beast rising from the land we have an unholy trinity. The dragon is the *anti-Father*, the beast rising from the sea is the *anti-Christ*, and the beast rising from the land is the *anti-Holy Spirit*.

2. (12-15) The second beast's "job description."

And he exercises all the authority of the first beast in his presence, and causes the earth and those who dwell in it to worship the first beast, whose deadly wound was healed. He performs great signs, so that he even makes fire come down from heaven on the earth in the sight of men. And he deceives those who dwell on the earth by those signs which he was granted to do in the sight of the beast, telling those who dwell on the earth to make an image to the beast who was wounded by the sword and lived. He was granted *power* to give breath to the image of the beast, that the image of the beast should both speak and cause as many as would not worship the image of the beast to be killed.

a. **He exercises all the authority of the first beast**: The beast rising from the earth is essentially a Satanic prophet, who leads the world to **worship** the beast and the dragon.

i. It may seem fantastic to some that the world will be led into worship of a man and of the devil. But by nature, men have an undeniable religious impulse, and they also have an undeniable rebellion against God. What men want most is not the elimination of religion, but their *own* religion. They say they want the kingdom, but they don't want God in it.

b. **He performs great signs**: The beast rising from the sea has the "signs and wonders" to back up his false teaching. A specific miracle of the false prophet is described: **he makes fire come down from heaven on the earth in the sight of men**. It is important that John highlights *this* miracle. In the eyes of the deceived world, it answers the miracle of the two witnesses, who minister during this period and are persecuted by the Antichrist and his false prophet (Revelation 11:5). To the deceived world, this also puts this false prophet in the class of Elijah (1 Kings 18). We can imagine the false prophet as saying, "Let the true God answer with fire" and then performing his deceptive wonder.

i. "There is a supernatural power which is *against* God and truth, as well as one *for* God and truth. A miracle, simply as a work of wonder, is not necessarily of God. There has always been a devilish supernaturalism in the world, running alongside of the supernaturalism of divine grace and salvation." (Seiss)

ii. In the days of the Exodus, Aaron performed miracles, and up to a point was matched miracle-for-miracle by the magicians of Egypt (Exodus 7-9).

iii. In Deuteronomy 13:1-5, God assumes there will be supernatural works on behalf of false prophets and idols, and He warns His people to judge a worker of miracles by their message, not only by their works.

iv. Jesus said that some who worked miracles - *even in His name* - were false followers and would perish in hell (Matthew 7:22-23).

v. Jesus said that in the end times, false prophets would emerge and *show great signs and wonders to deceive* (Matthew 24:24).

vi. Paul said that the Antichrist will come *with all power, signs, and lying wonders* (2 Thessalonians 2:9).

vii. Knowing all this, the emphasis on *signs and wonders* among some Christians is frightening. Some Christians say or think, "You can really know where God is and where His power is by signs and wonders." Thinking this way is to leave yourself wide open to deception. Years ago there was a large, multi-denominational conference of people who thought this way, and their slogan - on a huge banner over the conference platform - read "Unity Under Signs and Wonders." That's a unity that Satan, the Antichrist, and the false prophet could all join in. Signs and wonders will be present among Christians, but the real marks of God's work are love and truth.

c. **He was granted power to give breath to the image of the beast, that the image of the beast should both speak and cause as many as would not worship the image of the beast to be killed**: The beast rising from the earth will use a deceptive, animated **image** as the focus point of the worship of the beast.

i. It may seem strange to us to have the whole world give this kind of worship to the image of a man, but the personality cults of totalitarian governments in the twentieth century are a good example of this kind of worship. All we have to do is remember totalitarian states like the Soviet Union or Communist China, and their omnipresent pictures of Stalin or Mao and we see a pattern that will be ultimately fulfilled by the Antichrist.

ii. The image of the beast is animated in some way, in that it has **breath** and can **speak**. Whether the image is animated supernaturally or technologically, the result will be impressive. The Psalmist mocked idol worshippers because *the idols of the heathen are silver and gold, the work of men's hands. They have mouths, but they speak not; eyes have they, but they see not* (Psalm 135:15-16). This image of the Antichrist will be a different kind of idol, because **the image of the beast should both speak and cause as many as would not worship the image of the beast to be killed.**

iii. This idolatrous image is what Jesus, Daniel, and Paul spoke of as *the abomination of desolation* (Daniel 9:27, Matthew 24:15, and 2 Thessalonians 2:3-4). It is an idolatrous image set up in the holy place of a rebuilt temple; it is an *abomination* in the sense of being supreme idolatry, and it is *desolation* in the sense that it will bring the judgment described by the seals, trumpets, and bowls.

iv. This is the summation of the power of the Antichrist, whose authority ends after forty-two months (Revelation 13:5). This marks the halfway point of the final seven years of man's rule of this planet. The Antichrist's power ends as soon as it peaks.

v. This is not a recent understanding of this passage. The first commentary we have on the Book of Revelation, written by Victorinus in the early church, says of this Revelation 13:15: "He shall cause also that a golden image of Antichrist shall be placed in the temple at Jerusalem, and that the apostate angel should enter, and thence utter voices and oracles."

3. (16-17) The economic strategy of the first beast and the second beast.

He causes all, both small and great, rich and poor, free and slave, to receive a mark on their right hand or on their foreheads, and that no one may buy or sell except one who has the mark or the name of the beast, or the number of his name.

a. **He causes all . . . to receive a mark:** Under the government of the beast and his associate, all will be given a mark. Without the mark, one will not be able to participate in the economy (**no one may buy or sell except one who has the mark of his name**).

i. Since the ancient Greek word for **mark** (*charagma*) isn't generally applied to people, some have taken this as a symbolic mark. But a literal mark needed to buy or sell is certainly conceivable and practical.

ii. The technology to give people a mark that enables them to buy and sell in the electronic economy is available. There are many different ways it could happen. One interesting possibility from a company named Applied Digital Solutions, which is developing a product called "Digital Angel." Digital Angel™ is a microchip implanted in the body powered by the body's own biomechanical electricity and able to communicate with satellites. This is from a real, legitimate company whose stock is traded on major exchanges. The company plans a significant test of their technology in October 2000. In a press release, Digital Angel's Dr. Peter Zhou commented: "I'm particularly excited about Digital Angel's ability to save lives by remotely monitoring the medical conditions of at-risk patients and providing emergency rescue units with the person's exact location. I also see great potential for Digital Angel in the area of 'location-aware' e-commerce. This is a whole new wireless and Web-enabled frontier in which a purchaser's actual location is integral to making a successful sale or providing a valuable, location-critical service." It isn't hard to see how this kind of "mark" can become commonplace, simply as the logical step in the course of the electronic economy. Digital Angel's slogan is also interesting: "Digital Angel: Technology that Cares."

b. **A mark on their right hand or on their foreheads**: Satan is not a creative being, all he can do is imitate God. We are not surprised to find that this too is a Satanic parody of something God will do; it imitates God's mark upon his people (Revelation 7:3-4).

c. **The number of his name**: This was a common concept in the ancient world. In Greek (and Hebrew as well), letters were assigned a numerical value, such as "A" equaling 1, "B" equaling 2, and so forth. For example, graffiti in the ruins of Pompeii reads "I love her whose number is 545."

4. (18) The number of the beast.

Here is wisdom. Let him who has understanding calculate the number of the beast, for it is the number of a man: His number *is* 666.

a. **His number is 666**: Does this tell us who the beast is, by figuring out the numerical value of a name and seeing if it adds up to 666? Using this method, many candidates for Antichrist have been suggested, such as the Pope or the Papacy, John Knox, Martin Luther, Napoleon, Hitler, Mussolini,

Stalin, and so forth. But the schemes for unlocking the **number of the beast** are as confusing as they are endless.

i. "That as 12, the square root of 144, is God's number, so 25 is the square root of antichrist's number 666; and by this enigmatical expression we are taught that antichrist should be a political body, that should as much affect the number 15, as God seemeth to have his church affected the number 12." (Poole)

ii. "The year of Rome's ruin is by some held to be 1666. It is plain, saith one, Satan shall be tied up 1000 years; 666 is the number of the beast; Antichrist shall so long reign; these two together make the just number." (Trapp)

iii. "Here is the solution of this mystery: *let him that hath a mind* for investigations of this kind, find out a kingdom which contains precisely the number 666, for this must be infallibly the *name* of the beast. Ἡ Λατινη βασιλεια, The Latin Kingdom, has exclusively this number." (Clarke)

iv. Some commentators observe that there are six Roman numerals (I, V, X, L, C, and D). If you add them all up, you get 666. Some take this to say that the Antichrist will be a Roman. Or, they point out that all the numbers from 1 to 36 add up to 666. *Beast* in the evil sense appears 36 times in the Bible.

b. **It is the number of a man**: One persistent opinion, especially in the early church, was that this number identified the Antichrist with Caesar Nero. But to make the name "Caesar Nero" fit, one must take a variant spelling of the Greek form of a Latin name, transliterated into Hebrew characters.

c. The letters of "Jesus" in Greek add up to 888. **666** may be a Satanic counterpart to the name of Jesus, or **666** may be God's evaluation of such a Satanic counterpart - it falls short.

i. As compared to the number 888, the number 666 may signify an unholy trinity. It may be a human and demonic imitation of God, inherently falling short of the perfect and true. Seven is the number of completion and totality, and 6 doesn't quite make it.

d. Or, the number 666 may harken back to Solomon's wages. 1 Kings 10:14 says that Solomon received *yearly six hundred and sixty-six talents of gold*. Perhaps this suggests that the Antichrist, like Solomon, is a good man who becomes corrupted.

i. Modern interpretations of the idea of the Antichrist are full of the idea of some demon-child, marked by obvious evil from his birth, such as in the *Omen* movies. But the Antichrist may be someone whose evil is only seen *after* his rise to power.

e. Christians need not *fear* the number 666 in a superstitious way; but it interesting to see the way the world has an attachment to this number - even with things like "666" brand cough syrup.

5. The two beasts are Satanic imitations. We are presented with a false "Christ" and a false "John the Baptist" who promotes the false Christ. Satan can't create, but he can effectively deceive with imitation.

a. "Imitations have ever formed the gravest perils in the history of the Church and the world, and the devil's final attempt to gain the government of the race will thus be an appalling attempt to imitate." (Morgan)

b. Imitations work precisely because *they are similar*; if they were so obviously different, it would be easy to tell the difference. We must beware and be familiar with the genuine.

c. Instead of obsessing with fear and interest about the imitation - the Antichrist - how much more appropriate is it for Christians to be interested in the genuine: Jesus Christ.

Revelation 14 - Images of God's Victory and the Beast's Defeat

A. The fate of the 144,000.

1. (1-3) The Lamb and the 144,000 on Mount Zion.

Then I looked, and behold, a Lamb standing on Mount Zion, and with Him one hundred *and* forty-four thousand, having His Father's name written on their foreheads. And I heard a voice from heaven, like the voice of many waters, and like the voice of loud thunder. And I heard the sound of harpists playing their harps. They sang as it were a new song before the throne, before the four living creatures, and the elders; and no one could learn that song except the hundred *and* forty-four thousand who were redeemed from the earth.

a. **A Lamb standing on Mount Zion, and with Him one hundred and forty-four thousand**: These 144,000 were last seen in Revelation 7, where they were identified as a group of Jewish believers who minister during the great tribulation and are given a seal of protection throughout that period. Since they stand **on Mount Zion** with the **Lamb**, it shows that they emerge victorious from the great tribulation. The beast of Revelation 13 certainly has not defeated the 144,000; here they are triumphant, worshipping, and standing firm with Jesus.

i. Revelation 14 will answer two important questions raised by Revelation 13. The beast of Revelation 13 was terrifying and awesome; he even can *make war against the saints and overcome them* (Revelation 13:7). So it is fair to ask, "Is the beast completely victorious over all God's people?" The presence of the 144,000 on **Mount Zion** with the **Lamb** emphatically says "no." The second question has to do with this Satanic dictator himself: "What happens to the beast and his followers?" The rest of Revelation 14 will answer that question.

ii. In Revelation 7, the 144,000 are seen at the beginning of the Great Tribulation. In Revelation 14, it shows them in triumph at the end of the Great Tribulation.

b. **Standing on Mount Zion**: Why are they gathered on **Mount Zion**? **Zion** - the ancient name for the hills that make up Jerusalem - is the place where the Messiah gathers His redeemed and reigns over the earth (Psalm 48, Isaiah 24:23, Joel 2:32, Obadiah 17 and 21, Micah 4:1, 4:7).

i. Some commentators see this **Mount Zion** as the *heavenly Zion* referred to in Galatians 4:26. In this thinking, the 144,000 are *victims* of this beast, and are now in heaven with Jesus. But that view doesn't seem to match with the context at all. It also makes us wonder what good God's *seal* on the 144,000 amounted to (Revelation 7:4).

ii. The 144,000 are like the young Jewish men who survived the fiery furnace in Daniel 3:19-25. They prove God's ability to preserve His people.

c. **Having His Father's name written on their foreheads**: The followers of Satan and the beast may have a mark on their hand or forehead (Revelation 13:16-17). But this mark is just a copy of the idea behind the identifying mark on the foreheads of each one of the 144,000, showing that they belong to the Father.

i. "And who were these people, 'having his Father's name written in their foreheads?' Not *Bs* for 'Baptists,' not *Ws* for 'Wesleyens' not *Es* for 'Established Church.' They had their Father's name and nobody else's. What a deal of fuss is made on earth about our distinctions! We think such a deal about belonging to this denomination, and the other. Why, if you were to go to heaven's gates, and ask if they had any Baptists there, the angel would only look at you, and not answer you, if you were to ask if they had any Wesleyans, or members of the Established Church, he would say, 'Nothing of the sort;' but if you were to ask him whether they had any Christians there, 'Ay,' he would say, 'an abundance of them: they are all one now - all called by one name; the old brand has been obliterated, and now they have not the name of this man or the other, they have the name of God, even their Father, stamped on their brow.' " (Spurgeon)

d. **The voice of many waters, and like the voice of loud thunder**: This is the voice of God (Revelation 1:15 and 4:5). Perhaps God spoke here to proclaim His approval of these 144,000 faithful servants in the spirit of Matthew 25:21: *Well done, good and faithful servant.*

e. **And I heard the sound of harpists playing their harps**: We remember that the elders of Revelation 5:8 have harps. Perhaps this is where their music is heard, to accompany the worshipful singing of the 144,000 as they sing a **new song**, unique to them.

f. **And they sang as it were a new song before the throne**: In Revelation 14:1, the 144,000 have their feet firmly planted on an earthly Mount Zion. Yet their praise takes them right to the presence of God, right **before the throne**. In our praise and worship, we really can transport ourselves and be heard in heavenly places.

> i. "To be rapt in praise to God is the highest state of the soul. To receive the mercy for which we praise God for is something; but to be wholly clothed with praise to God for the mercy received is far more. Why, praise is heaven, and heaven is praise! To pray is heaven below, but praise is the essence of heaven above. When you bow in adoration, you are at your very highest." (Spurgeon)

> ii. "Heaven is not the place to learn that song; it must be learned on the earth. You must learn here the notes of free grace and dying love; and when you have mastered their melody, you will be able to offer to the Lord the tribute of a grateful heart, even in heaven, and blend it with the harmonies eternal." (Spurgeon)

2. (4-5) The description of the 144,000.

These are the ones who were not defiled with women, for they are virgins. These are the ones who follow the Lamb wherever He goes. These were redeemed from *among* men, *being* firstfruits to God and to the Lamb. And in their mouth was found no deceit, for they are without fault before the throne of God.

a. **For they are virgins**: Many take the virginity of the 144,000 as simply a symbol of their general purity (as in 2 Corinthians 11:2). Nevertheless, Paul recommended celibacy in distressing times (1 Corinthians 7:25-35), and Jesus spoke of woes upon those with children and families in that day (Matthew 24:19-21). It isn't hard to see that God would call these 144,000 to a literal celibacy for the kingdom's sake during the great tribulation.

> i. Some most commonly apply the term **virgins** to women, not men. So does the use of **virgins** here mean that all the 144,000 are women? Not at all, according to the great Greek scholar A.T. Roberston: "*Parthenos* can be applied to men as well as women."

> ii. If the term **virgins** is a picture of purity in general, it reinforces the connection of the 144,000 with Israel. "Israel is referred to frequently in the Bible as 'the virgin the daughter of Zion' (2 Kings 19:21; Isaiah 37:22), as 'the virgin daughter of Zion' (Lamentations 2:13), and as 'the virgin of Israel' (Jeremiah 18:13; 31:34, 21; Amos 5:2)." (Walvoord)

b. **These are the ones who follow the Lamb wherever He goes**: These 144,000 are of Jewish heritage (Revelation 7:4-8). Yet they are also clearly believers in Jesus, otherwise they would not stand with the Lamb, **follow the Lamb wherever He goes**, and could not be **without fault before the throne of God**.

i. Each of the vast multitude saved during the Tribulation will be saved in exactly the same manner as anyone today: by grace, through a personal faith in Jesus Christ unto salvation. Even though the rapture of the church ends God's dealings with the church as such on the earth, it certainly does not change the way people come to salvation or become part of the larger family of God, which includes all the redeemed, before and after the church.

c. **These were redeemed from among men, being firstfruits to God and to the Lamb**: The 144,000 are the beginnings of a greater harvest; they are **firstfruits**, the "godly nucleus of Israel which is the token of redemption of the nation." (Walvoord)

i. Because they are described as **firstfruits**, many have thought that they themselves will be instrumental in God's plan for bringing in a great harvest during the tribulation. Revelation 7:9 describes an innumerable company saved out of the Great Tribulation, and these 144,000 described as **firstfruits**, may be used to preach the gospel to those who will be saved in this period.

B. Proclamations from heaven.

1. (6-7) An angel preaches the gospel.

Then I saw another angel flying in the midst of heaven, having the everlasting gospel to preach to those who dwell on the earth; to every nation, tribe, tongue, and people; saying with a loud voice, "Fear God and give glory to Him, for the hour of His judgment has come; and worship Him who made heaven and earth, the sea and springs of water."

a. **Then I saw another angel flying in the midst of heaven, having the everlasting gospel to preach to those who dwell on the earth**: The angel preaches the gospel, but also announces judgment (**the hour of His judgment has come**). Because the judgment of God is so evident on the earth in great tribulation, it is no wonder why the crowd of those saved through the great tribulation can't be numbered (Revelation 7:9-14).

i. Some today like to identify their ministry or technology with this **angel flying in the midst of heaven**. One prominent television

ministry named the satelite they use "Angel One" in a hoped-for fulfillment of this verse. The desire to connect contemporary technology or events with this **angel** is nothing new. Adam Clarke, writing
from the late 18th century says, "But the vision seems truly descriptive
of a late institution, entitled THE BRITISH AND FOREIGN BIBLE SOCIETY,
whose object it is to print and circulate the Scriptures of the Old and
New Testaments, through all the habitable world, and in all the lan-
guages spoken on the face of the earth."

ii. John Trapp, writing in the late 17th century, saw a fulfillment of his
own: "This is held to be John Wicliff, who wrote more than two hundred volumes against the pope, and was a means of much good to
many."

b. **Fear God and give glory to Him**: This is what the angel tells the
whole world to do. They can do this and **give glory** to God and **worship
Him** willingly in this life, or be compelled to **give glory** to Him later.

i. It is certain that one day all will **give glory** to God. Philippians 2:9-
11 says, *Therefore God also has highly exalted Him and given Him the name
which is above every name, that at the name of Jesus every knee should bow, of
those in heaven, and of those on earth, and of those under the earth, and that
every tongue should confess that Jesus Christ is Lord, to the glory of God.*

ii. "Here is the bitter irony of their lot: though they damn themselves
eternally by their refusal to face the truth, one day they will be forced
to face it. Sooner or later the 'glory' they refuse to 'give' the Creator
willingly will be torn from them by the spectacle of His wrath." (Kiddle)

iii. John says this is the **everlasting gospel**, and it may sound different that the gospel we hear preached today. It isn't all that different,
but it is preached to a different, specific time - to those in the latter
part of the great tribulation. "Hence still something of a Gospel message sounds . . . It is *Gospel*, but it is the Gospel in the form it takes
when the hour of judgment has set in. It is one of the very last calls
of grace to an apostate world." (Seiss)

c. **To every nation, tribe, tongue, and people**: This can be a valid fulfillment of Jesus' promise in Matthew 24:14 that the gospel would be preached
to all the world before His second coming. But this can never be a valid
excuse for neglecting the urgency of missions. God has not given the
responsibility for spreading the Gospel to angels, but unto His people.

i. However, this is the only place in the New Testament where we see
angels preaching the Gospel. In God's sublime wisdom, He has chosen to give that responsibility to people alone, apart from the rarest of
exceptions.

2. (8) An angel announces Babylon's fall.

And another angel followed, saying, "Babylon is fallen, is fallen, that great city, because she has made all nations drink of the wine of the wrath of her fornication."

> a. **Babylon is fallen**: More on **Babylon** will come in Revelation 17. For now, it is enough to see it representing mankind in organized rebellion against God.
>
> > i. "Prophetically, 'Babylon' sometimes refers to a literal city, sometimes to a religious system, sometimes to a political system, all stemming from the evil character of historic Babylon." (Walvoord)
>
> b. **Because she has made all nations drink of the wine of the wrath of her fornication**: When we are told that **Babylon** has led all nations into **fornication**, the main idea is *spiritual* fornication - the worship of other gods. However, we are never surprised to see spiritual fornication accompanied with literal immorality.

3. (9-11) A third angel warns of coming judgment.

Then a third angel followed them, saying with a loud voice, "If anyone worships the beast and his image, and receives *his* mark on his forehead or on his hand, he himself shall also drink of the wine of the wrath of God, which is poured out full strength into the cup of His indignation. He shall be tormented with fire and brimstone in the presence of the holy angels and in the presence of the Lamb. And the smoke of their torment ascends forever and ever; and they have no rest day or night, who worship the beast and his image, and whoever receives the mark of his name."

> a. **If anyone worships the beast and his image, and receives his mark on his forehead or on his hand**: This reminds us that there is a connection between worshipping **the beast and his image** and receiving **his mark on his forehead or on his hand**. No one will "casually" or "accidentally" take the mark. The connection between worshipping the beast and taking the mark will be clear enough.
>
> > i. Although, receiving the mark may *seem* innocent enough to those who dwell on the earth. In their eyes it may not seem like much more that a mere pledge of allegiance and devotion to the Antichrist and his government. It was the same way in the first few centuries of Christianity, when burning a pinch of incense to an image of Caesar, and pledging "Caesar is Lord" was regarded as an innocent act of civic duty to the ancient pagans.

b. He himself shall also drink of the wine of the wrath of God, which is poured out full strength into the cup of His indignation: Those who worship the Antichrist are forced to drink **the wine of the wrath of God**. This cup of God's wrath is like undiluted wine, mixed with spices to make it still stronger (**full strength**).

> i. The idea that God holds a cup of wrath, which He makes those under judgment drink is expressed more than thirteen times in the Bible (Psalm 75:8 and Jeremiah 25:15 are examples). This is the idea behind the cup that Jesus wanted to avoid if it were possible (Matthew 26:39). Jesus willingly took the cup of the Father's wrath that we deserved; here, the enemies of Jesus have no choice - the cup is *forced* upon them.

c. The wine of the wrath of God . . . the cup of His indignation: The wine in the cup is associated with **wrath** (the ancient Greek word *thymos*), which describes a *passionate* anger. The cup itself is associated with **indignation** (the ancient Greek word *orge*) which is anger from a *settled disposition*.

> i. The ancient Greek word *orge* is the common word for God's anger in the New Testament. The ancient word *thymos* is used only 11 times, and 10 of the 11 are in Revelation. Usually, God's anger towards sinners does not flash against them; it is simply His settled opposition against sin and unrighteousness. But in the Book of Revelation, which so clearly describes God's ultimate judgment, the term for *passionate anger* is used much more often.

d. He shall be tormented with fire and brimstone in the presence of the holy angels and in the presence of the Lamb. And the smoke of their torment ascends forever and ever; and they have no rest day or night: This passage teaches several important truths about hell and the eternal destiny of the damned.

> i. **He shall be tormented with fire and brimstone**: This shows that the suffering of hell is *real torment*, that it is *painful* and *repulsive*. "The modern vogue for dispensing with hell has no counterpart in Revelation." (L. Morris)

> ii. **In the presence of the holy angels and in the presence of the Lamb**: This shows that God is not absent from hell. He is there in all His holiness and righteous judgment. Those who are in hell will *wish* God were absent, but He will not be. It is wrong to say that hell will be devoid of the presence of God; but it will be devoid of His love. The presence of Jesus will be there, but only the presence of His holy justice and wrath against sin.

iii. **The smoke of their torment ascends forever and ever; and they have no rest day or night**: Those who worship the Antichrist and receive his mark will endure this *wrath* and *indignation* for eternity in hell. Here, the fact of *eternal* torment is plainly stated; **forever and ever** means "forever and ever." If the only consequences for sin are in this life, or if the only penalty for sin is temporary, then clever sinners have won out over God. Walvoord says of the phrase **forever and ever**: "Literally 'into the ages of ages,' the strongest expression of eternity of which the Greek is capable."

iv. "Would to God men would everywhere think and talk more of hell, and of that eternity of extremity that they shall never else be able to avoid or to abide. Surely one good means to escape hell is to take a turn or two in hell by our daily meditations." (Trapp)

v. "In describing the worshippers of the beast, the word *worship* as well as the word *receive* in verse 11 is in the present tense emphasizing continued worship of the beast over a long period of time . . . the same present tense is used in describing their torment. As the worship of the beast is not interrupted by repentance, so their torment is not interrupted when repentance is too late." (Walvoord)

4. (12-13) The blessedness of the saints, even in the Great Tribulation.

Here is the patience of the saints; here *are* those who keep the commandments of God and the faith of Jesus. Then I heard a voice from heaven saying to me, "Write: 'Blessed *are* the dead who die in the Lord from now on.' " "Yes," says the Spirit, "that they may rest from their labors, and their works follow them."

a. **Here is the patience of the saints . . . Blessed are the dead who die in the Lord from now on . . . that they may rest from their labors**: We can easily contrast the **rest** of the saints with the continual torment of the wicked (Revelation 14:11). The **rest** comes through patient endurance and faithfulness to God and His Word (**here are those who keep the commandments of God and the faith of Jesus**).

i. We can only imagine what courage and comfort this passage will give embattled, persecuted saints during the Great Tribulation. Clearly, God wants to encourage His people to be steadfast in times of trial, focused on what blessed rest and reward awaits them in eternity.

ii. **Blessed are the dead who die in the Lord**: "These are the only *glorious* dead . . . they die in the cause of God, they die under the smile and approbation of God, and they die to live and reign with God for ever and ever." (Clarke)

b. **Their works follow them**: The patient endurance and work of these saints is remembered in heaven. Our work for the Lord goes with us into heaven, giving dignity and significance to all work here below.

C. The earth's harvest.

1. (14-16) Time for Jesus to bring in the harvest.

Then I looked, and behold, a white cloud, and on the cloud sat *One* like the Son of Man, having on His head a golden crown, and in His hand a sharp sickle. And another angel came out of the temple, crying with a loud voice to Him who sat on the cloud, "Thrust in Your sickle and reap, for the time has come for You to reap, for the harvest of the earth is ripe." So He who sat on the cloud thrust in His sickle on the earth, and the earth was reaped.

a. **On the cloud sat One like the Son of Man, having on His head a golden crown, and in His hand a sharp sickle**: Many have difficulty identifying Jesus as the one harvesting here. They have a hard time with Jesus responding to **another angel** who **came out of the temple**. But it is unlikely that anyone called **the Son of Man**, and wearing **a golden crown** is anyone but Jesus.

i. **Having on His head a golden crown**: "How different it will be to see him with a crown of gold upon his head from what it was to see him wearing that terrible crown of thorns which the cruel soldiers plaited, and thrust upon his brow! The word used here does not usually refer to the diadem of power, but to the crown won in conflict; and it is very remarkable that it should be said that, when Christ comes to judge the world, he will wear the garland of victory, the crown which he has won in the great battle which he has fought. How significant of his final triumph will that crown of gold be about those brows that were once covered with bloody sweat when he was fighting the battle for our salvation!" (Spurgeon)

b. **For the harvest of the earth is ripe**: This ancient Greek word for **ripe** has a negative sense, "to become dry or withered." The idea is of something that is *over*-ripe. This means that God will judge the earth only when it is *over*-ripe for judgment. He doesn't rush into judgment.

i. "It must be remembered that evil has its harvest as well as good. There is a harvest of misery and woe, - a harvest for the gathering, binding, and burning of the tares, - as well as for the gathering of the wheat into the garner of heaven." (Seiss)

2. (17-20) The winepress of God.

Then another angel came out of the temple which is in heaven, he also having a sharp sickle. And another angel came out from the altar, who had power over fire, and he cried with a loud cry to him who had the sharp sickle, saying, "Thrust in your sharp sickle and gather the clusters of the vine of the earth, for her grapes are fully ripe." So the angel thrust his sickle into the earth and gathered the vine of the earth, and threw *it* into the great winepress of the wrath of God. And the winepress was trampled outside the city, and blood came out of the winepress, up to the horses' bridles, for one thousand six hundred furlongs.

a. **Another angel who came out from the altar, who had power over fire**: "These allusions seem to indicate that the angel is acting in response to the prayers of the saints for divine judgment on wickedness." (Walvoord)

b. **The great winepress of the wrath of God**: This vivid picture of judgment was the inspiration for *The Battle Hymn of the Republic*.

Mine eyes have seen the glory of the coming of the Lord,
He is trampling out the vineyard where the grapes of wrath are stored,
He hath loosed the fateful lightning of His terrible swift sword,
His truth is marching on!

c. **Thrust in your sharp sickle and gather the clusters of the vine of the earth, for her grapes are fully ripe**: The image of the Second Coming of Jesus as a harvest is also communicated in Matthew 13:24-30 and 13:36-43, with the parable of the wheat and the tares. The implication is that true believers will not be separated from those who merely go to church until the final harvest.

i. **Fully ripe** "pictures grapes fully grown in the prime almost bursting with juice . . . The spurting of the grape juice from under the bare feet of those treading the grapes in the winepress is compared to the spurting of blood and speaks of the awful human carnage." (Walvoord)

ii. "What strength have grapes against the weight and power of a man when he comes to set his feet upon them? And the riper they are, the more helpless . . . The heel of Omnipotence is upon them, and they can only break and sink beneath it." (Seiss)

d. **Blood came out of the winepress, up to the horses' bridles, for one thousand six hundred furlongs**: This probably describes blood *splattering* **up to the horses' bridles**, a picture of tremendous carnage in the battle of Armageddon described in Revelation 16:16 and 19:11-19. It is not likely a description of a river of blood running the length of the

Promised Land and as high as a horse's bridle is. This would be an almost incomprehensible river of blood.

i. In ancient times, a battle area extending **one thousand six hundred furlongs** (approximately 200 miles) was incomprehensible - but not in modern warfare. "The area covered, 1,600 furlongs, is approximately 200 miles, and specifies that the area within a 200-mile radius from Jerusalem will be gathered at the time of the second coming of Christ." (Walvoord)

ii. But this vivid, powerful description shows how complete the judgment of God is. Revelation 14 is the perfect answer to Revelation 13. At the end of Revelation 13, it almost seemed like Satan and the Antichrist might win. But Revelation 14 shows who is really triumphant, powerful, and in control: God, His Messiah, and His people; not Satan, his messiah (the Antichrist) and his followers.

Revelation 15 - Prelude to the Bowl Judgments

A. Those victorious over the beast.

1. (1) Seven angels with seven plagues.

Then I saw another sign in heaven, great and marvelous: seven angels having the seven last plagues, for in them the wrath of God is complete.

a. Revelation 14 seemed to describe the consummation of all things, ending with the fury of the Battle of Armageddon. But now John will go back and describe God's judgment in more detail. This idea of stating and restating in more detail is common with prophecy, and with Hebrew literature in general (see Genesis 1:1-2:7 and Genesis 2:8-25).

i. "As is the plan of the prophet, he reviews, he recapitulates, he enlarges upon the scene he has already sketched." (Erdman)

ii. Remember, we already "saw the end" in Revelation 6:12-17. Then John took us over the same material in greater detail again. This reminds us that Revelation is not strictly *chronological* in its arrangement.

b. **Seven angels having the seven last plagues**: This idea is also in Leviticus 26:21: *Then, if you walk contrary to Me, and are not willing to obey Me, I will bring on you seven times more plagues, according to your sins.* These **seven last plagues** are God's judgment on a disobedient and contrary world.

c. **For in them the wrath of God is complete**: The ancient Greek word for **wrath** is *thymos*. As was the case in Revelation 14:10, there are two words for wrath or anger in Biblical Greek: *thymos* (a volatile, passionate anger) and *orge* (anger from a settled disposition). This is a place where God's anger flashes hot.

i. *Orge* is the more common word for God's anger in the New Testament. *Thymos* is used only 11 times, and 10 of the 11 are in Revelation. It is the book that reveals the judgment of God against a Jesus-rejecting world.

d. **Is complete**: **Complete** (the ancient Greek word *etelesthe*) means, "to reach an end or an aim." Here, the "hot" wrath of God will fulfill an eternal purpose. God isn't just blowing off steam.

2. (2) A multitude on the sea of glass.

And I saw *something* like a sea of glass mingled with fire, and those who have the victory over the beast, over his image and over his mark *and* over the number of his name, standing on the sea of glass, having harps of God.

a. **I saw something like a sea of glass**: The sea of glass is **mingled with fire**. This may be a reminder of the "fires" of judgment.

i. "The sea is designed to reflect the glory of God. In chapter 4 its description 'like unto crystal' speaks of the holiness of God. Here the sea mingled with fire speaks of divine judgment proceeding from God's holiness." (Walvoord)

ii. Because images from the Exodus abound in this chapter, some simply see an indication of the color red, with it an allusion to the Red Sea and the deliverance from bondage. Also in this chapter we see plagues, Moses, the tabernacle, and the cloud of God's glory. This chapter shows the ultimate Exodus, the freedom of God's people from a sinful and persecuting world.

b. **Those who have victory over the beast**: These are those who are victorious over the beast through their faithfulness unto death. They are the tribulation martyrs, described in Revelation 7:9-17.

i. They are not those who *survive* the tribulation. As much as we can discern any sort of chronology from Revelation (which is difficult), we are still very much in the tribulation - the bowl judgments still wait.

ii. Therefore, even though the Antichrist kills them, they **have victory over the beast** - they are *not* losers. The early church consistently described the day of martyrdom as "a day of victory."

c. **Standing on the sea of glass**: The ancient Greek word for **on** (*epi*) can mean *on, over* or *beside*. Many believe that in the "architecture" of heaven, the sea of glass is a physical representation of the Word of God, connecting to the idea of the tabernacle's laver and the *washing of water by the word* (Ephesians 5:26). Perhaps we could say that these saints are "standing on the Word."

d. **Having harps of God**: The only people we saw with **harps** before were the twenty-four elders (Revelation 5:8). These tribulation martyrs are given the blessing of worshipping God with music in heaven.

3. (3-4) Their song of praise.

They sing the song of Moses, the servant of God, and the song of the Lamb, saying: "Great and marvelous *are* Your works, Lord God Almighty! Just and true *are* Your ways, O King of the saints! Who shall not fear You, O Lord, and glorify Your name? For *You* alone *are* holy. For all nations shall come and worship before You, For Your judgments have been manifested."

a. **They sing the song of Moses**: Only one song is sung, but this song goes by two titles (**the song of Moses** and **the song of the Lamb**). The two titles refer to a single song. Here is a perfect union between law and love, between the Old Covenant and the New Covenant.

b. This song, deeply rooted in the Old Testament, gives praise to:

- God's works (**Great and marvelous are Your works**)

- God's ways (**Just and true are Your ways**)

- God's worthiness (**Who shall not fear You, O Lord, and glorify Your name? For You alone are holy**)

- God's worship (**all nations shall come and worship before You**)

c. **Your . . . Your . . . You . . . Your . . . You . . . You . . . Your**: These martyrs are only focused on God. They don't even focus on their own costly and glorious victory. They have the heart of true worship: It's all about *God*, not about us.

B. Seven angels are given seven bowls of judgment.

1. (5-6) Seven angels, distinctively clothed.

After these things I looked, and behold, the temple of the tabernacle of the testimony in heaven was opened. And out of the temple came the seven angels having the seven plagues, clothed in pure bright linen, and having their chests girded with golden bands.

a. **The temple of the tabernacle of the testimony in heaven**: Exodus 25:8-9 and Hebrews 8:9 remind us that the tabernacle God told Moses to build was based on a heavenly pattern. This here refers to the heavenly reality of the **tabernacle**, not the earthly copy.

b. **Out of the temple came the seven angels having the seven plagues**: These angels bring God's judgment. It is significant that they come directly from heavenly temple, from the presence and throne of God. They do not act on their own authority, but God's.

c. Their clothing (**pure bright linen . . . their chests girded with golden bands**) is a reminder that God's judgment is always completely pure and righteous. They are not like the modern anti-hero or vigilante, who sink to the level of the criminals they fight.

2. (7-8) The bowls are given; the cloud of God's glory fills the temple.

Then one of the four living creatures gave to the seven angels seven golden bowls full of the wrath of God who lives forever and ever. The temple was filled with smoke from the glory of God and from His power, and no one was able to enter the temple till the seven plagues of the seven angels were completed.

a. **Seven golden bowls**: These **bowls** are broad, flat bowls or saucers used ritually for drinking or for pouring libations in sacrifice. The contents of such a shallow bowl were quickly, easily, and completely poured out.

i. The King James Version says that the angels had *seven golden vials full of the wrath of God.* The word *vials* is really a poor translation. They are really "shallow, pan-like, golden bowls, or censers, such as were used in the temple to hold the fire when incense was burned." (Seiss)

b. **The temple was filled with smoke from the glory of God and from His power**: When the cloud of glory fills the temple in heaven, no one can enter. It was the same when Moses could not enter the Tabernacle when the smoke of the cloud of God's glory, sometimes called the *Shekinah* filled the tent (Exodus 40:34-35).

c. Both the **bowls** and the cloud come **from the glory of God and from His power**. This is a reminder of God's special presence and glory, even in the midst of devastating judgment.

d. **No one was able to enter the temple till the seven plagues of the seven angels were completed**: This declares that judgment is now irreversible. Nothing can hinder it any more, because access to this temple in heaven will not long be denied.

Revelation 16 - The Bowl Judgments

A. Bowls directed against natural phenomenon.

1. (1) A voice from the temple.

Then I heard a loud voice from the temple saying to the seven angels, "Go and pour out the bowls of the wrath of God on the earth."

a. Since no one could enter the temple (Revelation 15:8), this **loud voice from the temple** must be God Himself, who personally initiates the horrific judgment of the bowls.

b. **Go and pour out the bowls of the wrath of God on the earth**: These bowls of judgment are the *third woe* described in Revelation 11:14. Because they are described as **the wrath of God**, they are *chastisements* (with the purpose of bringing repentance) as much as *punishments* (with the purpose of dispensing justice).

    i. As such, we usually think of these as occurring at the end of the seven-year period, immediately before Jesus' return.

c. Images from Israel's Exodus are prominent in the bowl judgments. In the days of Moses, God sent plagues upon Egypt that included plagues of boils (Exodus 9:8-12), waters turning to blood (Exodus 7:14-25), and darkness (Exodus 10:21-29).

d. Are the plagues described in this chapter symbolic? Perhaps we can't envision *all* that these words mean. However, God's judgment of this world will not be a symbolic judgment. We can remember that the reality behind a symbol is always more real - and in this case therefore more terrifying - than the symbol itself.

e. **On the earth**: Those who believe the Book of Revelation is all fulfilled in history have a hard time with this. In Poole's commentary, his suggestions on what **earth** might mean show how difficult it is to make sense of Revelation this way.

- Poole says **earth** might mean *some parts of the earth*
- Poole says **earth** might mean *the common people*
- Poole says **earth** might mean *The Roman Empire*
- Poole says **earth** might mean *The Roman Catholic clergy*

    i. The point is clear. If **earth** doesn't mean **earth**, then no one can tell what it means, and God may as well not have written it.

2. (2) The first bowl: **foul and loathsome** sores.

So the first went and poured out his bowl upon the earth, and a foul and loathsome sore came upon the men who had the mark of the beast and those who worshiped his image.

   a. **A foul and loathsome sore came upon the men who had the mark of the beast**: Those who worshipped the beast and received his **mark** are now "marked" by God with **loathsome** sores.

3. (3) The second bowl: the sea turned to blood.

Then the second angel poured out his bowl on the sea, and it became blood as of a dead *man;* and every living creature in the sea died.

   a. **The sea . . . became blood**: Revelation 8:8-9 described a partial contamination of the sea. Here the contamination is made complete (**every living creature in the sea died**).

   b. **Blood as of a dead man**: The sea doesn't necessarily *become* blood, but **as of** a corpse's blood. It will match the appearance and sickening character of the blood in a dead body.

4. (4) The third bowl: fresh waters polluted.

Then the third angel poured out his bowl on the rivers and springs of water, and they became blood.

   a. **The rivers and springs of water, and they became blood**: This *complete* contamination is in contrast to the partial (one-third) pollution of fresh waters shown in Revelation 8:10-11.

   b. When these judgments come, the time must be very short until the return of Jesus. With ecological disaster such as this, the human race cannot survive long.

      i. "They thirsted after blood and massacred the saints of God; and now they have got blood to drink!" (Clarke)

5. (5-7) The righteousness of God's judgments.

And I heard the angel of the waters saying: "You are righteous, O Lord, the One who is and who was and who is to be, because You have judged

these things. **For they have shed the blood of saints and prophets, and You have given them blood to drink. For it is their just due." And I heard another from the altar saying, "Even so, Lord God Almighty, true and righteous** *are* **Your judgments."**

> a. **You are righteous . . . For they have shed the blood of saints and prophets, and You have given them blood to drink**: It is completely fitting that those who delighted in shedding the blood of the saints should now be forced to drink "blood." They have refused the Living Water, and now will be given the water of death.
>
> b. Even in the midst of judgment, it is right that the angel declares **You are righteous, O Lord**. Not only is God's justice *fair*, it is also *pure* and *appropriate*. There is no "vigilante justice" with God.
>
> c. **I heard another from the altar saying**: This voice is either an angel speaking from the **altar**, or the **altar** personified, representing the corporate testimony of the martyrs (Revelation 6:9) and the prayers of the saints (Revelation 8:3-5).
>
> > i. This "speaking altar" may be *God's altar* - the cross, where His greatest sacrifice was made, and which here testifies of His righteous judgment, both in the past and soon to come. This is the altar where God in His love offered a way of escape from these judgments.

6. (8-9) The fourth bowl: the sun scorches men.

Then the fourth angel poured out his bowl on the sun, and power was given to him to scorch men with fire. And men were scorched with great heat, and they blasphemed the name of God who has power over these plagues; and they did not repent and give Him glory.

> a. **The sun, and power was given to him to scorch men with fire**: What is normally taken for granted as a blessing - the warmth of the shining **sun** - is now a curse.
>
> b. **They did not repent and give Him glory**: The failure of men to respond with repentance shows that knowledge or experience of *judgment* will not change man's sinful condition. Those who are not won by *grace* will never be won.
>
> > i. "The wishful thinking of some that men would repent if they only knew the power and righteous judgment of God is shattered by frequent mention in this chapter of the hardness of the human heart in the face of the most stringent and evident divine discipline." (Walvoord)

B. Bowls directed against the beast and his government.

1. (10-11) Fifth bowl: a plague of darkness.

Then the fifth angel poured out his bowl on the throne of the beast, and his kingdom became full of darkness; and they gnawed their tongues because of the pain. They blasphemed the God of heaven because of their pains and their sores, and did not repent of their deeds.

a. **His kingdom became full of darkness**: Some see this as a symbolic darkness. Caird calls the last three plagues a "triad of political disaster" - internal anarchy, invasion, and irreparable collapse.

i. But it isn't necessary to see this darkness as a symbolic political darkness. The ninth plague on Egypt was a literal darkness, with spiritual overtones. It could be *felt*, as described in Exodus 10:21-22.

b. **They gnawed their tongues because of the pain**: The darkness of the fifth bowl is a preview of hell itself, which is described by Jesus as *the outer darkness* (Matthew 25:30). Those under the judgment of this fifth bowl stand, as it were, on the shores of the lake of fire.

c. **And did not repent of their deeds**: In man's sinful condition, he *increases* his sin when under God's judgment, the very time he should *forsake* his sin.

i. "Judgment may produce a carnal repentance - a repentance that is of the flesh, and after the manner of the sinful nature of men. In this repentance the depravity of the heart remains the same in essence, though it takes another form of showing itself. Though the man changes, he is not savingly changed: he becomes another man, but not a new man. The same sin rules in him, but it is called by another name, and wears another dress. The stone is carved into a more sightly shape, but it is not turned into flesh. The iron is cast into another image, but it is not transformed into gold. This carnal repentance is caused by fear. Does not every thief repent of robbery when he is convicted and sent to jail? Does not every murderer repent of his crime when he stands under the fatal tree?" (Spurgeon)

ii. "This is real penitence, when the man gives glory to the justice of God, even though it condemns him. O my hearer, do you thus repent? Is sin really sinful to you? Do you see its desert of hell? If not, your repentance needs to be repented of." (Spurgeon)

2. (12-16) The sixth bowl: Armies are gathered for a great battle.

Then the sixth angel poured out his bowl on the great river Euphrates, and its water was dried up, so that the way of the kings from the east might be prepared. And I saw three unclean spirits like frogs *coming* out of the mouth of the dragon, out of the mouth of the beast, and out of

the mouth of the false prophet. For they are spirits of demons, performing signs, *which* go out to the kings of the earth and of the whole world, to gather them to the battle of that great day of God Almighty. "Behold, I am coming as a thief. Blessed *is* he who watches, and keeps his garments, lest he walk naked and they see his shame." And they gathered them together to the place called in Hebrew, Armageddon.

a. **The great river Euphrates**: The Romans considered the **Euphrates** River a secure barrier against invasion from the empires of the east. In that day it was 1,800 miles long and anywhere from 300-1200 yards wide.

b. **Its water was dried up, so that the way of the kings of the east might be prepared**: If the Euphrates were dried up and made a road, massive armies from the east (nations such as China, India, and Japan) could move westward with ease.

> i. Why do these armies come? Is it to wipe out Israel? Is it to rebel against a European-based world leader (the Antichrist)? Ultimately, they come to do battle against God and His Messiah (Psalm 2).

c. **I saw three unclean spirits like frogs coming out of the mouth of the dragon**: The spirits are **like frogs** in form. The ancient Jewish people regarded frogs as unclean and repulsive, but the Egyptians revered a frog-goddess.

> i. "We can only explain the similitude from the uncleanness, and the pertinacious noise, of the frog." (Alford)

> ii. "Christ expelled unclean spirits, but His enemies send them forth." (Swete)

> iii. The frogs are "a devastating caricature of the failure of evil. That which men fear most because it appears to be mighty and eternally entrenched becomes at long last only a ridiculous spawning of sickly creatures of the night." (Love)

> iv. These demons are like the "lying spirit" who led Ahab into battle (1 Kings 22:19-23).

d. **They are spirits of demons, performing signs**: Again, signs and wonders are used by demons as tools of deception. The **false prophet** here is the second beast of Revelation 13.

e. **Gather them to the battle**: This battle is not nation against nation, but the nations against God (Psalm 2:2). This is one of three important battles mentioned in prophecy.

> i. The battle of Gog, Magog and her allies come against Israel (Ezekiel 38 and 39).

ii. The battle of **Armageddon**, when the Antichrist leads the world system against a returning Jesus (Revelation 17:12-16, 17:14, 19:19).

iii. The final battle, when Satan and his allies, after the millennium, make war against God (Revelation 20:7-10).

f. **That great day of God Almighty**: The winner of this battle is apparent. It is the **great day of** *God*, not the great day of man, not the great day of the Antichrist, not the great day of the dragon.

g. **Behold, I am coming as a thief. Blessed is he who watches, and keeps his garments, lest he walk naked and they see his shame**: In the midst of the description of the coming battle, there is a warning to be prepared in light of Jesus' assured victory.

i. **Garments** are pictures of spiritual and practical righteousness. We are given the righteousness of Jesus as a garment (Galatians 3:27), but we are also called to "put on" the nature of Jesus in terms of practical holiness (Ephesians 4:20-24). Above all, we must not be "**naked**" - that is, without a covering, or trying to provide our own covering like Adam and Eve (Genesis 3:7), which is like filthy rags in the sight of God (Isaiah 64:6).

h. **And they gathered them together to the place called in Hebrew, Armageddon**: This great battle happens at a place called **Armageddon** (*Har-Megiddo*).

i. Those who believe the Book of Revelation is all fulfilled in history have a hard time with this battle. "Some say it is the great Valley of the Mississippi. A few years ago some said it was Sebastopol, or the Crimea. Others think it is France. Whilst many take it as a mere ideal place, for an ideal assemblage, having no existence in fact. To such wild, contradictory, and mutually destructive notions are men driven once they depart from the letter of what is written." (Seiss)

ii. Since there is no specific mount (*Har*) Megiddo (Megiddo is actually a valley), many see this as a symbolic mountain or hill of slaughter. But Seiss makes a good point: "Whether we take it as the mount or the valley, it makes no difference, for the mount and the valley are counted as one, each belonging to the other."

iii. Megiddo is in a region frequently associated with decisive battles: Deborah over Sisera (Judges 5:19); Gideon over the Midianites (Judges 7); Pharaoh over Josiah (2 Kings 23:29; 2 Chronicles 35:22). It is also a place of end-times mourning (Zechariah 12:11).

iv. The vast Valley of Megiddo has seen tremendous battles through the centuries. Over 200 battles have been fought in the region, from

1468 B.C. (with Pharaoh Tuthmosis III) to 1917 (with Lord Allenby of the British).

v. It is best to see the place as literal, as the region of Megiddo and the valley of Esdraelon. Revelation 16:14, 17:14 and 19:19 described an organized battle that must center *somewhere*, even if it extends much further.

vi. "But what is the *battle of Armageddon?* How ridiculous have been the conjectures of men relative to this point! Within the last twenty years this battle has been fought at various places, according to our purblind seers and self-inspired prophets! At one time it was *Austerlitz*, at another *Moscow*, at another *Leipsic*, and now *Waterloo!* And thus they have gone on, and will go on, confounding and being confounded." (Clarke)

3. (17-21) The seventh bowl: the final judgments.

Then the seventh angel poured out his bowl into the air, and a loud voice came out of the temple of heaven, from the throne, saying, "It is done!" And there were noises and thunderings and lightnings; and there was a great earthquake, such a mighty and great earthquake as had not occurred since men were on the earth. Now the great city was divided into three parts, and the cities of the nations fell. And great Babylon was remembered before God, to give her the cup of the wine of the fierceness of His wrath. Then every island fled away, and the mountains were not found. And great hail from heaven fell upon men, *each hailstone* about the weight of a talent. Men blasphemed God because of the plague of the hail, since that plague was exceedingly great.

a. **It is done**: This announcement, coming from the throne itself tells us that there will be no more delay. In mercy, God has stretched out this scene as much has He could. The seals were followed by trumpets; the trumpets were followed by bowls; but there will be no more judgments upon the earth after this - **it is done**.

b. **Poured out his bowl into the air**: The fact that the bowl is poured into the air may show judgment against the *prince of the power of the air* (Ephesians 2:2) and his allies.

c. **There was a great earthquake, such a mighty and great earthquake as had not occurred since men were on the earth**: In these final judgments, God shakes the earth with a tremendous earthquake. The same is promised in Hebrews 12:26: *Now He has promised, saying, "Yet once more I shake not only the earth, but also heaven."* Yet, what cannot be shaken will remain.

d. **Great Babylon was remembered before God, to give her the cup of the wine of the fierceness of His wrath**: The fall of Babylon (**the great city**) is more explicitly described in Revelation 17 and 18. Here, it is enough to say that God gives her **the cup of the wine of the** *fierceness* (the ancient Greek word *thymos*, describing a passionate outburst of anger) **of His** *wrath* (the ancient Greek word *orge*, describing a standing state of anger).

i. "The combination of *thymos* and *orge* connotes the strongest kind of outpouring of divine judgment." (Walvoord)

e. **Great hail from heaven fell upon men, each hailstone about the weight of a talent**: Giant hailstones fall, weighing up to 100 pounds. Men respond in utter, unrepentant depravity (**men blasphemed God because of the plague of the hail**).

i. **Hail** is frequently a tool of judgment against God's enemies, as seen against Egypt (Exodus 9:24), the Canaanites (Joshua 10:11), apostate Israel (Isaiah 28:2), and Gog and Magog (Ezekiel 38:22).

ii. In each of these instances, **hail** rained down from heaven as a tool of judgment, not as a corrective chastisement of God's own children.

iii. Despite all their suffering, many still will not repent. "I have known people say, 'Well, if I were afflicted I might be converted. If I lay sick I might be saved.' Oh, do not think so. Sickness and sorrow of themselves are no helps to salvation. Pain and poverty are not evangelists; disease and despair are not apostles. Look at the lost in hell. Suffering has effected no good in them. He that was filthy here is filthy there. He that was unjust in this life is unjust in the life to come. There is nothing in pain and suffering that, by their own natural operation, will tend to purification." (Spurgeon)

4. We might say that Revelation 16 is a "great" chapter.

a. It describes great evil: a *great city*, *great Babylon* (Revelation 16:19).

b. It describes great tools of judgment: *great heat* (Revelation 16:9), a *great river* dried up (Revelation 16:12), a *great earthquake* (Revelation 16:18), *great hail* and *great* plagues (Revelation 16:21).

c. It describes a great God: His great voice (*loud* is the same Greek word for *great*; verses 1; 17), and His *great day* of victory (Revelation 16:14).

Revelation 17 - The Fall of Religious Babylon

A. The concept of Babylon.

1. Revelation 16:19 and 14:8 have already declared Babylon's fall. In Revelation 17 and 18, the fall of Babylon is carefully detailed.

2. Babylon is mentioned 287 times in the Scriptures, more than any other city except Jerusalem.

a. Babylon was a literal city on the Euphrates River. Genesis 11:1-10 shows that right after the flood, Babylon "was the seat of the civilization that expressed organized hostility to God." (Tenney)

b. Babylon was later the capitol of the empire that cruelly conquered Judah. "Babylon, to them (the Jews), was the essence of all evil, the embodiment of cruelty, the foe of God's people, and the lasting type of sin, carnality, lust and greed." (Tenney)

c. To those familiar with the Old Testament, the name *Babylon* is associated with organized idolatry, blasphemy and the persecution of God's people.

i. "In John's day Rome epitomized all the antagonism and opposition to the Christian faith." (Mounce) In some ways, the city of Rome was the clearest fulfillment of the Babylon attitude. If we had to pick one city today that most exemplifies the world system, perhaps we would say that Los Angeles is the Babylon of today.

3. The concept of Babylon is greater than Revelation 17-18 and the Antichrist's reign. Babylon was present in John's day (typified by Rome), in our day, and throughout history, as the "world system." But under the Antichrist, Babylon (in both its religious and commercial aspects) will hold sway over the earth as never before.

B. The great harlot (religious Babylon) is described.

1. (1-2) Described by the angel.

Then one of the seven angels who had the seven bowls came and talked with me, saying to me, "Come, I will show you the judgment of the great harlot who sits on many waters, with whom the kings of the earth committed fornication, and the inhabitants of the earth were made drunk with the wine of her fornication."

a. **I will show you the judgment of the great harlot**: Her **judgment** is assured at the outset. There is never any doubt regarding the fate - and ultimate failure - of Babylon.

> i. As a religious system, Babylon came into being long before Chris-
> tianity, but in Satanic imitation it anticipated the coming true Messiah.
> According to religious history and legend, the Babylonian religion was
> founded by the wife of Nimrod (a great-grandson of Noah), named
> Semiramis. She was a high priestess of idol worship, and she gave
> birth to a son who she claimed was conceived miraculously. The son,
> named Tammuz, was considered a savior. Many ancient artifacts re-
> main with the familiar motif of the mother Semiramis holding the
> savior-infant Tammuz, which predate Christianity. It was also said that
> Tammuz was killed by a wild beast and then miraculously brought
> back to life. Baal was the local, Canaanite name for the Babylonian
> Tammuz.

> ii. The Bible makes specific mention of some of the features of the
> classic religion of Bablyon:

>> • Ezekiel protests against the ceremony of weeping for Tammuz
>> (Ezekiel 8:14)

>> • Jeremiah mentions the heathen practice of making cakes for the
>> queen of heaven (Jeremiah 7:18) and offering incense to the queen
>> of heaven (Jeremiah 44:17-19, 44:25)

b. **Who sits on many waters**: Here, Babylon **sits on many waters**; that is, she presides over many nations (compare with Revelation 17:15). She has a universal, international character.

> i. This is unification of all false, idolatrous religion, with representa-
> tives from apostate Catholicism, Protestantism, as well as a smorgas-
> bord of other religions of the world.

> ii. "The woman pictures false religion that will dominate the world in
> the tribulation period." (Hocking) Many people like to identify this
> **great harlot** with the Roman Catholic Church, but false religion is
> not limited to any one church.

> iii. "That Rome and the Romish system are involved, may readily be
> admitted; but that this is all, and that the sudden fall of Great Babylon

is simply the fall of Romanism, or the utter destruction of the city of Rome, must be emphatically denied." (Seiss)

c. **The inhabitants of the earth were made drunk**: Religious Babylon intoxicates kings and peoples. Karl Marx was *partly* right when he said, "Religion is the opiate of the masses." He was partly right because *empty* religion *is* the opium of the masses.

d. **Made drunk with the wine of her fornication**: The idea of **fornication** often has strong associations throughout the Bible with idolatry. Since this is a well-accepted religious system, it is likely to appear as attractive and spiritual, though not necessarily moral.

2. (3-6) What John saw.

So he carried me away in the Spirit into the wilderness. And I saw a woman sitting on a scarlet beast *which was* full of names of blasphemy, having seven heads and ten horns. The woman was arrayed in purple and scarlet, and adorned with gold and precious stones and pearls, having in her hand a golden cup full of abominations and the filthiness of her fornication. And on her forehead a name *was* written: MYSTERY, BABYLON THE GREAT, THE MOTHER OF HARLOTS AND OF THE ABOMINATIONS OF THE EARTH. I saw the woman, drunk with the blood of the saints and with the blood of the martyrs of Jesus. And when I saw her, I marveled with great amazement.

a. **He carried me away in the Spirit into the wilderness**: John is carried away into the **wilderness**; the desolate nature of the wilderness is an appropriate setting for a vision of judgment.

b. **Sitting on a scarlet beast**: The harlot rides the same beast (**seven heads and ten horns**) that was previously seen in Revelation 13:1 - the Antichrist and his dictatorship.

   i. "Her position, that of riding the beast, indicates on the one hand that she is supported by the political power of the beast, and on the other that she is in a dominant role and at least outwardly controls and directs the beast." (Walvoord)

   ii. Her association with blasphemy and the dragon's beast are clearly seen from God's perspective. But to the people of the earth she will look quite religious, and have the "faith" everybody wants.

c. The woman is clothed with emblems of luxury (**purple . . . gold and precious stones**) and government (**scarlet**). Yet she offers idolatry (**abominations**) and impurity (**filthiness of her fornication**) in this sumptuous setting.

i. **Purple** and **scarlet** were colors of splendor and magnificence; the dyes to make fabric these colors were rare and costly.

ii. "We find in the course of church history that one of the deadliest marks of ecclesiastical corruption is the lust for temporal power." (Barnhouse) Purple and scarlet were the colors of *rulers*, whether economic or political.

d. **On her forehead a name was written**: The name on her forehead identifies her in more ways than one. Roman prostitutes frequently wore a headband with their name engraved upon it.

i. "In spite of all her glamour she is nothing but a prostitute." (Johnson)

ii. There is a stark contrast between the woman of Revelation 12 (representing Israel, God's people), and this woman (representing idolatrous, false religion).

Characteristics: each are	Woman of Revelation 12	Harlot of Revelation 17
Mothers	Of the Man-Child	Mother of harlots
Notably dressed	In heavenly glories	In worldly splendor
Influential	Moon under her feet	Over earthly kings
Suffering	Attacked by Satan	Attacked by kings

iii. "These two Women, thus related, and set over one against the other as opposites and rivals, must necessarily be interpreted in the same way. As Antichrist corresponds to Christ as a rival and antagonist of Christ, so Great Babylon corresponds to the Woman that bears the Man-child, as *her* rival and antagonist." (Seiss)

e. **MYSTERY, BABYLON THE GREAT**: This title is not for *literal* Babylon; but its *spiritual* (**mystery**) representation, which is the source (**mother**) of all idolatry (**abominations**) and spiritual adultery (**harlots**).

i. This harlot must be larger than any one branch of a religious institution. She is the embodiment of Satan's own ecumenical movement - the religion of the world system.

ii. Our world, with its "it doesn't matter what you believe as long as you believe" philosophy, is ripe for the harlot's seductions. We see the casual disregard for the truth crippling the church today.

f. **Drunk with the blood of the saints and with the blood of the martyrs of Jesus**: The woman not only persecutes, she *revels* in her persecution of the godly as a drunk revels in wine.

g. **I marveled with great amazement**: Why is John amazed? Because this isn't pagan persecution (such as he knew in his day), but religious error and persecution. This is a *psuedo-church*, thirsty for the blood of the saints. "False religion is always the worst enemy of true religion." (Walvoord)

i. We should never forget that some of the most vicious persecution conducted against true Christians has been done in the name of the church. In the days when the Roman Catholic Queen Mary ruled England (known as "Bloody Mary"), some 288 Christians were burnt at the stake for their stand for Christian truth between 1555 and 1558. The first of these martyrs was a man named John Rogers, who, as he stood chained to a stake, and the fire rose around him, up to his legs and shoulders, he rubbed his hands in the flames as if he were washing his hands in cold water. Then he lifted his hands to the heavens and held them high until he was completely consumed by fire. Rogers went to the stake with such calm and dignity that the French Ambassador wrote that he went to his death "as if he was walking to his wedding." His courage was so evident that the huge crowd burst into applause when they saw him walking to the stake.

C. The great harlot is interpreted.

1. (7) The angel tells John that the harlot will be explained to him.

But the angel said to me, "Why did you marvel? I will tell you the mystery of the woman and of the beast that carries her, which has the seven heads and the ten horns."

a. **I will tell you the mystery of the woman and of the beast that carries her**: The focus of the explanation is on the **beast**. It appeared that the harlot ruled (*rode*) the Antichrist's system, but he is the dynamic factor, using her as tyrants have always used religion - as a mere tool to accomplish their purposes.

2. (8) The beast carrying the woman is plainly connected with the beast of Revelation 13.

The beast that you saw was, and is not, and will ascend out of the bottomless pit and go to perdition. And those who dwell on the earth will marvel, whose names are not written in the Book of Life from the foundation of the world, when they see the beast that was, and is not, and yet is.

3. (9) Seven mountains associated with the beast.

Here *is* the mind which has wisdom: The seven heads are seven mountains on which the woman sits.

a. **The seven heads are seven mountains**: Many quickly associate the **seven mountains** with Rome and the Papacy, because Rome is well known as the city on seven hills. Yet literally, the Greek word means **mountains**, not *hills*.

> i. Many commentators - especially those who see all of Revelation fulfilled in history - regard the **seven mountains** as an irrefutable connection with Rome. Clarke is a good example of this when he writes, "This verse has been almost universally considered to allude to the seven hills upon which Rome originally stood."

> ii. But in the Bible mountains are sometimes a figure of governments (such as in Daniel 2:35) and the city of Rome is built on hills, not mountains.

b. It is probably better to see the **seven mountains** as representing the seven kings and kingdoms described in Revelation 17:10. Many people find the connection between religious Babylon and Roman Catholicism irresistible, yet it is flawed in the sense that there is no doubt that religious Babylon will incorporate a strong Roman Catholic element, but it will be *much bigger* than Roman Catholicism.

> i. Indications about Roman Catholicism's ultimate partnership with a one-world religion are evident in Pope John Paul II's bizarre involvement with and approval of other anti-Christian religions.

> ii. In addressing a "prayer gathering" of Christians, Muslims, Jews, Buddhists and others, Pope John Paul II told participants that their efforts were "unleashing profound spiritual energies in the world and bringing about a new climate of peace." The Pope pledged that "the Catholic Church intends to 'share in and promote' such ecumenical and inter-religious cooperation."

> iii. The *Catholic Review* commented on this and said, "The unity of religion promoted by the Holy Father Pope John Paul II and approved by His Holiness the Dalai Lama is not a goal to be achieved immediately, but a day may come when the love and compassion which both Buddha and Christ preached so eloquently will unite the world in a common effort to save humanity from senseless destruction, and lead toward the light in which we all believe."

4. (10) Seven kings and kingdoms.

There are also seven kings. Five have fallen, one is, *and* the other has not yet come. And when he comes, he must continue a short time.

a. **Five have fallen, one is, and the other has not yet come**: This is one of the more difficult passages in the Book of Revelation. Some explain these **seven kings**, five past, one present, and one to come in the succession of Roman Emperors in John's era, but there are many historical difficulties with this approach. More likely, it is a reference to:

- **Five have fallen** refers to the five world empires before John's day: Egypt, Assyria, Babylonia, Medo-Persia, and Greece

- **One is** refers to the world empire of John's day: Rome

- **The other has not yet come** refers to the one world empire to come: a revival of the Roman Empire

b. **When he comes, he must continue a short time**: This seventh will quickly be taken over by an eighth - and will become the state of the Antichrist (Revelation 17:11).

  i. There are problems with this viewpoint as well (so some have taken the seven as symbolic). This plainly is a difficult passage!

5. (11) The beast (the Antichrist) is clearly identified as the eighth king.

And the beast that was, and is not, is himself also the eighth, and is of the seven, and is going to perdition.

a. **Is himself also the eighth**: He is **of the seven** in the sense that he shares characteristics with all previous world empires, but his fate is clear. **Perdition** means "destruction," and the **beast** will be destroyed.

6. (12-15) Ten kings to come, allies of the Antichrist.

"The ten horns which you saw are ten kings who have received no kingdom as yet, but they receive authority for one hour as kings with the beast. These are of one mind, and they will give their power and authority to the beast. These will make war with the Lamb, and the Lamb will overcome them, for He is Lord of lords and King of kings; and those *who are* with Him *are* called, chosen, and faithful." Then he said to me, "The waters which you saw, where the harlot sits, are peoples, multitudes, nations, and tongues."

a. **Ten kings who have received no kingdom as yet**: This probably alludes to a ten-nation confederation (as in the toes of the Daniel 2:24-45 image), but some take **ten** as a symbolic number.

  i. "They are ten kingdoms which shall arise out of the fourth great kingdom there: ten European powers, which in the last time, in concert with and subjugation to the antichristian power, shall make war against Christ. In the precise number and form here indicated, they have not yet arisen . . . What changes in Europe may bring them into the required tale and form, it is not for us to say." (Alford, 1866)

b. Many have seen the European Economic Community as the potential fulfillment of this. Perhaps, but now there are more than ten nations in this revived European power, and more on the way.

> i. There is little doubt of the credentials of the EEC to claim itself a successor to the ancient Roman Empire. The EEC started in 1957, when six European nations met to talk about combining their nuclear, coal, and economic resources. They met together in Rome and signed the treaty of Rome - the beginnings of the present EEC. In many places in Europe, the EEC flag is just as prominent as any national flag. In the spiritual dynamic of things, it's no accident that on the back of the Eurodollar coin is a woman riding a multi-headed beast.

> ii. We could still say what Alford wrote in 1866: "In the precise number and form here indicated, they have not yet arisen . . . What changes in Europe may bring them into the required tale and form, it is not for us to say." But it *will* happen, and this confederation of nations will emerge as an heir to the ancient Roman Empire.

c. **These are of one mind, and they will give their power and authority to the beast**: Whatever their exact identity, their actions are clear. They ally with the Antichrist in the war against Christ, in the battle alluded to in the sixth and seventh bowls (Revelation 16:12-21).

d. The harlot presides over **peoples, multitudes, nations, and tongues**. This tells us that the harlot's influence is worldwide, through her connection to the beast. This will be a truly one-world religion.

e. The interpretation of the harlot focuses on her relation to the beast: she is utterly connected to the beast and his government. If this sounds unthinkable, remember that throughout history, religion - not true Christianity - has often been the willing servant and supporter of tyrants.

D. The great harlot is judged.

1. (16) Antichrist's allies turn on the great harlot.

And the ten horns which you saw on the beast, these will hate the harlot, make her desolate and naked, eat her flesh and burn her with fire.

a. **These will hate the harlot, make her desolate and naked, eat her flesh and burn her with fire**: This violence probably takes place at the mid-point of the tribulation period. Here, apostate religion discovers the true nature of the beast.

> i. Ultimately, the Antichrist will not tolerate any worship except of himself: *The son of perdition, who opposes and exalts himself above all that is called God or that is worshipped, so that he sits in the temple of God, showing himself that he is God* (2 Thessalonians 2:3-4).

b. Once his power has been consolidated, the Antichrist no longer needs the help of religious Babylon. He will then work to dismantle and destroy her and her one-world religion.

i. This has always been the goal of tyrants - and most politicians - to *use* religion for their purposes, then discard it.

2. (17) God's hand ultimately directs all this.

For God has put it into their hearts to fulfill His purpose, to be of one mind, and to give their kingdom to the beast, until the words of God are fulfilled.

a. **God has put it into their hearts**: God has directed the judgment against religious Babylon. God will sometimes use a wicked group (here, the ten kings) to be an instrument of His judgment against another wicked group (here, religious Babylon).

b. **To be of one mind, and to give their kingdom to the beast**: God will ordain the political support of these ten kings for the Antichrist. God will give the world just what it wants: godless religion and godless rulers.

3. (18) The great harlot is identified with Rome.

And the woman whom you saw is that great city which reigns over the kings of the earth.

a. **That great city**: In John's day, there was no doubt which city **reigns over the kings of the earth**. Rome was the political, economic, and religious center of the world in John's day.

i. But *Babylon* - in the sense of the world system - has always been **that great city which reigns over the kings of the earth**. The question for Christians is, "Does it reign over me? Or am I the citizen of a better city, the Jerusalem above?" (Galatians 4:26)

b. Again, the association of this harlot - of religious Babylon - with Rome doesn't mean that the Roman Catholic Church is identical to religious Babylon, though apostate Roman Catholics will definitely be a part of this great harlot.

i. "It is most direct in Paganism; but it is in Mohammedanism, in Papalism, in the degenerate Catholicism of the Eastern churches, and in all the heretical isms, infidelities, and mere goodishness which afflict our Protestant Christianity as well." (Seiss)

c. Rather, Rome was the ready personification of Babylon - the world in rebellion against God - in John's day. Today, idolatry is just as strong, but more dispersed. Today, which city in the world is most readily identified with the world system? Hollywood? Wall Street? Washington?

Revelation 18 - The Fall of Commercial Babylon

A. Announcing the fall of Babylon.

    1. Introduction: is this the same Babylon as is described in chapter 17?

        a. Good scholars see the issue differently. Some point to two manifestations of Babylon, one religious and one commercial or material. Others see the two as one, both being judged at the same time.

        b. There are definite similarities between Babylon as described in Revelation 17 and Revelation 18. Both are under the rule of Antichrist, and have ruling queens; both are filled with blasphemy; both hate the saints, and shed their blood; both are associates with kings in fornication; and both are under judgment and destroyed.

        c. However, there are also some significant differences:

Religious Babylon (Rev. 17)	Commercial Babylon (Rev. 18)
1. Mystery Babylon	1. Great Babylon; Babylon the Great
2. Symbol: a harlot woman	2. Symbol: a great city
3. Identified with Rome (inland)	3. Identified with a port city
4. Woman, whore, and mother	4. Habitation, great city, market place
5. Guilty of religious abominations	5. Guilty of greed, self-indulgence
6. Destroyed by a political power that previously supported her	6. Destroyed by a sudden act of God

        d. In my view, it is best to see them as intertwined, yet somewhat distinct. Religious Babylon of Revelation 17 is judged at the mid-point of the seven-year period of tribulation. Commercial Babylon is judged at the end of that period.

i. This breadth in prophecy shouldn't surprise us. Think of what the Old Testament says about the first coming of the Messiah:

- Micah said that Messiah would *come* out of Bethlehem (Micah 5:2)
- Hosea said that Messiah would come out of Egypt (Hosea 11:1)
- Malachi said that Messiah would *come* to the temple (Malachi 3:1)
- Zechariah said that Messiah would *come* to Zion (Zechariah 9:9)
- Isaiah said that Messiah would *come* to Galilee (Isaiah 9:1-2)

ii. Which of these is true? They are all true. So it isn't strange at all to say, "Babylon is falling" and to mean it in two senses (religious Babylon and commercial Babylon) at two different times (the middle of the Great Tribulation and the end of the Great Tribulation).

e. This passage is very much in the style of Old Testament prophecies of doom regarding wicked cities. Two examples of this are Babylon (Isaiah 13-14, Isaiah 21 and Jeremiah 50-51) and Tyre (Ezekiel 26-28).

i. "John has caught the spirit of the prophetic doom songs." (L. Morris)

2. Is Babylon of Revelation 18 a literal or symbolic city?

a. Some have thought it to be a future rebuilt Babylon on the Euphrates River in the Middle East. This is now a desolate desert in modern day Iraq.

i. Sudam Hussein has been outspoken in his desire to resurrect the ruined city of Babylon in all of its glory. He may in fact do this, and it is conceivable that a rebuilt Babylon could be a world economic center, especially with the wealth of Mideast oil. But so far, Hussein has not made good on his dream to rebuild Babylon.

b. But most likely, commercial Babylon is symbolic, like religious Babylon. "When the Lord was here on earth He spoke of the great hatred that 'the world' had for Him and His own (John 15:18,19). What is this world but a combination of religion, government and commerce? In other words, Babylon in all its parts stands for that which Christ called 'the world.' " (Barnhouse)

i. "In portraying the destruction of a (symbolic) city, he describes God's judgment on the great satanic system of evil that has corrupted the earth's history." (Johnson)

ii. "In chapter 18, the context seems to indicate that Babylon here is viewed in its political and economic character rather than its religious aspect." (Walvoord)

3. (1-3) Announcement of the glorious angel.

After these things I saw another angel coming down from heaven, having great authority, and the earth was illuminated with his glory. And he cried mightily with a loud voice, saying, "Babylon the great is fallen, is fallen, and has become a dwelling place of demons, a prison for every foul spirit, and a cage for every unclean and hated bird! For all the nations have drunk of the wine of the wrath of her fornication, the kings of the earth have committed fornication with her, and the merchants of the earth have become rich through the abundance of her luxury."

a. **Illuminated with his glory**: This angel **coming down from heaven** is so "fresh" from God's presence that he glows. "So recently has he come from the Presence (of God) that in passing he flings a broad belt of light across the dark earth." (Swete)

i. "It is a matter of no great moment, whether by this *angel* we understand Christ, or a created angel; the description agreeth to Christ, and may agree to a created angel." (Poole)

ii. "The term 'another' (Gr., *allon*) makes it clear that this angel is the same in kind as the angel of 17:1." (Walvoord)

b. **Babylon the great is fallen, is fallen**: He announces that Babylon is **fallen, fallen**; the phrase is "repeated like a solemn dirge of the damned." (Robertson)

c. The city has **become a dwelling place of demons**: This is "a prophetic picture of absolute desolation where the proud achievements of man become the demonic haunts of unclean and horrible creatures." (Mounce)

d. **Abundance of her luxury**: Babylon's sin is not only idolatry (referred to with the term **fornication**), but also pride, greed, and selfishly held wealth.

4. (4-5) A call to God's people to separate from Babylon.

And I heard another voice from heaven saying, "Come out of her, my people, lest you share in her sins, and lest you receive of her plagues. For her sins have reached to heaven, and God has remembered her iniquities."

a. **Come out of her, my people, lest you share in her sins**: It is inconceivable that a child of God could be a part of religious Babylon (though elements may creep in). But commercial Babylon, with its materialistic lure, is a constant threat to be guarded against.

b. **Lest you receive of her plagues**: The warning is focused towards saints who are in the position Lot was in while he lived in the city of

Sodom (Genesis 19). These are God's people in a place they shouldn't be, a place ripe for destruction.

c. The call to depart from Babylon and the worldliness that it represents is a theme repeated frequently in the Scriptures.

> i. *Depart! Depart! Go out from there, touch no unclean thing; go out from her, be clean, you who bear the vessels of the* LORD. (Isaiah 52:11)
>
> ii. *Flee from the midst of Babylon, and everyone save his life!* (Jeremiah 50:8)
>
> iii. *My people, go out of the midst of her! And let everyone deliver himself from the fierce anger of the* LORD. (Jeremiah 51:45)
>
> iv. *Do not be unequally yoked together with unbelievers. For what fellowship has righteousness with lawlessness?* (2 Corinthians 6:14)
>
> v. *And have no fellowship with the unfruitful works of darkness, but rather expose them.* (Ephesians 5:11)

d. Their sins **have reached to heaven**: The sins of commercial Babylon have piled up like a tower - the tower of Babel.

e. **God has remembered her iniquities**: This is the destiny of the materialistic world, but towards believers, God says, *I will remember their sins no more* (Hebrews 8:12).

5. (6-8) A call to those who will carry out Babylon's judgment.

"Render to her just as she rendered to you, and repay her double according to her works; in the cup which she has mixed, mix double for her. In the measure that she glorified herself and lived luxuriously, in the same measure give her torment and sorrow; for she says in her heart, 'I sit *as* queen, and am no widow, and will not see sorrow.' Therefore her plagues will come in one day; death and mourning and famine. And she will be utterly burned with fire, for strong *is* the Lord God who judges her."

a. **Render to her just as she rendered to you**: The ancient Greek word for **render** (*apodidomi*) means literally "to pay a debt" or "to give back that which is due." God will give Babylon exactly what she deserves.

b. **Repay her double according to her works . . . mix for her double**: Double restitution was required in the Old Testament in cases of theft (Exodus 22:4-9). This perhaps is a commentary on how Babylon has made her wealth - through dishonest dealings.

c. This passage presents a three-fold sin. First, *self-indulgence* (**lived luxuriously**). Second, *pride* (**glorified herself . . . sits as a queen**). Third, *avoidance of suffering* (**am no widow, and will not see sorrow**). All these things are characteristic of worldliness and materialism.

d. **Therefore her plagues will come in one day**: The destruction of commercial Babylon will come suddenly and with completeness (**utterly burned with fire**).

B. Lament for commercial Babylon.

1. (9-10) Lament of the kings.

"The kings of the earth who committed fornication and lived luxuriously with her will weep and lament for her, when they see the smoke of her burning, standing at a distance for fear of her torment, saying, 'Alas, alas, that great city Babylon, that mighty city! For in one hour your judgment has come.'"

a. **Standing at distance for fear of her torment**: So great is the heat and **smoke of her burning** that these kings must stand **at a distance**. Some think this may be an indication that nuclear weapons are used in the judgment of these commercial centers.

i. "Whether this is to be understood of the literal destruction of the city of Rome by fire, is surely doubtful, considering the mystical character of the whole prophecy." (Alford)

b. **Alas, alas, that great city Babylon, that mighty city!** "With a touch of grim humour he paints them as standing at a safe distance from the conflagration, and contenting themselves with idle lamentations." (Swete)

2. (11-17a) Lament of the merchants.

"And the merchants of the earth will weep and mourn over her, for no one buys their merchandise anymore: merchandise of gold and silver, precious stones and pearls, fine linen and purple, silk and scarlet, every kind of citron wood, every kind of object of ivory, every kind of object of most precious wood, bronze, iron, and marble; and cinnamon and incense, fragrant oil and frankincense, wine and oil, fine flour and wheat, cattle and sheep, horses and chariots, and bodies and souls of men. The fruit that your soul longed for has gone from you, and all the things which are rich and splendid have gone from you, and you shall find them no more at all. The merchants of these things, who became rich by her, will stand at a distance for fear of her torment, weeping and wailing, and saying, 'Alas, alas, that great city that was clothed in fine linen, purple, and scarlet, and adorned with gold and precious stones and pearls! For in one hour such great riches came to nothing.'"

a. **Merchandise of gold and silver**: This long list needs little explanation, except to note these are all luxuries, not necessities. It is plain that the mourning is rooted in self-interest: **for no one buys their merchandise anymore**.

i. "The combined picture is one of complete abandonment to the wealth of this world and complete disregard of the God who gave it." (Walvoord)

b. **And bodies and souls of men**: The profits of commercial Babylon have come through cruelly using others. They sold the **bodies and souls of men**. This idea has many applications, none less so than today's widespread prostitution and pornography.

c. Those who lived for the luxuries of commercial Babylon will be tormented by hell all the more: **you shall find them no more at all**. Ultimately, hell will be a place of unfulfilled desire.

3. (17b-19) Lament of the sea-captains.

"Every shipmaster, all who travel by ship, sailors, and as many as trade on the sea, stood at a distance and cried out when they saw the smoke of her burning, saying, 'What is like this great city?' They threw dust on their heads and cried out, weeping and wailing, and saying, 'Alas, alas, that great city, in which all who had ships on the sea became rich by her wealth! For in one hour she is made desolate.' "

a. **Alas, alas, that great city, in which all who had ships on the sea became rich by her wealth**: Again, little comment needs to be made on this, other than to notice that their sorrow at commercial Babylon's fall is selfish.

4. (20) Call to the heavens and the people of God: rejoice!

"Rejoice over her, O heaven, and *you* holy apostles and prophets, for God has avenged you on her!"

a. **Rejoice over her**: Should God's people rejoice when judgment comes? Yes, but we don't rejoice in the destruction in judgment. Rather, we rejoice in the righteous resolution God's judgment brings.

C. Finale: commercial Babylon's death knell.

1. (21) An angel graphically shows Babylon's fall.

Then a mighty angel took up a stone like a great millstone and threw *it* into the sea, saying, "Thus with violence the great city Babylon shall be thrown down, and shall not be found anymore."

a. **A mighty angel took up a stone like a great millstone and threw it into the sea**: This is reminiscent of Jeremiah's instructions to Seraiah to bind a stone to a text of Jeremiah and cast it into the Euphrates. *Thus shall Babylon sink, and shall not rise from the evil that I will bring upon her: and they shall be weary* (Jeremiah 51:61-64).

i. But it also reminds us of what Jesus said in Matthew 18:6: *But whoever causes one of these little ones who believe in Me to sin, it would be better for him if a millstone were hung around his neck, and he were drowned in the depth of the sea.* This applies to Babylon in Revelation 18, because *she led others into sin.* It is a terrible thing to sin unto yourself; it is even more terrible to lead others into sin.

b. **The great city Babylon shall be thrown down, and shall not be found anymore**: Some day, this world system will pass away, like a great stone falls to the bottom of the sea.

i. Will this fall hurt us? We will only be hurt to the extent that we invest ourselves in the mentality of commercial Babylon's materialism and worldliness.

2. (22-23) Babylon is left desolate and powerless.

"The sound of harpists, musicians, flutists, and trumpeters shall not be heard in you anymore. No craftsman of any craft shall be found in you anymore, and the sound of a millstone shall not be heard in you anymore. The light of a lamp shall not shine in you anymore, and the voice of bridegroom and bride shall not be heard in you anymore. For your merchants were the great men of the earth, for by your sorcery all the nations were deceived."

a. **Shall not be heard . . . shall be found anymore . . . shall to be heard in you anymore . . . shall not shine in you anymore**: In graphic and poetic language, John describes how the industry and commerce of Babylon come to an end.

b. **For by your sorcery all the nations were deceived**: **Sorcery** is the Greek word *pharmakia*, which means, "to prepare drugs." The lure of commercial Babylon is like a drug addiction, fed by deceptive advertising.

3. (24) The ultimate reason for commercial Babylon's judgment: She has killed the prophets and saints.

"And in her was found the blood of prophets and saints, and of all who were slain on the earth."

a. **The blood of prophets and saints, and of all who were slain on the earth**: The extent of this charge is an indication that this great city is symbolic of the world system at large. There is no one literal city that is responsible for **all who were slain on the earth**.

b. God takes the persecution of His people as a personal offense. Those who attack His people really attack Him.

Revelation 19 - Jesus Returns as Conquering Lord

A. Praise in heaven.

1. (1-5) Praise for the judgment of Babylon.

After these things I heard a loud voice of a great multitude in heaven, saying, "Alleluia! Salvation and glory and honor and power *belong* to the Lord our God! For true and righteous *are* His judgments, because He has judged the great harlot who corrupted the earth with her fornication; and He has avenged on her the blood of His servants *shed* by her." Again they said, "Alleluia! Her smoke rises up forever and ever!" And the twenty-four elders and the four living creatures fell down and worshiped God who sat on the throne, saying, "Amen! Alleluia!" Then a voice came from the throne, saying, "Praise our God, all you His servants and those who fear Him, both small and great!"

a. **A great multitude in heaven**: Back in Revelation 7:9-14, we saw a *great multitude* saved out of the Great Tribulation, ready for the end of the world system and the Antichrist's reign on earth. Here, this **great multitude**, the **twenty-four elders and the four living creatures** all join in celebrating the fall of the Antichrist and the world system that supported him.

i. A part of this **great multitude** - those martyred saints who fell at the hand of Antichrist during the Great Tribulation - cried out for God's righteous judgment in Revelation 6:10. Here, finally, their prayer is answered.

b. **Alleluia . . . Alleluia . . . Alleluia**: This wonderful word, borrowed from Hebrew, occurs four times in Revelation 19, but nowhere else in the New Testament. It belongs here - because God's people rejoice without restraint at His victory over Babylon.

i. **Alleluia** is Hebrew for "Praise the Lord," saying it in the *imperative* sense. It is an encouragement and an exhortation to *Praise the Lord!*

ii. Some seem afraid of saying **Alleluia**, but we'll all be saying it in heaven. It's such a wonderful word that we should never use it without thinking.

iii. "Anselm of Canterbury, considers it an angelic word, which cannot be fully reproduced in any language of man, and concurs with Augustine that the feeling and saying of it embodies all the blessedness of heaven." (Seiss)

c. **For true and righteous are His judgments**: This section is really the climax of Revelation 18. In Revelation 18, Babylon's friends mourned her fall; but here, God's people celebrate it.

d. **He has judged the great harlot . . . He has avenged on her the blood of His servants shed by her**: Here, the focus of worship is on the great *works* of God, specifically, His work of righteous judgment.

e. **Then a voice came from the throne**: This voice from the throne of God might be Jesus, but more likely it is the voice of one of the angels that serve at the throne of God.

2. (6-9) Praise for the marriage of the Lamb.

And I heard, as it were, the voice of a great multitude, as the sound of many waters and as the sound of mighty thunderings, saying, "Alleluia! For the Lord God Omnipotent reigns! Let us be glad and rejoice and give Him glory, for the marriage of the Lamb has come, and His wife has made herself ready." And to her it was granted to be arrayed in fine linen, clean and bright, for the fine linen is the righteous acts of the saints. Then he said to me, "Write: 'Blessed *are* those who are called to the marriage supper of the Lamb!' " And he said to me, "These are the true sayings of God."

a. **The voice of a great multitude, as the sound of many waters and as the sound of mighty thunderings**: The height of praise on earth is only a dim shadow of what these verses describe. At this point, Revelation approaches the consummation of God's plan for all history, so we also come to a summit of praise.

i. This is obviously *loud, enthusiastic* praise. While it is certainly possible to make praise and worship a self-indulgent focus on our feelings or a disorderly expression of the flesh, there is nothing wrong with *loud, enthusiastic* praise. And while there is something precious and irreplaceable about quiet times alone with God, there is also something absolutely thrilling about a large number of Christians worshipping God with sincere enthusiasm.

ii. "We ought not to worship God in a half-hearted sort of way; as if it were now our duty to bless God, but we felt it to be a weary business, and we would get it through as quickly as we could, and have done with it; and the sooner the better. No, no; 'All that is within me, bless his holy name.' Come, my heart, wake up, and summon all the powers which wait upon thee! Mechanical worship is easy, but worthless. Come rouse yourself, my brother! Rouse thyself, O my own soul!" (Spurgeon)

iii. "All Christian duties should be done joyfully; but especially the work of praising the Lord. I have been in congregations where the tune was dolorous to the very last degree; where the time was so dreadfully slow that one wondered whether they would ever be able to sing through the 119 Psalm; whether, to use Watt's expression, eternity would not be too short from them to get through it; and altogether, the spirit of the people has seemed to be so damp, so heavy, so dead, that we might have supposed that they were met to prepare their minds for a hanging rather than for blessing the ever-gracious God." (Spurgeon)

iv. "Heaven is always heaven, and unspeakably full of blessedness; but even heaven has its holidays, even bliss has its overflowings; and on that day when the springtide of the infinite ocean of joy shall have come, what a measureless flood of delight shall overflow the souls of all glorified spirits . . . We do not know yet, beloved, of what happiness we are capable." (Spurgeon)

b. **The marriage of the Lamb has come**: One reason this great multitude is so filled with praise is because the time has come for the **Lamb** of God to be joined unto His people, in a union so close it can only be compared to the **marriage** of a man and a woman.

i. The **marriage of the Lamb**, who is the Messiah, is a picture used frequently throughout the Scriptures. In the Old Testament, Israel is presented as God's wife, who is often unfaithful (Hosea 2:19-20, Isaiah 54:5, Ezekiel 16). In the New Testament, the church is presented as the fiancé of Jesus, waiting for this day of marriage (2 Corinthians 11:2, Ephesians 5:25-32).

ii. "In Biblical times a marriage involved two major events, the betrothal and the wedding. These were normally separated by a period of time during which the two individuals were considered husband and wife and as such were under the obligations of faithfulness. The wedding began with a procession to the bride's house, which was followed by a return to the house of the groom for the marriage feast. By analogy, the church, espoused to Christ by faith, now awaits the *parousia* when the heavenly groom will come for his bride and return to heaven for the marriage feast which lasts throughout eternity." (Mounce)

c. **And His wife has made herself ready**: What do we do to make ourselves ready for this wedding? There *is* much for us to do, but it is ultimately a work God does in us (Ephesians 5:25-27). This point is emphasized when John notes, **to her it was *granted* to be arrayed in fine linen, clean and bright**.

> i. In this perfect union with Jesus, His people will be **clean and bright** before Him. "Clean (*katharos*) reflects purity, loyalty and faithfulness, the character of the New Jerusalem . . . Bright (*lampros*) is the color of radiant whiteness that depicts glorification." (Johnson)

> ii. **For the fine linen is the righteous acts of the saints**: Believers are created for divinely prepared good works. These "righteousnesses" (**righteous acts**) are what fill the "hope chest" of the bride of Jesus.

> iii. Paul spoke of his desire that Christians would be presented before the Lord pure: *For I am jealous for you with godly jealousy. For I have betrothed you to one husband, that I may present you as a chaste virgin to Christ.* (2 Corinthians 11:2) This should be the desire of every Christian worker.

d. **Blessed are those who are called to the marriage supper of the Lamb!** Blessed indeed; Jesus Himself eagerly anticipates this marriage supper. He spoke longingly of the day when He will drink of the fruit of the vine again, with His disciples in the kingdom (Matthew 26:29).

> i. In Jewish culture, the **marriage supper** was the best banquet or party anyone knew; it always was an occasion of tremendous joy. According to Rabbinical teaching, obedience to the commandments was suspended during a wedding celebration if obeying a commandment might lessen the joy of the occasion.

> ii. On that day, *everyone* will see the church for what she really is: the precious bride of Jesus. "The Bride of Christ is a sort of Cinderella now, sitting among the ashes. She is like her Lord, 'despised and rejected of men'; the watchmen smite her, and take away her veil from her; for they know her not, even as they knew not her Lord. But when he shall appear, then shall she appear also, and in his glorious manifestation she also shall shine forth as the sun in the kingdom of the Father." (Spurgeon)

e. **These are the true sayings of God**: This is a necessary note of assurance for us. This anticipated consummation *will* take place, and though it seems too good to be true, it will happen.

3. (10) John worships an angel, and is corrected.

And I fell at his feet to worship him. But he said to me, "See *that you do not do that!* I am your fellow servant, and of your brethren who have the testimony of Jesus. Worship God! For the testimony of Jesus is the spirit of prophecy."

a. **I fell at his feet to worship him**: Why would such a godly man like John make such a blunder as this? "John either felt that the angel represented God or he was beside himself with excitement over the glorious consummation." (Robertson)

b. **See that you do not do that!** No created being should be worshipped. This is in contrast to Jesus, who receives the worship of angels (Hebrews 1:6) and of men (Matthew 8:2, Matthew 14:33, John 9:38).

c. **I am your fellow servant**: There are important differences between humans and angels, but both are servants of the same Lord.

d. **For the testimony of Jesus is the spirit of prophecy**: The true spirit of prophecy always shows itself in bearing witness to Jesus. "Any teaching of prophecy that takes our minds and hearts away from Him is not being properly communicated." (Hocking)

i. "This means that prophecy at its very heart is designed to unfold the beauty and loveliness of our Lord and Saviour Jesus Christ." (Walvoord)

B. Jesus Christ returns to a hostile earth.

1. (11-16) Jesus returns to earth with an army from heaven.

Now I saw heaven opened, and behold, a white horse. And He who sat on him *was* called Faithful and True, and in righteousness He judges and makes war. His eyes *were* like a flame of fire, and on His head *were* many crowns. He had a name written that no one knew except Himself. He *was* clothed with a robe dipped in blood, and His name is called The Word of God. And the armies in heaven, clothed in fine linen, white and clean, followed Him on white horses. Now out of His mouth goes a sharp sword, that with it He should strike the nations. And He Himself will rule them with a rod of iron. He Himself treads the winepress of the fierceness and wrath of Almighty God. And He has on *His* robe and on His thigh a name written: KING OF KINGS AND LORD OF LORDS.

a. **Now I saw heaven opened, and behold**: There is a sense in which everything before this in the Book of Revelation is an introduction to this *revelation* (unveiling) of Jesus Christ. Now He returns to earth in power and glory.

i. According to Zechariah 14:3-4, when Jesus returns He will come first to the Mount of Olives in Jerusalem. The plea of Isaiah 64:1-2 is now fulfilled: *Oh, that You would rend the heavens! That You would come down! That the mountains might shake at Your presence; as fire burns brush wood, as fire causes water to boil; to make Your name known to Your adversaries that the nations may tremble at Your presence!*

ii. This prayer for deliverance will be on the lips of the Jewish people surviving through the Great Tribulation. Unlikely as it may seem now, they will cry out to Jesus their Messiah for deliverance, and as a whole they will embrace Him as their Savior. As Jesus said in Matthew 23:39 *I say to you, you shall see Me no more till you say, "Blessed is He who comes in the name of the LORD!"* Hard pressed by the terrible persecution of the Antichrist, Israel as a whole will turn their hearts towards Jesus, and He will deliver them at this late hour.

iii. When Jesus comes, He comes on a **white horse**. In Biblical times - especially among Israel - most soldiers were *foot soldiers*. To have a **horse** in battle was a significant advantage. A horse spoke of *honor*, of *power*, and of *speed*; the color of this horse speaks of *victory*.

b. **Faithful and True**: This glorious title shows Jesus is the keeper of promises, including His promises of judgment.

c. **In righteousness He judges and makes war**: Jesus comes as a judge and a general to make **war**. The world that rejected Him before rejects Him again, but this time Jesus judges those who reject Him.

i. "The world likes a complacent, reasonable religion, and so it is always ready to revere some pale Galilean image of Jesus, some meager anemic Messiah, and to give Him a moderate rational homage." (Torrance)

ii. "Any view of God which eliminates judgment and his hatred of sin in the interest of an emasculated doctrine of sentimental affection finds no support in the strong and virile realism of the Apocalypse." (Mounce)

iii. This is a Jesus we can't control. Here we see Jesus as someone who demands not only our attention, but also our submission.

iv. It's good for us to remember that this dramatic display of judgment comes *only at the end* of a long time of grace, patience, and mercy. This is no "rush to judgment." Jesus has *amply* displayed His nature of mercy, forgiveness and grace to this fallen world. He comes now to judge a world hardened and totally given over to their rebellion against Him.

v. "All of these passages point to the sad conclusion that in the day of judgment it is too late for men to expect the mercy of God. There is nothing more inflexible than divine judgment where grace has been spurned. The scene of awful judgment which comes from this background is in flat contradiction of the modern point of view that God is dominated entirely by His attribute of love." (Walvoord)

vi. Remember that He does it all in **righteousness**. "The wars which *he* wages are from no principle of ambition, lust of power, or extension of conquest and dominion; they are *righteous* in their *principle* and in their *object*. And this is perhaps what no earthly potentate could ever say." (Clarke)

vii. "Jesus is the only king who always wars in this fashion. There have been brilliant exceptions to the general rule, but war is usually as deceitful as it is bloody, and the words of diplomatists are a mass of lies. It seems impossible that men should deliberate about peace and war without straightway forgetting the meaning of words and the bonds of honesty: War still seems to be a piece of business in which truth would be out of place; it is a matter so accursed that falsehood is there most at home, and righteousness quits the plain. But as for our King, it is in righteousness that he doth judge and make war. Christ's kingdom needs no deception: the plainest speech and the clearest truth - these are the weapons of our warfare." (Spurgeon)

d. **His eyes were like a flame of fire**: "Why are they like flames of fire? Why, first, to discern the secrets of all hearts. There are no secrets here that Christ does not see. There is no lewd thought, there is no unbelieving scepticism, that Christ does not read. There is no hypocrisy, no formalism, no deceit, that he does not scan as easily as a man reads a page in a book. His eyes are like a flame of fire to read us through and through, and know us to our inmost soul." (Spurgeon)

e. **On His head were many crowns**: The last time this earth saw Jesus He wore a crown of thorns, but not in Revelation 19. Now, He wears **many crowns**. The ancient Greek word used for **crowns** here is the *diadema*, the crown of royalty and authority, not the *stephanos*, the crown of achievement.

i. The fact that there are **many crowns** means that Jesus is the ultimate in royal authority and power. It is a visible manifestation of what we mean when we say KING OF KINGS. It is an expression of unlimited sovereignty.

f. **He was clothed with a robe dipped in blood**: His robe is **dipped** (or sprinkled) **in blood**. Bible students debate whether this is His own blood (reminding us of the cross) or the blood of His enemies. Either is quite possible.

g. **The armies in heaven**: These are God's people (Revelation 17:14, Jude 14-15). There is little doubt that angels will also accompany Jesus and His people, but the main idea is that the Son of God leads the people of God from heaven against earth.

> i. There is no mention of any kind of armor or weapon for any soldier in the great army that follows Jesus. The only armor or weapon they have is the only one they need: **clothed in fine linen, white and clean**.

h. **Now out of His mouth goes a sharp sword**: The idea isn't that Jesus holds a sword in his mouth like a buccaneer, or that He is "spitting swords." This is a dramatic way of referring to the power of His Word. "Christ conquers by the power of His Word" (Johnson). Five times in the Book Revelation, John emphasizes that Jesus' sword comes out of **His mouth**.

i. **And He Himself will rule them with a rod of iron**: Jesus comes to rule and to reign in triumph, to rule the nations with a **rod of iron** as predicted in Psalm 2. He comes as **KING OF KINGS** to displace every king reigning on this earth.

> i. "It does not mean the leavening of existing governments with Christian principles, the spiritual conversion of countries and empires, leaving them in existence, and simply Christianizing them so as to exhibit something of Christ's spirit in their administrations; but the total displacement of all this world's sovereigns and governments, the taking of all dominion and authority out of their hands and putting it in the hands of Christ, as the true and only King of the world." (Seiss)

j. **He has on His robe and on His thigh a name written: KING OF KINGS AND LORD OF LORDS**. The name is on His **thigh** for prominence, being easily visible when seated on a horse. At the same time, **no one knew [the name] except Himself** - that is, no one can comprehend Him perfectly.

> i. Clarke is among those who believe that the **name written that no one knew except Himself** is actually the tetragrammaton, the four letters YHWH that make up the name *Yahweh*, the sacred and secret name of God.

2. (17-18) Invitation to the great supper.

Then I saw an angel standing in the sun; and he cried with a loud voice, saying to all the birds that fly in the midst of heaven, "Come and gather together for the supper of the great God, that you may eat the flesh of

kings, the flesh of captains, the flesh of mighty men, the flesh of horses and of those who sit on them, and the flesh of all *people,* free and slave, both small and great."

a. **An angel standing in the sun**: This shows how *bright* this angels shines with the glory of God. The angel can be seen, even though it stands before the sun. "The angel is standing in the light of the sun with the angel himself possibly shining with even greater brilliance." (Walvoord)

b. **Saying to all the birds that fly**: This is a preparation for a great slaughter of Armageddon, "presented in a picture of almost repellent realism." (Erdman)

c. **The flesh of kings, the flesh of captains**: The repetition of **flesh** (5 times) is revealing. "The race has walked in carnal enmity against God, living after the flesh, and now the day of His patience is at an end." (Barnhouse)

i. It also shows that men of *all stations* are judged. The high and the low together, if they remain hardened in their rejection of Jesus, will be judged. "The divine judgment upon the wicked is no respecter of persons or station, and is the great equalizer of all." (Walvoord)

d. **Gather together for the supper of the great God**: Newell points to four different suppers described in the Bible.

- The supper of salvation, alluded to in Jesus' parable (Luke 14:16-24)
- The Lord's supper, a commemoration of Jesus' sacrifice
- The marriage supper of the Lamb
- The supper of the great God

i. If you reject the first supper, the second supper will mean nothing to you. Then you will not be present at the third supper, but will be present at the fourth supper. Everybody gets to attend at least one of these suppers, but some will eat and others are eaten at the suppers.

3. (19-21) War and the victory of Jesus Christ.

And I saw the beast, the kings of the earth, and their armies, gathered together to make war against Him who sat on the horse and against His army. Then the beast was captured, and with him the false prophet who worked signs in his presence, by which he deceived those who received the mark of the beast and those who worshiped his image. These two were cast alive into the lake of fire burning with brimstone. And the rest were killed with the sword which proceeded from the mouth of Him who sat on the horse. And all the birds were filled with their flesh.

a. **Armies, gathered together to make war against Him who sat on the throne**: Some find it hard to understand how man could be so foolish to try and keep Jesus and this heavenly army off the earth in a pitched battle. They suggest that these armies initially gather to battle against each other, and then turn their fury on the returning Jesus. This may be the case, but we should never underestimate man's folly and hatred of God.

i. "This is the *incurable insanity* of sin, which wars away in spite of defeat after defeat, against a holy God." (Newell)

ii. **To make war against Him**: This is just the logical extension of man's constant war against God since the fall. It is no more unbelievable than the idea that God came to earth and men murdered Him.

b. John says nothing about a battle. This is an entirely one-sided affair, more of a simple act of judgment than an actual war. "The battle of Armageddon is the laughter of God against the climax of man's arrogance." (Barnhouse)

c. **Then the beast was captured, and with him the false prophet**: The **beast** and the **false prophet** receive special treatment. They are cast alive into the **lake of fire** *before* the Great White Throne of judgment holds court (Revelation 20:11-15).

i. "A lake of burning brimstone would not only be intensely hot, but malodorous and fetid as well." (Mounce)

ii. The **lake of fire** is what we normally consider *hell*. It is *real*, and there is nothing more important than avoiding it.

Revelation 20 - Satan, Sin and Death are Finally Eliminated

A. Satan bound for a thousand years.

1. (1) A nameless angel comes to bind Satan with a great chain.

Then I saw an angel coming down from heaven, having the key to the bottomless pit and a great chain in his hand.

a. **An angel coming down from heaven**: The angel that will subdue Satan is anonymous. It is not Jesus Himself, nor is it Michael or Gabriel or any other high-ranking angel.

i. "The final importance of Satan is perhaps indicated in the fact that it is not the Father who deals with him, nor the Christ, but only an unnamed angel." (L. Morris)

b. This is a dramatic declaration that Satan is *not* God's opposite or equal; and that God could easily stop Satan's activity at any time. Yet God allows Satan to continue, because even in his evil, he indirectly serves the purposes of God.

2. (2-3) Satan is imprisoned for 1,000 years.

He laid hold of the dragon, that serpent of old, who is *the* Devil and Satan, and bound him for a thousand years; and he cast him into the bottomless pit, and shut him up, and set a seal on him, so that he should deceive the nations no more till the thousand years were finished. But after these things he must be released for a little while.

a. **Laid hold . . . bound him . . . cast him . . . shut him up . . . set a seal on him**: Satan tried to imprison Jesus in a tomb, but couldn't. Here, God has no problem restraining Satan, and this incarceration is not for punishment, but restraint. By implication, Satan's demonic armies are also restrained and imprisoned.

i. "Is this a literal transaction? Certainly it is. The battle is literal; the taking of the Beast and the False Prophet is literal; the slaying of the kings and their armies is literal; Satan is literal; and his binding must be equally literal. It will not resolve itself into anything else." (Seiss)

ii. Some people ask, "What kind of chain can hold the devil?" We don't know, but God can fashion a chain for that exact purpose. We know that right now there are demonic spirits who are imprisoned and chained (Jude 6). If God can chain them now, He can chain Satan for 1,000 years.

iii. "The elaborate measures taken to insure his custody are most easily understood as implying the complete cessation of his influence on earth (rather than a curbing of his activities)." (Mounce)

iv. Some take this as Satan's binding on a personal level, believing that is refers to how Satan's work can be restrained in the life of an individual. But this view does not take the text seriously. If God *did* want to tell us of the total inactivity of Satan, how could He have said it any stronger?

v. This is no man who simply "binds" Satan with his prayer. This is a work done on divine initiative. "One very important detail is to notice that the conquest of Satan and his powers does not come by any human effort." (Barnhouse)

b. **That he should deceive the nations no more**: This shows us Satan's main mode of attack is revealed. Satan is a deceiver, so the most potent defense and weapon against Satan is the truth of God's Word.

i. "The truth is ever against him; therefore falsehood is his particular recourse and instrument. But naked falsehood is only repulsive. What we know to be a lie cannot command our respect . . . Untruth can only gain credence and acceptance by being so disguised as to appear to be the truth. Falsehood can have no power over us until we are led to believe and conclude that it is the truth. And this deluding of men, getting them to accept and follow lies and false hopes, under the persuasion that they are accepting and following the truth, is the great work and business of Satan in every age." (Seiss)

ii. Since Satan's work of deception continues today, we know that he is not bound in the way that this passage describes. We know that Satan was not bound at the finished work of Jesus on the cross, at the resurrection, or at the founding of the church. We know this because Peter said that Satan was free to walk about as a roaring lion, seeking whom he may devour (1 Peter 5:8).

iii. Satan continues to effectively deceive. "People not only make false-hoods, speak falsehoods, print falsehoods, and believe falsehoods; but they eat them, and drink them, and wear them, and act them, and live them, and make them one of the great elements of their being." (Seiss)

c. **Till the thousand years were finished**: This thousand-year period is often known as the *Millennium*. Through church history, there has been many different ways of understanding the Millennium.

i. The Bible speaks powerfully to other aspects of the millennial earth. Tragically, the Church through history has often ignored or denied the promise of the millennial reign of Jesus Christ. The early church until Augustine almost universally believed in an earthly, historical reign of Jesus, initiated by His return. Tyconius (in the late 300's) was the first to influentially champion a spiritualized interpretation, saying that this Millennium is *now* (*amillennialism*) and must be understood as a *spiritual* reign of Jesus, not a literal reign. His view was adopted by Augustine, the Roman Catholic Church and most Reformation theologians.

ii. Growing out of *amillennialism* is the doctrine of *postmillennialsim*, saying the millennium will happen in *this* age, before Jesus' return - but that the church will bring it to pass. Yet the clear teaching of the Bible isn't *amillennialism* or *postmillennialism*, but what is called *premillennialism* - the teaching that Jesus Christ will return to this earth *before* the millennial earth, and *He* will establish and govern it directly.

iii. There is no need to say that Satan is only bound in a spiritual sense, and Jesus only rules in a spiritual sense. When we consider the rest of the Scriptures, the earthly reign of Christ and His people on this earth is plainly taught in the Old and New Testaments. In the Old Testament, we see it in Psalm 72, Isaiah 2:2-4, Isaiah 11:4-9, Jeremiah 23:5-6, and in many, many more passages. In the New Testament we see it in Luke 1:32-33, Matthew 5:18, Luke 19:12-27, among other passages. All in all, there are more than 400 verses in more than 20 different passages in the Old Testament which deal with this time when Jesus Christ will rule and reign personally over planet earth.

iv. Who will be on the earth in the Millennium? Even after the rapture and the vast judgments of the Great Tribulation, there will be many people left on earth. After Jesus returns in glory, He will judge those who survive the Great Tribulation in the judgment of the nations (Matthew 25:31-46). This is not a judgment unto salvation, but a judgment of moral worthiness, and entrance into the Millennial Kingdom of Jesus. The unworthy will be sent into eternal damnation, and the worthy will be allowed in Jesus' Millennial Kingdom.

d. Some of what we know of the Millennium from other passages of Scripture.

i. During the Millennium, Israel will be the superpower of the world the leading nation in all the earth, and the center of Israel will be *the mountain of the LORD's house* - the temple mount, which will be the "capital" of the government of the Messiah. *All nations shall flow to* the "capital" of Jesus' government (Isaiah 2:1-3, Ezekiel 17:22-24).

ii. During the Millennium, the citizens of earth will acknowledge and submit to the Lordship of Jesus. It will be a time of perfectly administrated enforced righteousness on this earth (Isaiah 2:1-5).

iii. During the Millennium, there will be no more war. There will still be conflicts between nations and individuals, but they will be justly and decisively resolved by the Messiah and those who reign with Him (Isaiah 2:1-5). It isn't the reign of the Messiah itself that will change the heart of man. Citizens of earth will still need to trust in Jesus and in His work on their behalf for their personal salvation during the millennium. But war and armed conflict will not be tolerated.

iv. During the Millennium, the way animals relate to each other and to humans will be transformed. A little child will be safe and able to lead a wolf or a leopard or a young lion or a bear. Even the danger of predators like cobras and vipers will be gone. In Genesis 9:2-3, the LORD gave Noah, and all mankind after him, the permission to eat meat. At the same time, the LORD put the *dread* of man in animals so they would not be effortless prey for humans. Now, in the reign of the Messiah, that is reversed. For this reason, many think that in the reign of the Messiah (the Millennium) humans will return to being vegetarians, as it seems they were before Genesis 9:2-3 (Isaiah 11:6-9).

v. During the Millennium, King David will have a prominent place in the millennial earth, ruling over Israel (Isaiah 55:3-5, Jeremiah 30:4-11, Ezekiel 34:23-31, Ezekiel 37:21-28, Hosea 3:5).

vi. During the Millennium, there will be blessing and security for national Israel (Amos 9:11-15).

vii. The Millennium will be a time of purity and devotion to God (Zechariah 13:1-9).

viii. During the Millennium, there will be a rebuilt temple and restored temple service on the earth as a memorial of God's work in the past. (Ezekiel 40-48, Ezekiel 37:26-28, Amos 9:11, Ezekiel 20:39-44).

ix. During the Millennium, saints in their resurrected state will be given responsibility in the Millennial Earth according to their faithful service (Luke 19:11-27, Revelation 20:4-6, Revelation 2:26-28; 3:12,22, 1 Corinthians 6:2-3).

e. **Thousand years**: Is it a literal 1,000 years? We should take a number literally *unless* there is clear reason or evidence to do otherwise. We should take this **thousand years** literally, because God has an important work to accomplish during the Millennium.

>   i. The Millennium is important because it will demonstrate Jesus' victory and worthiness to rule the nations.

>   ii. The Millennium is important because it will reveal the depths of man's rebellious nature in a perfect environment. Some people seem to believe that man is basically good, and deep down he really *wants* God's righteous rule. Many believe that man is really innocent, and corrupted only by a bad environment. The Millennium will answer these questions *before* the great judgment (Revelation 20:11-15).

>   iii. The Millennium is important because it will display the eternal depravity of Satan, who continues his evil as soon as he is released from his incarceration.

>   iv. The Millennium is important because it will show the invulnerability of the city of God and God's new order.

>   v. "Let us rejoice that Scripture is so clear and so explicit upon this great doctrine of the future triumph of Christ over the whole world . . . We believe that the Jews will be converted, and that they will be restored to their own land. We believe that Jerusalem will be the central metropolis of Christ's kingdom; we also believe that all the nations shall walk in the light of the glorious city which shall be built at Jerusalem. We expect that the glory which shall have its center there, shall spread over the whole world, covering it as with a sea of holiness, happiness, and delight. For this we look with joyful expectation." (Spurgeon)

B. Saints reigning for a thousand years.

1. (4) The saints live and reign for 1,000 years.

And I saw thrones, and they sat on them, and judgment was committed to them. Then *I saw* the souls of those who had been beheaded for their witness to Jesus and for the word of God, who had not worshiped the beast or his image, and had not received *his* mark on their foreheads or on their hands. And they lived and reigned with Christ for a thousand years.

>   a. **And I saw thrones, and they sat on them**: Who sits on these **thrones**? Perhaps the twenty-four elders representing the church (Revelation 4:4)

or the apostles (Matthew 19:28) or the company of saints as a whole (1 Corinthians 6:2-3).

> i. **And judgment was committed to them**: Perhaps this is the "judging of angels" mentioned in 1 Corinthians 6:2-3, but it is more likely that these are the saints ruling on and over the earth.

b. From these thrones, **they lived and reigned with Christ for a thousand years**. These saints reign with Jesus for the same period of time that Satan is bound (**a thousand years**). They administrate the kingdom of Jesus Christ over the earth, reigning over those who pass from the earth of the Great Tribulation to the earth of the Millennium.

c. **Who had been beheaded for their witness to Jesus . . . who had not worshipped the beast or his image, and had not received his mark**: *All* those who overcome in Jesus will rule and reign with Him (Revelation 2:26-28, 3:12,22, 1 Corinthians 6:2-3). Why does John only mention the Tribulation saints?

> i. They are specifically mentioned so as to encourage them, while not implying others will be left out. This is special vindication for Tribulation saints. They suffered under Antichrist who had said, "*I* will rule the earth;" now *they* are in authority and Antichrist is destroyed. So, these martyrs are literal, but also representative of all that give their lives in faithfulness to Jesus.

> ii. **Beheaded** is actually a broader word than we might think. The ancient Greek word really means "executed."

2. (5-6) The first resurrection.

But the rest of the dead did not live again until the thousand years were finished. This *is* the first resurrection. Blessed and holy *is* he who has part in the first resurrection. Over such the second death has no power, but they shall be priests of God and of Christ, and shall reign with Him a thousand years.

> a. **This is the first resurrection**: This **first resurrection** is the granting of resurrection life in resurrection bodies to all those dead in Jesus.
>
> • This is a resurrection of *blessing* (**blessed and holy is he**)
>
> • This is a resurrection of *power* (**over such the second death has no power**)
>
> • This is a resurrection of *privilege* (**they shall be priests of God . . . shall reign with Him a thousand years**)

b. **The rest of the dead**: Those who *do not* have part in the *first resurrection* are *not* blessed, they are *under the power* of the **second death**, and they are without privilege.

i. In John 5:28-29, Jesus described two resurrections: *Do not marvel at this; for the hour is coming in which all who are in the graves will hear His voice and come forth - those who have done good to the resurrection of life, and those who have done evil, to the resurrection of condemnation.*

ii. The two events are separated by this 1,000 year period because the **rest of the dead** are not given their resurrection bodies until **the thousand years were finished**.

c. If the **first resurrection** is a singular event, it argues well for a post-tribulation rapture, because it implies that all saints receive their resurrection bodies at the same time, immediately before the rule and reign of Jesus Christ.

d. If the **first resurrection** is an "order" or "class" encompassing previously dead believers (who are at once with the Lord), the raptured church (already in heaven), and saints from the Great Tribulation, then the idea fits in a pre-tribulation framework.

i. Donald Barnhouse says of the phrase **first resurrection**: "It must be especially emphasized that our phrase in the Apocalypse covering this resurrection is a retrospect that looks back over all three phases (of resurrection)."

ii. " 'The 'first resurrection' is not an event but an order of resurrection including all the righteous who are raised from the dead before the millennial kingdom begins." (Walvoord)

C. The final battle after the thousand-year reign of Jesus.

1. (7-8) Satan is released and gathers an army.

Now when the thousand years have expired, Satan will be released from his prison and will go out to deceive the nations which are in the four corners of the earth, Gog and Magog, to gather them together to battle, whose number *is* as the sand of the sea.

a. **Satan will be released**: For the thousand years of the direct reign of Jesus over this earth, Satan was bound and inactive. But after the thousand years are over, he will be released and successfully organize many people of the earth in another rebellion against God.

i. If Jesus has reigned so wonderfully for a thousand years, then why will the earth rebel? They will do it, and God will allow it, as a final demonstration of man's rebellion and depravity. *Outward* conformity to Jesus' rule will be required during His reign, but seemingly, an inward embrace of His Lordship will still be up to the individual.

ii. In this we see more of the important reason God has for the Millennial Kingdom and allowing this final rebellion. For all of human history, man has wanted to blame his sinful condition on his *environment.* "Of course I turned out the way I did. Did you see the family I came from? Did you see the neighborhood I grew up in?" With the Millennial Kingdom of Jesus, God will give mankind *a thousand years* of a perfect environment - with no Satan, no crime, no violence, no evil, or other social pathology. But at the end of the 1,000 years, man will still rebel against God at his first opportunity. This will powerfully demonstrate that the problem is in *us*, not only in our environment.

iii. "It will be proved once more that man, whatever his advantages and environment, apart from the grace of God and new birth, remains at heart only evil and at enmity with God." (Hoste)

b. **Gather them together to battle**: Who will these rebels be? They will be those who survive the Great Tribulation, enter into the Millennial Kingdom, and their descendants. "Infants born during the millennium will live to its conclusion and will not be required to make a choice between the devil and Christ until the end." (Walvoord)

c. Who are **Gog and Magog**? These are prophetic enemies of Israel in Ezekiel 38-39, but the battle described in those chapters of Ezekiel seems to be distinct and different from this final battle.

i. John seems to borrow the term and use it as a symbol. Seemingly, the battles described in Ezekiel 38-39 take place before the return of Jesus, perhaps right before or during the tribulation. This final battle clearly takes place at the end of the thousand-year reign of Jesus.

2. (9-10) A battle ends before it begins.

They went up on the breadth of the earth and surrounded the camp of the saints and the beloved city. And fire came down from God out of heaven and devoured them. The devil, who deceived them, was cast into the lake of fire and brimstone where the beast and the false prophet *are*. And they will be tormented day and night forever and ever.

a. **Surrounded the camp of the saints and the beloved city**: We don't know if the **saints** referred to here are glorified saints who reign with Jesus, or earth-inhabitants who come to faith in Jesus during the Millennium. Either way, the strategy of this vast Satanic army is clear: to destroy

God's people, and the "headquarters" or "capital city" of His administration, Jerusalem (**the beloved city**).

b. **Fire came down from God out of heaven and devoured them**: We shouldn't even call this a final battle, because there is no battle. The fight is over before it begins. At this point, God finally deals with the devil and his followers forever.

c. **Cast into the lake of fire . . . they will be tormented day and night forever and ever**: After this aborted battle, Satan is then judged and **tormented** forever - together with the **beast and the false prophet**, who were cast into the lake of fire at the beginning of the thousand years (Revelation 19:20).

> i. The presence of the beast and the false prophet in the lake of fire after a thousand years argues against annihilationism. In eternal punishment, a thousand years is just the beginning. It never ends. Commentator John Trapp thought this eternal aspect of hell so terrible that he called it "another hell in the midst of hell."

d. **Forever and ever**: Is this really *eternal* punishment? Yes it is; the words mean exactly what they appear to mean. "There would be no way possible in the Greek language to state more emphatically the everlasting punishment of the lost than here in mentioning both day and night and the expression 'forever and ever,' literally 'to the ages of ages.' " (Walvoord)

D. Judgment at the Great White Throne.

1. (11) An awesome throne.

Then I saw a great white throne and Him who sat on it, from whose face the earth and the heaven fled away. And there was found no place for them.

a. **I saw a great white throne**: **Great** in status, power and authority; **white** in purity and holiness; and a **throne** in kingly sovereignty.

b. **And Him who sat on it**: Who is this? The Bible tells us that the Judge is Jesus (John 5:22-27); or more likely, the fullness of the Triune God.

c. **Earth** and **heaven** flee from this throne, but **there was found no place for them**. There is absolutely no hiding from this throne. No one can escape the judgment that it represents.

> i. Many - even most - Bible scholars believe that Christians will never appear before this **great white throne**. It isn't because we can *hide* from it - no one can. The idea is that we are spared from this awesome throne of judgment because our sins are *already judged* in Jesus at the cross. We don't escape God's judgment; we satisfy it in Jesus.

ii. However, Christians will have to stand before another throne - the *judgment seat of Christ*. 2 Corinthians 5:10 says, *For we must all appear before the judgment seat of Christ, that each one may receive the things done in the body, according to what he has done, whether good or bad.*

iii. Therefore, when we pass from these bodies to the world beyond, we must each give account *according to what he has done, whether good or bad*. This describes a judgment of works of believers.

iv. At the judgment seat of Christ, *what we have done* will be judged. Our *motives* for what we have done will be judged. Paul presents essentially the same idea in 1 Corinthians 3:12-15, where he speaks of a coming assessment of each one's work before the Lord. In that passage, he makes it clear that what we have done, and our motive for doing it, will be tested by fire, and the purifying fire of God will burn up every-thing that was not of Him. We won't be *punished* for what was not done rightly unto the Lord, it will simply be *burned up*, and it will be as if we never did those things. We will simply be rewarded for what remains. Sadly, some will get to heaven *thinking* they have done great things for God, and will find out at the judgment seat of Christ that they really did nothing.

2. (12-13) The judgment of condemnation.

And I saw the dead, small and great, standing before God, and books were opened. And another book was opened, which is *the Book* of Life. And the dead were judged according to their works, by the things which were written in the books. The sea gave up the dead who were in it, and Death and Hades delivered up the dead who were in them. And they were judged, each one according to his works.

a. **Standing before God**: This is not a *trial*, trying to determine what the facts are. The facts are in; here is the sentencing of someone already con-demned. "Their standing posture means that they are now about to be sentenced." (Walvoord)

i. Because this is a sentencing and not a trial, those who stand before the throne have nothing to say. Many think they will "tell God a thing or two" at the final judgment, as reflected in this letter to *Dear Abby*:

Dear Abby: I am troubled with something a reader wrote: "What right do we mortals have to demand an explanation from God?" Abby, that writer has never known the gut-wrenching pain of losing a child . . .

God didn't answer my prayers, and I resent being told that I have no right to question God. If there is a God, and if I ever get to meet him face to face, you can bet your life I will have plenty of whys for him to answer.

I want to know why my little girl died and why that drunk was allowed to go on living. I love her more than my life, and I miss her so. I am mad that I am having to live in a world where she no longer lives, and I want to know why. Why shouldn't I have the right to ask God?

Aren't we supposedly created in his image? If so, surely he has a heart and soul capable of hurting just as I hurt. Why would he not expect to be questioned if he has anything to do with miracles?

I don't fear the Lord. And I don't fear hell, either. I know what hell is like. I've already been there since the day my precious daughter was killed.

Please sign me . . . A Bereaved Mother

ii. Of course, there will be no criticism of God on that day. This desperate woman will see not only the righteousness and goodness of God, but she will also see her own sin and rejection of Him more clearly than ever. How we wish she knew how the Father Himself knows what she has gone through!

b. **And the dead were judged according to their works**: If people are *not* listed in the **Book of Life**, *then* each one is judged **according to his works**. Those who refuse to come to God by faith will, by default, be judged (and condemned) by their works.

i. "The issue is not salvation by works but works as the irrefutable evidence of a man's actual relationship with God." (Mounce)

ii. There are degrees of punishment for unbelievers, according to their works (Matthew 11:20-24). Here is where they are sentenced to their specific eternal punishment.

c. **The sea gave up the dead who were in it**: Why does the *sea* give up its dead? It represents the place of unburied bodies; the emphasis is on the universal character of judgment - *everybody* is included.

3. (14-15) Death and Hades are cast into the lake of fire.

Then Death and Hades were cast into the lake of fire. This is the second death. And anyone not found written in the Book of Life was cast into the lake of fire.

a. **Then Death and Hades were cast into the lake of fire**: The last echoes of sin are now eliminated. **Death** is the result of sin, and it is gone. **Hades** is the result of death, and it is gone. The last vestiges of sin's unlawful domination are done away with.

b. **The lake of fire**: When a person refers to "hell," **the lake of fire** is what they usually have in mind. The Bible uses three main words to describe where the ungodly may go when they die.

i. *Sheol* is a Hebrew word with the idea of the "place of the dead." It has no direct reference to either torment or eternal happiness. The idea of *Sheol* is often accurately expressed as "the grave."

ii. *Hades* is a Greek word used to describe the "world beyond." In the Bible, it has generally the same idea as *Sheol*. Revelation 9:1 speaks of the *bottomless pit*; this place called the *abyssos* is a prison for certain demons (Luke 8:31; 2 Peter 2:4; Jude 6). Or more generally, it is considered part of the realm of the dead (Romans 10:7 uses it in the sense of *Hades*).

iii. *Gehenna* is a Greek word borrowed from the Hebrew language. In Mark 9:43-44, Jesus speaks of *hell* (*gehenna*). *Hell is a* Greek translation of the Hebrew "Valley of Hinnom," a place outside Jerusalem's walls desecrated by Molech worship and human sacrifice (2 Chronicles 28:1-3; Jeremiah 32:35). It was also a garbage dump where rubbish and refuse were burned. The smoldering fires and festering worms of the Valley of Hinnom made it a graphic and effective picture of the fate of the damned. This is **the lake of fire** prepared for the devil and his angels (Matthew 25:41). Men only go to this place prepared for the devil and his angels if they reject God's salvation and condemn themselves.

c. **This is the second death**: "As there is a second and higher life, so there is also a second and deeper death. And as after that life there is no more death, so after that death there is no more life." (Alford)

i. "The devil and the damned have punishment without pity, misery without mercy, sorrow without succor, crying without comfort, mischief without measure, torments without end and past imagination." (Trapp)

Revelation 21 - A New Heavens, a New Earth, and a New Jerusalem

A. All things made new.

1. (1) The new heaven and the new earth.

Now I saw a new heaven and a new earth, for the first heaven and the first earth had passed away. Also there was no more sea.

a. **Now I saw**: We can say that Revelation chapter 21 begins a new section of the Book of Revelation:

- Jesus, the *Lord of the Churches* (Revelation 1:1 to 3:22)
- Jesus, the *Lion over the nations* (Revelation 4:1 to 20:15)
- Jesus, the *Lamb among believers* (Revelation 21:1 to 22:21)

i. The new perspective of this last section is glorious. "From the smoke and pain and heat it is a relief to pass into the clear, clean atmosphere of the eternal morning where the breath of heaven is sweet and the vast city of God sparkles like a diamond in the radiance of his presence." (Moffatt)

b. **A new heaven and a new earth**: The idea of a new earth, with a new atmosphere and sky is a familiar theme in the Scriptures. Many of the prophets, both Old and New Testaments, spoke to this **new heaven** and **new earth**.

i. *For behold, I create new heavens and a new earth; and the former shall not be remembered or come to mind. But be glad and rejoice forever in what I create; for behold, I create a Jerusalem as a rejoicing, and her people a joy.* (Isaiah 65:17-19)

ii. *Of old, You laid the foundation of the earth, and the heavens are the work of Your hands. They will perish, but You will endure; yes all of them will grow old like a garment, like a cloak You will change them, and they will be changed. But You are the same, and Your years will have no end.* (Psalm 102:25-27)

iii. *Looking for and hastening the coming of the day of God, because of which the heavens will be dissolved being on fire, and the elements will melt with fervent heat . . . Nevertheless we, according to His promise, look for a new heaven and a new earth in which righteousness dwells.* (2 Peter 3:12-13)

iv. It's worth remembering that the **new heaven** referred to doesn't mean the *heaven* where God is enthroned. The Bible uses the word *heaven* in three senses. The *first heaven* is the earth's atmosphere, the "blue sky." The *second heaven* is outer space, the "night sky." The *third heaven* is the place where God lives in glory. When the Scriptures speak of a **new heaven**, they mean a new "blue sky" and a new "night sky," not a new heaven where God dwells.

c. **New heaven . . . new earth**: The ancient Greek word translated **new** here (*kaine*) means "new in character, 'fresh'." It doesn't mean "recent" or "new in time." This isn't just the *next* heaven and the *next* earth; this is the *better* heaven and *better* earth replacing the old (**the first earth had passed away**).

i. Though some disagree, such as Seiss, who argues passionately that this earth will *never* be destroyed - we should understand that this is truly a **new heaven** and a **new earth**, not merely a "remade" heaven and earth. We know this because Jesus said that heaven and earth *shall* pass away, but His Word would live forever (Luke 21:33). Also, in Isaiah 65:17 God says prophetically that He will create a new heaven and earth, and the ancient Hebrew word for "create" (*bara*) means to "create out of nothing," instead of re-fashioning existing material.

ii. Some take this "newness" as only a spiritual and moral change. But there seems to be a genuine physical transformation in mind: **there was no more sea.**

d. Is this **new heaven** and **new earth** the Millennial earth shown in Revelation 20, or is it something beyond? It definitely seems to be past the Millennial earth. This is what we think of as "heaven" and "eternity."

i. "In this chapter we see that the history of time is finished; the history of eternity is about to begin." (Barnhouse)

ii. "The eternal state is clearly indicated in the absence of sea, for frequent mention of bodies of water occur in millennial passages (cf. Psalm 72:8; Isaiah 11:9, 11; Ezekiel 47:10, 15, 17, 18, 20; 48:28; Zechariah 9:10; 14:8). The evidence of Revelation 21:1 is so specific that most commentators do not question that the eternal state is in view." (Walvoord)

e. **No more sea**: To the Jewish mind, the sea was a place of separation and evil. Already in the Book of Revelation it is shown to be the source of the Satanic beast (Revelation 13:1) and the place of the dead (Revelation 20:13).

> i. In other passages of Scripture, the **sea** is associated with the heathen (Isaiah 57:20) and in a more general sense, with the opponents of the Lord that must be conquered (Psalm 89:9).

2. (2-4) The New Jerusalem descends from heaven.

Then I, John, saw the holy city, New Jerusalem, coming down out of heaven from God, prepared as a bride adorned for her husband. And I heard a loud voice from heaven saying, "Behold, the tabernacle of God *is* with men, and He will dwell with them, and they shall be His people. God Himself will be with them *and be* their God. And God will wipe away every tear from their eyes; there shall be no more death, nor sorrow, nor crying. There shall be no more pain, for the former things have passed away."

a. **The holy city, New Jerusalem**: This is the Jerusalem of hope (Hebrews 12:22), the Jerusalem above (Galatians 4:26), the place of our real citizenship (Philippians 3:20).

> i. The terms **holy** and **new** distinguish the city. Because it is **holy** and **new**, it is different from any earthly city. The name **Jerusalem** gives it continuity with earth, especially with the place of our redemption.

> ii. It is significant that this glorious dwelling place of God and His people is described as **the holy *city***. Cities are places where there are many people, and people interact with each other. This isn't isolation, but a perfect *community* of the people of God.

> iii. The Christian concept of heaven as a city - a place of life, activity, interest, and people - is very different from Hindu conception of a blank "Nirvana." "The consummation of the Christian hope is supremely social. It is no 'flight of the alone to the Alone' but life in the redeemed community of heaven." (Hunter)

> iv. Man has never known a community unmarred by sin. Adam and Eve only knew a limited community, and community in a larger context only came long after the Fall. Here, in the **New Jerusalem**, we have something totally unique: a sinless, pure, community of righteousness, a **holy city**.

> v. Problems arise when believers expect this kind of community *now*, or fail to realize that it *only comes* **down out of heaven**. This city is not, and never can be, the achievement of man, but only a gift from God.

b. **Prepared as a bride adorned for her husband**: John uses the most striking, beautiful image he can think of. The most beautiful thing a man will ever see is his bride coming down the aisle, ready to meet him. John says that this is how beautiful the New Jerusalem will be.

c. **The tabernacle of God is with men, and He will dwell with them**: Moses' tabernacle represented the dwelling place of God on earth. This is past the *representation* of the dwelling place of God; this is the reality of His presence.

i. **He will dwell with them, and they shall be His people**: This succinctly states essence of *God's desire* and *man's purpose*. Simply, God's desire is to live in close fellowship with man, and man's purpose is to be a people unto God.

ii. *This* is the greatest glory of heaven, and the ultimate restoration of what was lost in the Fall. "I do not think the glory of Eden lay in its grassy walks, or in the boughs bending with luscious fruit-but its glory lay in this, that the 'Lord God walked in the garden in the cool of the day.' Here was Adam's highest privilege, that he had companionship with the Most High." (Spurgeon)

d. **The former things have passed away**: The New Jerusalem is distinguished by what it does *not* have - no tears, no sorrow, no death or pain. Later it will be shown that the New Jerusalem has no temple, no sacrifice, no sun, no moon, no darkness, no sin, and no abomination.

i. "Man comes into the world with a cry; and goes out of it with a groan, and all between is more or less intoned with helpless wailing . . . But the Halleluias of the renewed world will drown out the voice of woe forever." (Seiss)

e. **God will wipe away every tear from their eyes**: " '*Every tear*,' for they be many; - tears of bereaved affection, such as Mary, and Martha, and the widow of Nain wept; - tears of sympathy and mercy, such as Jeremiah and Jesus wept over the sins and the calamities of Jerusalem; - tears of persecuted innocence, tears of contrition and penitence for faults and crimes against the goodness and majesty of heaven; - tears of disappointment and neglect; - tears of yearning for what cannot now be ours; - these, and whatever others ever course the cheeks of mortals, shall then be dried forever." (Seiss)

i. But the idea of "tears in heaven" should never be used as some kind of guilt-manipulation on this earth. "There is no just ground for imagining from this text that the saints will shed tears in heaven concerning the failures of their former life on earth. The emphasis here is on the comfort of God, not on the remorse of the saints." (Walvoord)

3. (5) All things new.

Then He who sat on the throne said, "Behold, I make all things new." And He said to me, "Write, for these words are true and faithful."

a. **He who sat on the throne said**: This is an authoritative announcement, coming from the throne of God itself. This is one of the few times in Revelation where we clearly see God speaking directly from His throne.

b. **Behold, I make all things new**: This statement is in the present tense, "*I am making everything new.*" This is the consummation of God's work of renewal and redemption, having *begun* here and now in our present time.

   i. Paul saw this transformation at work on *this side* of eternity: *Therefore we do not lose heart. Even though our outward man is perishing, yet the inward man is being renewed day by day . . . Therefore, if anyone is in Christ, he is a new creation; old things have passed away; behold, all things have become new.* (2 Corinthians 4:16, 5:17)

c. **All things new**: This is a brief glance at the thinking behind God's eternal plan - to allow sin and its destruction in order to do a greater work of making **all things new**. At this point in His plan of the ages, the plan is complete. **All things** are **new**.

   i. Our instinct is to romantically consider innocence as man's perfect state, and wish Adam would have never done what he did. But we fail to realize that redeemed man is greater than innocent man, that we gain more in Jesus than we ever lost in Adam. God's perfect state is one of redemption, not innocence.

   ii. When God finally completes this work of making **all things new**, they will *stay* **new**. "Presumably this means not only that everything will be made new, but also that everything will stay then new. The entropy law will be 'repealed.' Nothing will wear out or decay, and no one will age or atrophy anymore." (H. Morris)

d. **Write, for these words are true and faithful**: John is probably so astounded by these words that he forgot to **write** - and must be told to do so.

4. (6-8) The invitation and a warning.

And He said to me, "It is done! I am the Alpha and the Omega, the Beginning and the End. I will give of the fountain of the water of life freely to him who thirsts. "He who overcomes shall inherit all things, and I will be his God and he shall be My son. But the cowardly, unbelieving, abominable, murderers, sexually immoral, sorcerers, idolaters, and all liars shall have their part in the lake which burns with fire and brimstone, which is the second death."

a. **It is done!** God's eternal purpose in Jesus is now accomplished. Ephesians 1:10 has been fulfilled: *that in the dispensation of the fullness of the times He might gather together in one all things in Christ, both which are in heaven and which are on earth; in Him.* At this point, all things have been resolved or "summed up" in Jesus - **it is done!**

b. **I will give of the fountain of the water of life freely to him who thirsts**: Drinking and thirst are common pictures of God's supply and man's spiritual need. Drinking is an action, but an action of receiving - like faith, it is *doing* something, but it is not a merit-earning work in itself.

> i. "What does a thirsty man do to get rid of his thirst? He drinks. Perhaps there is no better representation of faith in all the Word of God than that. To drink is to receive-to take in the refreshing draught-and that is all. A man's face may be unwashed, but yet he can drink; he may be a very unworthy character, but yet a draught of water will remove his thirst. Drinking is such a remarkably easy thing, it is even more simple than eating." (Spurgeon)

c. **He who overcomes shall inherit all things**: Those who overcome (by faith in Jesus, as in 1 John 5:5) enjoy a special relationship with God (**I will be his God and he shall be My son**).

d. **But the cowardly, unbelieving, abominable . . . have their part in the lake which burns with fire and brimstone**: But the Jesus-rejecting and apostate are specifically prohibited from entering the New Jerusalem.

> i. **Cowardly**: Is cowardice enough to send a person to hell? "John is not speaking of natural timidity, but of that cowardice which in the last resort chooses self and safety before Christ." (L. Morris) John Trapp spoke of these "Cowardly recreants, white-livered milk-sops, that pull in their horns for every pile of grass that toucheth them, that are afraid of every new step."

B. The nature of the New Jerusalem.

1. (9-10) An angel will show John the city in greater detail.

Then one of the seven angels who had the seven bowls filled with the seven last plagues came to me and talked with me, saying, "Come, I will show you the bride, the Lamb's wife." And he carried me away in the Spirit to a great and high mountain, and showed me the great city, the holy Jerusalem, descending out of heaven from God,

a. **I will show you the bride . . . showed me the great city, the holy Jerusalem**: Passages like this make some wonder if the New Jerusalem is a literal *place* at all. Some suggest that it is really just an exotic symbol of the Church, the Bride of Christ.

b. This heavenly city is literal, but it is called **the bride, the Lamb's wife** because it is the place where all God's people are gathered. In this sense the New Jerusalem is certainly *like* the bride; but this association doesn't diminish the reality behind the image. The city is associated with the bride to awe us with a sense of its beauty.

2. (11-14) The city's brilliance, wall, gates and foundation.

Having the glory of God. Her light *was* like a most precious stone, like a jasper stone, clear as crystal. Also she had a great and high wall with twelve gates, and twelve angels at the gates, and names written on them, which are *the names* of the twelve tribes of the children of Israel: three gates on the east, three gates on the north, three gates on the south, and three gates on the west. Now the wall of the city had twelve foundations, and on them were the names of the twelve apostles of the Lamb.

a. **Her light was like a most precious stone**: John is first struck by the *glory* of this city. She shares in the **glory of God**, and it is expressed in the radiant line that shines from her.

b. **She had a great and high wall**: The wall is not needed for defense, because there are no more enemies. But the **great and high wall** gives the city perimeters (this is no cosmic nirvana) and shows us that some will be excluded from the city (only the righteous can enter).

c. **Twelve gates . . . and names written on them, which are the names of the twelve tribes of the children of Israel**: The names of the tribes on the gates communicate the unity and heritage that the people of God have with Israel. God will never forget the tribes of Israel, even unto eternity.

i. **Three gates on the east, three gates on the north**: Some have thought the arrangement of gates looks back to the camp layout used during the Exodus (Numbers 2).

d. **The wall of the city had twelve foundations, and on them were the names of the twelve apostles of the Lamb**: The foundations are an eternal testimony to the apostles, and their permanent place in God's plan. If it isn't build on the foundation of the apostles, it's isn't the right place for God's people.

i. The New Jerusalem and the church are founded upon the apostles (Ephesians 2:20).

3. (15-17) The dimensions of the city.

And he who talked with me had a gold reed to measure the city, its gates, and its wall. The city is laid out as a square; its length is as great as its breadth. And he measured the city with the reed: twelve

thousand furlongs. Its length, breadth, and height are equal. Then he measured its wall: one hundred *and* forty-four cubits, *according* to the measure of a man, that is, of an angel.

a. **The city is laid out as a square**: The New Jerusalem's length, height and width are equal. This means that it is either a cube or a pyramid. A cube is reminiscent of the Holy Place of the tabernacle, suggesting that the entire city is the Holy Place.

b. **He measured the city with the reed**: The size of the New Jerusalem is enormous; **twelve thousand furlongs** equals 1,500 miles. This is the same distance from Maine to Florida; the square footage would approximate the size of the moon.

i. "A city of this size is too large for the imagination to take in. John is certainly conveying the idea of splendour. And, more importantly, that of room for all." (L. Morris)

ii. Henry Morris, guessing that there will have been 100 billion people in the human race, and that 20% of them will be saved, calculates that each person would have a "block" with about 75 acres on each face to "call their own."

c. **According to the measure of a man, that is, of an angel**: In this case, the cubit measure of a man is the same as an angel's measure of a cubit.

4. (18-21) The beauty of its structure.

The construction of its wall was *of* jasper; and the city *was* pure gold, like clear glass. The foundations of the wall of the city *were* adorned with all kinds of precious stones: the first foundation *was* jasper, the second sapphire, the third chalcedony, the fourth emerald, the fifth sardonyx, the sixth sardius, the seventh chrysolite, the eighth beryl, the ninth topaz, the tenth chrysoprase, the eleventh jacinth, and the twelfth amethyst. The twelve gates *were* twelve pearls: each individual gate was of one pearl. And the street of the city *was* pure gold, like transparent glass.

a. When we read of **jasper** and **pure gold** and **all kinds of precious stones**, we should take these as literal representations; yet they express realities of another world. We can gain a brief glimpse of what John saw, but we can't even begin to see it in fullness until we see it with our own eyes.

i. John's use of riches in his description "is his way of bringing out the very great value of what God has for His people." (L. Morris)

b. **Jasper . . . sapphire . . . chalcedony:** The precise identification of these gemstones in modern terms is difficult, but the impression is of unending, staggering beauty.

i. "The symbolism is not meant to give the impression of wealth and luxury, but to point to the glory and holiness of God." (Johnson)

ii. If there is any Biblical reference point for this assortment of gemstones, it is probably the High Priest's breastplate (Exodus 28:15-21).

c. **Like clear glass . . . like transparent glass:** "The constant mention of transparency indicates that the city is designed to transmit the glory of God in the form of light without hindrance." (Walvoord)

d. If the dimensions and descriptions seem confusing or impossible, there are two main principles to keep in mind. First, we must understand the *ideas* communicated in the details (glory, beauty, splendor, and so forth). Second, we must understand that this is the city *whose architect and maker is God* (Hebrews 11:10). We should expect it to be beyond our comprehension.

C. The temple of the New Jerusalem.

1. (22-23) God is all in the New Jerusalem.

But I saw no temple in it, for the Lord God Almighty and the Lamb are its temple. The city had no need of the sun or of the moon to shine in it, for the glory of God illuminated it. The Lamb *is* its light.

a. **But I saw no temple in it:** In the ancient world, it was unthinkable to have a great city without many different temples. It's like saying today, "I saw a great city but I saw no bank in it" or "I saw a great city but I saw no shopping mall in it." Nevertheless, in this city there is **no temple in it.**

b. **For the Lord God Almighty and the Lamb are its temple:** Here, the temple is not removed, but expanded. Everything and every place is holy and the dwelling place of God.

i. Before Jesus the temple was a prophecy. In the Christian era God's people are His temple. In the Millennium the temple will be a memorial. Here the temple is everywhere.

ii. "The inhabitants need no place of worship or sacrifice, the object of all worship being present, and the great sacrifice Himself being there." (Alford)

c. **No temple . . . no need of the sun or of the moon:** This reminds us that heaven will be a place of *pure* worship. The things we use to help us worship, but often end up *distracting* us in worship (such as buildings, music systems, customs, and so forth) will no longer be an issue. Our focus will be totally on the Person we worship, **the Lord God Almighty and the Lamb**.

> i. In heaven, none of our joy, beauty, or knowledge will be based on *created things*, but only on the *Creator*. By faith, you can have it that way *now*. You can decide to trust in God so completely that your *joy*, what you consider *beauty*, and your foundation of *knowledge* are all based on Jesus, and not on anything created.

d. **The Lamb is its light**: Light speaks of *joy*, for in the Scriptures light and joy go together. Light speaks of *beauty*, because without light there is no beauty. Light speaks of *knowledge* and in heaven we will all know Him as He knows us.

2. (24-27) Access into the city.

And the nations of those who are saved shall walk in its light, and the kings of the earth bring their glory and honor into it. Its gates shall not be shut at all by day (there shall be no night there). And they shall bring the glory and the honor of the nations into it. But there shall by no means enter it anything that defiles, or causes an abomination or a lie, but only those who are written in the Lamb's Book of Life.

a. **The kings of the earth shall bring their glory and honor into it**: What about these **kings of the earth**? Who are they? This is difficult to understand, and different commentators have different suggestions.

> i. "How encouraging to note that not all were destroyed when the nations came to do battle against Jerusalem and the Lord Himself. There will also be 'kings of the earth' who will be a part of the eternal state." (Hocking)

> ii. "Among the mysteries of this new heaven and earth this is set forth to us: that, besides the glorified church, there shall still be dwelling on the renewed earth nations, organized by kings, and [xxii. 2] saved by means of the influences of the heavenly city." (Alford)

b. **There shall by no means enter it anything that defiles**: Does this mean that such people will threaten the city? It isn't necessary to say that this is the idea, because all sinners and death have been cast into the Lake of Fire (Revelation 20:11-15). Instead, "the exhortation warns present readers that the only way to participate in the future city is to turn one's loyalties to the Lamb now." (Johnson)

Revelation 22 - Come, Lord Jesus

A. The interior of the New Jerusalem.

1. (1) A river flowing from the throne of God.

And he showed me a pure river of water of life, clear as crystal, proceeding from the throne of God and of the Lamb.

a. **A pure river of water of life**: Through the Old Testament, prophets used the picture of a river as a powerful expression of richness, provision, and peace (Isaiah 48:18, Zechariah 14:8, Ezekiel 47:1-9).

i. Or, as expressed by the Psalmist in Psalm 46:4-5: *There is a river whose streams shall make glad the city of God, the holy place of the tabernacle of the Most High. God is in the midst of her, she shall not be moved; God shall help her, just at the break of dawn.*

ii. "One of the gladdest things on earth is water. There is nothing in all the world so precious to the eye and the imagination of the inhabitant of the dry, burning and thirsty East, as a plentiful supply of bright, pure, and living water." (Seiss)

iii. Poole says that this point of this river is "To let us know, that in heaven there shall be no want of any thing that can make the saints happy."

b. **Clear as crystal**: God's provision in the New Jerusalem is described with pure, absolutely unpolluted waters. "Its waters are literal waters, of a nature and quality answering to that of the golden city to which they belong. Man on earth never knew such waters, as men on earth never knew such a city; but the city is a sublime reality." (Seiss)

c. **From the throne of God and of the Lamb**: This river of provision comes right from God's throne. Because it comes from God, it cannot be anything other than pure and abundant.

i. Ezekiel saw a glorious river (Ezekiel 47) flow down from the temple in Jerusalem and into the sea, but that river belongs to the millennial earth. It is perhaps the final preview of this heavenly river. This is a better river with better trees.

2. (2) The tree of life.

In the middle of its street, and on either side of the river, *was* the tree of life, which bore twelve fruits, each *tree* yielding its fruit every month. The leaves of the tree *were* for the healing of the nations.

a. **The tree of life**: The Bible begins with a tree of life (Genesis 3:22-24) which man was not allowed to eat from after the sin at the tree of the knowledge of good and evil. Now we see **the tree of life** again.

i. **In the middle of its street, and on either side of the river**: It's a little hard to picture this heavenly landscaping. John may be describing a large street with a river flowing down the middle, and a large tree - or series of trees - that grows with roots on either side of the river.

ii. This is how John Walvoord sees it: "The visual picture presented is that the river of life flows down through the middle of the city, and the tree is large enough to span the river, so that the river is in the midst of the street, and the tree is on both sides of the river."

iii. Others see that the word **tree** as a collective reference, speaks of rows of trees that stand on either side of the river. "The picture presented to the mind's eye would appear to be that of a wide street, with a river flowing down the center, like some of the broader canals of Holland, with trees growing on either side, all of them of the same kind, all called the tree of life. I do not know how we can make the figure out in any other way." (Spurgeon)

iv. Seeing the **tree of life** again points to a restoration of all things. "Now at last, almost at the end of the great drama of the Bible, man may return and legitimately enjoy the blessing which he was banished for illegitimately desiring." (Preston/Hanson)

b. **Each tree yielding its fruit every month**: From all indications, this describes the world of the new heaven and the new earth, yet we are given a *time indicator*. Apparently, heaven will still mark time, but not be subject to it in the same way we are on this side of eternity.

i. Some people wonder if we will eat in heaven. The best answer is that we can eat, but will not have to. In His resurrection body, Jesus enjoyed food (Luke 24:41-43, John 21:12-14). Angels ate with Abraham (Genesis 18:6-8). The great heavenly reunion between Jesus and His people is described as a marriage supper (Revelation 19:9). Even though man fell by what he ate, God will still allow us to eat in heaven.

ii. "Like the golden table of showbread which ever stood in the ancient Tabernacle and Temple for the priests to eat, so the Tree of Life stands in all the golden streets of the New Jerusalem, with its monthly fruit for the immortal king-priests of heaven." (Seiss)

c. **The leaves of the tree were for the healing of the nations**: Why do the **nations** need **healing**? In the ancient Greek language, the word for **healing** can also mean "health-giving," and this may be the sense here.

i. "The word for 'healing' is *therapeian*, from which the English word *therapeutic* is derived, almost directly transliterated from the Greek. Rather than meaning 'healing,' it should be understood as 'health-giving,' as the word in its root meaning has the idea of serving or ministering." (Walvoord)

d. Are these pictures of heaven literal or symbolic? It may be that you can't describe another dimension like heaven without using symbols, but they are symbols *connected* to their reality. What John saw may or may not be exactly like a river on earth, but when we see it we will also say, "That looks like a river."

i. Even though this great chapter of the Bible tells us of heaven, we should think deeply about it and take in now what we can. "We do not suppose that a man is shooting at a target if he does not look that way; nor can we imagine that a man's ambition is fixed on heaven if he has no heavenward thoughts or aspirations." (Spurgeon)

3. (3-5) What it will be like and what the saints will do.

And there shall be no more curse, but the throne of God and of the Lamb shall be in it, and His servants shall serve Him. They shall see His face, and His name *shall be* on their foreheads. There shall be no night there: They need no lamp nor light of the sun, for the Lord God gives them light. And they shall reign forever and ever.

a. **There shall be no more curse**: In heaven, the curse is gone. Since the fall, man and creation have lived with the effect of the curse described in Genesis 3:16-19: sorrow and pain in childbirth for women, friction between the sexes, the necessity of hard and often futile work for man's sustenance, and most of all *death*.

i. These aspects of the **curse** will even be present during the Millennium, though they will be greatly mitigated by the perfect rule of Jesus. Isaiah 65:20 shows us that it is still possible for a sinner to be accursed in the millennial earth. But in the new heaven and new earth they are done away with forever. Instead of the **curse, the throne of God and of the Lamb shall be in it**. That's quite an exchange.

ii. **The throne of God and of the Lamb**: "Henceforth, eternal praises to his name, the throne of God is the throne of the Lamb. It is a throne of righteousness, but no less a throne of grace. There, on the throne of the Almighty, mercy reigns. According to the merit of the sacrifice and the virtue of the atonement all the statutes and decrees of the kingdom of heaven are issued. The altar and the throne have become identical. From that throne no fiery bolt can ever again be hurled against the believer, for it is the throne of the Lamb as well as the throne of God." (Spurgeon)

b. **His servants shall serve Him**: Heaven will be a place of work and service for God's people. However, this is a picture of the pure blessedness of service rather than arduous, curse-stained toil.

i. "Heaven is not a place of indolent leisure, but a place where service is done, centering on God." (L. Morris)

c. **They shall see His face**: Heaven will be a place where God's people **see His face**, a place of intimate, face to face fellowship with God. Moses was denied the privilege of seeing God face to face (Exodus 33:20-23), but everyone in heaven **shall see His face**.

i. **They shall see His face**: "By which I understand two things: first, that they shall literally and physically, with their risen bodies, actually look into the face of Jesus; and secondly, that spiritually their mental faculties shall be enlarged, so that they shall he enabled to look into the very heart, and soul, and character of Christ, so as to understand him, his work, his love, his all in all, as they never understood him before." (Spurgeon)

ii. Because of Jesus, we can know something of the face of God right now: *For it is the God who commanded light to shine out of darkness, who has shone in our hearts to give the light of the knowledge of the glory of God in the face of Jesus Christ* (2 Corinthians 4:6).

iii. Yet, Paul also anticipated a greater fulfillment of our seeing the face of God: *For now we see in a mirror, dimly, but then face to face. Now I know in part, but then I shall know just as I am also known* (1 Corinthians 13:12). In that day there will be nothing that obscures our vision of Jesus:

- We will see Jesus clearly because sin is done away with
- We will see Jesus clearly because care and worry are gone
- We will see Jesus clearly because idols are done away with

iv. This will be the greatest glory of heaven: to know God, to know Jesus, more intimately and wonderfully than we ever could on earth. "It is the chief blessing of heaven, the cream of heaven, the heaven of heaven, that the saints shall there see Jesus." (Spurgeon)

v. "To look into the face of Christ signifies to be well acquainted with his person, his office, his character, his work. So the saints in heaven shall have more knowledge of Christ than the most advanced below. As one has said, the babe in Christ admitted to heaven discovers more of Christ in a single hour than is known by all the divines of the assemblies of the church on earth." (Spurgeon)

d. **His name shall be on their foreheads**: Heaven will be a place where God's people will forever be identified with their God, and there will never be any doubt that they belong to Him.

e. **There shall be no more night there**: Heaven will be a place where the darkness of this age will be forever gone. The light is not artificial, even from the sun - God Himself is the light.

f. **They shall reign forever and ever**: Heaven will be a place where God's people enjoy an eternal reign, in contrast to the limited duration of the Millennium. It will never end.

i. "As the Bible opens with the story of 'Paradise Lost,' so it here closes with the story of 'Paradise Regained.' " (Erdman) We see the return of Paradise in the ideas of a river, a tree of life, revocation of the curse, intimacy restored, and reigning resumed. It is a perfect consummation:

No more curse	Perfect *Restoration*
Throne in their midst	Perfect *Administration*
Servants shall serve	Perfect *Subordination*
Shall see His face	Perfect *Transformation*
Name on foreheads	Perfect *Identification*
God is the light	Perfect *Illumination*
Reigning forever	Perfect *Exultation*

B. Parting words.

1. (6-7) The angel and Jesus add words of verification

Then he said to me, "These words *are* faithful and true." And the Lord God of the holy prophets sent His angel to show His servants the things which must shortly take place. Behold, I am coming quickly! Blessed *is* he who keeps the words of the prophecy of this book."

a. In these last few verses of the Book of Revelation, we hear parting words from a variety of persons. It isn't always easy to know who is speaking, but the themes make sense no matter who speaks: verification, invitation, and warning.

b. **These words are faithful and true**: The angel that showed John all this reminds John that it isn't too good to be true. John is assured that it is in fact **faithful and true**.

c. **The things which must shortly take place . . . I am coming quickly!** As John reminds us of the suddenness of these events, Jesus Himself breaks in with a reminder to all that He is **coming quickly**. Why does it seem that it has been so long? Was Jesus wrong here?

   i. The word **quickly** in the ancient Greek isn't exactly the same as our word for "quickly." "The word 'quickly' might with accuracy be rendered 'suddenly.' " (Morgan)

   ii. Still, the early church expected Jesus' return *soon* - were they just wrong, or did Jesus mislead them? Not at all; they were not wrong and they were not misled by Jesus. God *wants* to keep all generations expectant, watching, and ready for His return.

   iii. We are not rushing towards a distant brink of the consummation of all things; we are running parallel along the edge of that brink, and have been since the time of the apostles. "Thus the time has always been at hand. The tension of imminence is endemic to that span of redemptive history lying between the cross and the *parousia*." (Mounce)

d. **Blessed is he who keeps the words of the prophecy of this book**: This blessing reminds us that prophecy gives us a word to keep, not merely material for interesting discussions and debates. The main intent of prophecy is to lead us to trust and obey God, and apply His truth to the way we *live*.

2. (8-9) John is corrected for worshipping an angel a second time.

Now I, John, saw and heard these things. And when I heard and saw, I fell down to worship before the feet of the angel who showed me these things. Then he said to me, "See *that you do* not *do that*. For I am your fellow servant, and of your brethren the prophets, and of those who keep the words of this book. Worship God."

a. **I fell down to worship before the feet of the angel**: As he did in Revelation 19:10, John is overwhelmed, and bows before an angel in worship. In the same way, the angel reminds John that only God is to be worshipped, and that they are both players on the same team - along with all who **keep the words of this book**.

i. No created being should ever be worshipped. This is in contrast with Jesus, who receives the worship of angels (Hebrews 1:6) and of men (Matthew 8:2, 14:33, John 9:38).

ii. "If it was wrong to worship this glorious heavenly messenger, in and through whom came forth the very voice of Jesus, how can it be right to worship and pray to the Virgin Mary, to whom is assigned no such dignity or office? The impulse and intention may be devout and good; but it is a great mistake." (Seiss)

b. **See that you do not do that**: It is striking that even someone who has received all these visions may go astray. Supernatural visions and revelations do not mean that someone is correct in their doctrine, teaching, or practice.

3. (10-11) A warning is given, either by the same angel or by Jesus.

And he said to me, "Do not seal the words of the prophecy of this book, for the time is at hand. He who is unjust, let him be unjust still; he who is filthy, let him be filthy still; he who is righteous, let him be righteous still; he who is holy, let him be holy still."

a. **Do not seal the words of this prophecy of this book, for the time is at hand**: Because the **time is at hand**, and history now runs parallel to the brink of the consummation of all things, this book *isn't* sealed. This is in contrast to Old Testament prophecy (Daniel 8:26); men seal the Book of Revelation in defiance of God's command.

b. **He who is unjust, let him be unjust still . . . he who is righteous, let him be righteous still**: The thought here is probably "since Jesus is coming so suddenly, there won't be time for change." There will be no time for last minute repentance, but there is time now. If what you have read in Revelation hasn't changed you, there isn't much hope!

i. "It is the hopelessness of the final state of the wicked which is here pictured. The states of both the evil and the good are now fixed forever. There is no word here about a 'second chance' hereafter." (Robertson)

ii. "If the warnings of this book are not sufficient, there is no more that God has to say." (Walvoord)

4. (12-13) Jesus declares: **I am coming quickly**.

"And behold, I am coming quickly, and My reward *is* with Me, to give to every one according to his work. I am the Alpha and the Omega, *the* Beginning and *the* End, the First and the Last."

a. **And behold, I am coming quickly**: We can never miss the note of urgency and warning in all what Jesus tells us about His coming. His message is always *be ready*! (Matthew 24:44)

b. **My reward is with Me**: If Jesus will **give to everyone according to his work**, does that mean we are saved by our works? No, but it does show that living faith will have works with it (James 2:20, Titus 3:8).

i. "It is the quality of a man's life which provides the ultimate indication of what he really believes." (Mounce)

c. **I am the Alpha and the Omega, the Beginning and the End, the First and the Last**: As an added incentive for us to do and be what is right, being ready for Jesus' return, He reminds us just who He is. If we really know and understood who Jesus is, we will not have any trouble being ready for His return.

i. The term **Alpha and Omega** is "Applied to God in 1:8; 21:6; and here alone to Christ, crowning proof in this book of Christ's deity." (Robertson)

ii. The title **the First and the Last** is also irrefutable proof that Jesus is Yahweh, the LORD: *I, the LORD, am the first; and with the last I am He.* (Isaiah 41:4)

iii. These terms together mean that Jesus is the beginning, middle, and end for the Christian. "Preach orthodoxy, or any form of doxy; if you have left out Christ, there is no manna from heaven, no water from the rock, no refuge from the storm, no healing for the sick, no life for the dead. If you leave out Christ, you have left the sun out of the day, and the moon out of the night, you have left the waters out of the sea, and the foods out of the river, you have left the harvest out of the year, the soul out of the body, you have left joy out of heaven, yea, you have robbed all of its all. There is no gospel worth thinking of, much less worth proclaiming in Jehovah's name, if Jesus be forgotten." (Spurgeon)

5. (14-15) A blessing and a curse is pronounced by someone (perhaps John, perhaps the angel, perhaps Jesus Himself).

Blessed *are* those who do His commandments, that they may have the right to the tree of life, and may enter through the gates into the city. But outside *are* dogs and sorcerers and sexually immoral and murderers and idolaters, and whoever loves and practices a lie.

a. **Blessed are those who do His commandments**: Doing His commandments does not earn us eternal life, but it is evidence that we have been granted eternal life. Besides, there is an *inherent* blessing in doing His commandments, because they are good and right for us.

i. Regarding the phrase **those who do His commandments** some translations have *those who have washed their robes* instead. The difference is between two ancient Greek words:

HOIPLUNONTESTASSTOLAS (*washed their robes*) or
HOIPOIOUNTESTASENTOLAS (**do His commandments**)

ii. This is a good example of how a copyist's error can cloud a text in rather minor ways, without affecting the essential meaning of the passage. Even allowing for the small percentage of disputed texts, we can trust our Bibles.

b. **But outside are dogs and sorcerers and sexually immoral and murderers**: What about those **outside**? We shouldn't think that outside the walls of heaven multitudes will throng, longing to get in. "The verse does not intend to teach that in the eternal state all manner of wicked men will be living just outside the heavenly city. It simply describes the future with the imagery of the present." (Mounce)

i. Why does it say that all **dogs** will be outside? Is this a refutation of the idea of "doggie heaven"? No, what is meant here is "Not literal dogs, but the morally impure . . . Dogs in the Oriental cities are scavengers and excite unspeakable contempt (Matthew 7:6; Philippians 3:2)." (Robertson)

6. (16) Jesus brings a word of verification.

"I, Jesus, have sent My angel to testify to you these things in the churches. I am the Root and the Offspring of David, the Bright and Morning Star."

a. **I, Jesus, have sent My angel to testify to you**: With these solemn words, Jesus authenticates the entire book. Much of the Book of Revelation is either fantastic or seems too good to be true, but it is all true.

i. "Thus the very God of all inspiration, and of all inspired men, reiterates and affirms the highest authority for all that is herein written. Either, then, this Book is nothing but a base and blasphemous forgery, unworthy of the slightest respect of men, and specially unworthy of a place in the Sacred Canon; or it is one of the most directly inspired and authoritative writings ever given." (Seiss)

b. **To testify to you these things in the churches**: The Book of Revelation is written to **the churches**. This book is not a private affair, knowable only by an elite - it is for all believers. It's also worth noting that this is the first reference to the *church* since the letters to the seven churches in Revelation 2-3.

c. **The Root and offspring of David**: This is a precious Messianic title (Isaiah 11:1). It shows that Jesus is both the *Creator* of King David and His *descendent*. Jesus spoke to this same idea in Matthew 22:41-46.

d. **Bright and Morning Star**: This is another Messianic title from the Old Testament (Numbers 24:17) and the New Testament (Revelation 2:28). Just as the **Morning Star** (generally held to be the planet Venus) shines and welcomes the new day, so does Jesus.

7. (17) The Spirit and the Bride say to all: **Come!**

And the Spirit and the bride say, "Come!" And let him who hears say, "Come!" And let him who thirsts come. Whoever desires, let him take the water of life freely.

a. **The Spirit and the bride say, "Come!"** Is this an invitation to Jesus, asking Him to return? Or is it an invitation to those with a spiritual thirst to come to Jesus? Either sense is certainly true.

b. Who can **come**? **Him who hears** can come to Jesus, but they can't come unless they hear. **Him who thirsts** can come to Jesus, but they can't come unless they feel their thirst. **Whoever desires** can come, but they can't come unless God works in their heart to desire Him.

i. So how do you know if God has worked in your heart? Go through a little checklist. Have you heard? Are you thirsty for God and eternal life? Do you want Him? Then **come!**

c. **Whoever desires, let him take the water of life freely**: This is an open invitation to receive salvation from Jesus. He will not exclude anyone who comes to Him. An invitation is both an opportunity *and* a responsibility. If we decline an invitation, we have only ourselves to blame.

i. "A similar invitation is extended in Isaiah 55:1. The invitation to come is an urgent command, for the day will arrive when it is too late to come. Now is the day of grace. The hour of judgment is impending." (Walvoord)

d. Glory in the greatness of the invitation: **whoever desires, let him take the water of life freely**! Anyone who **desires** salvation in Jesus Christ can **come** to Him and **take the water of life freely**.

i. One might say, "I don't understand all the Christian doctrine and theology" - come anyway, because it doesn't say *whoever understands, let him take the water of life freely*.

ii. One might say, "I can't repent the way I should. My heart is hard and I can't even weep over my sins or feel bad over them as I should" - come anyway, because it doesn't say *whoever feels, let him take the water of life freely.*

iii. One might say, "I don't know if I can live the Christian life the way that I should" - come anyway, because it doesn't say *whoever can, let him take the water of life freely.*

iv. One might say, "I don't know if I am worthy to live the Christian life" - come anyway, because it doesn't say *whoever is worthy, let him take the water of life freely.*

v. "But mark thee, sinner, it says, 'whosoever.' What a big word that is! Whosoever! There is no standard height here. It is of any height and any size. Little sinners, big sinners, black sinners, fair sinners, sinners double dyed, old sinners, aggravated sinners, sinners who have committed every crime in the whole catalogue, - whosoever." (Spurgeon)

vi. It is really this simple: do you **desire** Jesus and His salvation? Then **come**. Can you say, "Now, Lord, I desire to be saved, give me a new heart; I desire to give up my sins; I desire to be a Christian; I desire to believe and desire to obey. But I have no strength to do this. I have the desire, give me the power." If this is your desire, then you are freely invited to come, if you are only willing. There is no barrier between you and Jesus except your stubborn will.

e. **Let him take the water of life freely**: When you **desire**, when you **come**, then you must **take**. All of this world's religion can be summed up in the idea that you must *bring* something to *give* unto the gods. The essence of Christianity is summed up in the idea that God invites us to **take the water of life freely**. You can't *bring* anything to save or justify or commend yourself before God, but you can **take** the salvation He offers.

f. It is fitting that this great invitation closes the Book of Revelation and the Bible. "All the prophets of the Bible, all the apostles of the Bible, all the threatenings of the Bible, all the promises of the Bible, gather themselves up, and focus themselves into this one burning ray, 'Come to Jesus. Come, and take the water of life freely.' " (Spurgeon)

8. (18-19) Someone brings a warning - either Jesus, or an angel, or John.

For I testify to everyone who hears the words of the prophecy of this book: If anyone adds to these things, God will add to him the plagues that are written in this book; and if anyone takes away from the words of the book of this prophecy, God shall take away his part from the

Book of Life, from the holy city, and _from_ the things which are written in this book.

> a. **If anyone adds to these things, God will add to him the plagues that are written in this book**: This is another section at the end of the Book of Revelation where it is hard to tell exactly who speaks. In most red-letter editions, these words are in black, indicating that the translators believe that these are not the words of Jesus. But there may be good reason to believe Jesus gave this warning.
>
> > i. "The solemnity of the injunction suggests that the speaker is Christ Himself." (Mounce)
>
> b. **If anyone adds . . . if anyone takes away**: This means that there is a high price to pay for tampering with the Book of Revelation specifically, and the Scriptures in general.
>
> > i. "What a solemn warning this is to critics who have tampered with this book and other portions of Scripture in arrogant self-confidence that they are equipped intellectually and spiritually to determine what is true and what is not true in the Word of God." (Walvoord)
> >
> > ii. This solemn promise also implies that the Book of Revelation can be understood. Why would God assign such a strong rebuke for the addition to or subtraction from a book that just painted big ideas in wild pictures, or if no one could really understand the book anyway?
> >
> > iii. "Divines generally do further extend the sense of these two verses, considering this as the last portion of holy writ, not only placed last in our Bibles, but revealed and written last. They conceive these verses the seal of all canonical Scripture, and that God here denounces a curse to those who shall pretend any new revelations of his will . . . as also against all those who shall deny, corrupt, or deprave any part of them." (Poole)

9. (20-21) Last words.

He who testifies to these things says, "Surely I am coming quickly." Amen. Even so, come, Lord Jesus! The grace of our Lord Jesus Christ _be_ with you all. Amen.

> a. **Surely I am coming quickly**: To the very end, the Book of Revelation emphasizes readiness and watchfulness. If we miss this practical lesson from the Book of Revelation - the lesson of readiness - then we miss the essential message of the book.
>
> > i. If the statement "**I am coming quickly**" were not enough, Jesus puts emphasis on both sides - **surely** before and **amen** after.

b. **Even so, come, Lord Jesus!** With this phrase, John uses an Aramaic expression that was well known in the ancient church: *Maranatha!*

i. The Book of Revelation concerns many prophetic events, but the book closes with John's longing for the return of Jesus for His people - he wants the rapture of the church.

ii. "If the whole creation groans and travails together in pain for the manifestation of the sons of God, how much more those sons of God themselves!" (Seiss)

iii. "At the very close of the book is the confession that the answers to the problems of life do not lie in man's ability to create a better world but in the return of the One whose sovereign power controls the course of human affairs." (Mounce)

c. **The grace of our Lord Jesus Christ be with you all. Amen**: The book (and the Bible) ends with a word of **grace**, and **grace** for **all**. Paul also used this phrase as a final word in some of his letters (1 Corinthians 16:23, 2 Corinthians 13:14, 1 Thessalonians 5:28, 2 Thessalonians 3:18). In 2 Thessalonians 3:17-18, Paul even indicated that this signature - no doubt written with his own hand - was a mark that the letter was genuinely from him.

i. "It is a good word for the close of this marvelous picture of God's gracious provision for his people in earth and heaven." (Robertson)

ii. "Whatever you may miss, may the grace of our Lord Jesus Christ be always with you. In whatsoever points you or any of us may fail, may we never come short of the grace of our Lord Jesus Christ." (Spurgeon)

iii. The last verse of the Old Testament contains a curse: *Lest I come and strike the earth with a curse* (Malachi 4:6). Fittingly, the last words of the New Testament speak of **grace**, because **grace** describes God's dealing with man on the basis of the New Covenant.

The Book of Revelation - Bibliography

This is a bibliography of books cited in the commentary. Of course, there are many other worthy books on Revelation, but these are listed for the benefit of readers who wish to investigate sources more thoroughly.

Alford, Henry *The New Testament for English Readers, Volume II, Part II* (London: Rivingtons, 1866)

Barclay, William *Letters to the Seven Churches* (Nashville, Tennessee: Abingdon Press, 1957)

Barclay, William *The Revelation of John, Volumes 1 and 2* (Philadelphia: Westminster Press, 1976)

Barnhouse, Donald Grey *Revelation* (Grand Rapids, Michigan: Zondervan, 1982)

Bunch, Taylor G. *The Seven Epistles of Christ* (Washington D.C: Review and Herald Publishing, 1947)

Clarke, Adam *The New Testament with A Commentary and Critical Notes, Volume III* (New York: Eaton & Mains, 1831)

Erdman, Charles R. *The Revelation of John* (Philadelphia: Westminster Press, 1936)

Hocking, David *The Coming World Leader* (Portland, Oregon: Multnomah Press, 1988)

Hughes, Philip Edgcumbe *The Book of the Revelation* (Leicester, England: Inter-Varsity Press, 1990)

Johnson, Alan F. *The Expositor's Bible Commentary, Volume 12: Revelation* (Grand Rapids, Michigan: Zondervan, 1981)

Morgan, G. Campbell *An Exposition of the Whole Bible* (Old Tappan, New Jersey: Fleming H. Revell, 1959)

Morris, Henry *The Revelation Record* (Wheaton, Illinois: Tyndale, 1983)

Morris, Leon *The Book of Revelation* (Grand Rapids, Michigan: Eerdmans, 1988)

Mounce, Robert H. *The Book of Revelation* (Grand Rapids, Michigan: Eerdmans, 1979)

Newell, William R. *The Book of The Revelation* (Chicago: Moody Press, 1935)

Poole, Matthew *A Commentary on the Holy Bible, Volume III: Matthew-Revelation* (London: Banner of Truth Trust, 1969, first published in 1685)

Ries, Raul A. *Hear What the Spirit Is Saying* (Diamond Bar, California: Logos Media Group, 1993)

Robertson, Archibald T. *Word Pictures in the New Testament*, Volume VI (Nashville: Broadman Press, 1933)

Seiss, Joseph A. *The Apocalypse (Lectures on Revelation)* (Grand Rapids, Michigan: Kregel Publications, 1987)

Smith, Chuck *What the World is Coming To* (Costa Mesa, California: Maranatha House Publishers)

Spurgeon, Charles Haddon *The New Park Street Pulpit, Volumes 1-6* and *The Metropolitan Tabernacle Pulpit, Volumes 7-63* (Pasadena, Texas: Pilgrim Publications, 1990)

Talbot, Louis T. *The Revelation of Jesus Christ* (Grand Rapids, Michigan: Eerdmans, 1962)

Tenney, Merrill C. *Interpreting Revelation* (Grand Rapids, Michigan: Eerdmans, 1970)

Trapp, John *A Commentary on the Old and New Testaments, Volume Five* (Eureka, California: Tanski Publications, 1997)

Victorinus *Commentary on the Apcalypse of the Blessed John; The Ante-Nicean Fathers Volume VII*; Roberts and Donaldson Editors (Grand Rapids, Michigan: Eerdmans, 1985)

Walvoord, John F. *The Revelation of Jesus Christ* (Chicago: Moody Press, 1966)

Much thanks to the many who helped prepare this commentary. My wife Inga-Lill and our children give so much support in this and all the ministry. Aan-Sofie - this one's for you! Martina Patrick did an outstanding job as proofreader - thank you Martina and Tim, not only for the help with this book but for your long friendship over the years. Craig Brewer created the cover and helped with the layout. Kara Valeri helped with graphic design. Gayle Erwin provided both inspiration and practical guidance. I am often amazed at the remarkable kindness of others, and thanks to all who give the gift of encouragement. With each year that passes, faithful friends and supporters become all the more precious. Through you all, God has been better to me than I have ever deserved.

David Guzik is the Pastor of Calvary Chapel of Simi Valley.   David and his wife Inga-Lill live in Simi Valley with their children Aan-Sofie, Nathan, and Jonathan. You can e-mail David at david@enduringword.com

For more resources by David Guzik, go to www.enduringword.com

More Bible Study Resources from Enduring Word Media

Ask for these works from your local Christian bookstore, or order directly from Enduring Word Media.

Books

Genesis Commentary (ISBN: 1-56599-049-8)

Acts Commentary (ISBN: 1-56599-047-1)

1 Corinthians Commentary (ISBN: 1-56599-045-5)

Software

Commentary CD-ROM (ISBN: 1-56599-048-X)

This CD-ROM gives immediate access to thousands of pages of verse-by-verse Bible commentary through all of the New Testament and some Old Testament books. For ease of use, commentary is available in both Acrobat and HTML format.

Audio Resources

David Guzik's teaching is available on cassette tape and on mp3 cd-rom. Contact Enduring Word Media for a catalog.

Enduring Word Media

www.enduringword.com

ewm@enduringword.com

23 West Easy Street, #204

Simi Valley, CA 93065

(805) 582-6545

CPSIA information can be obtained
at www.ICGtesting.com
Printed in the USA
FSOW02n0802111214
3808FS

9 781565 990432